IMAGES
of America

LEWIS COUNTY

IMAGES
of America

LEWIS COUNTY

William M. Talley, Ph.D.,
and Paula Franke

ARCADIA
PUBLISHING

ISBN 978-0-7385-1813-8

Published by Arcadia Publishing
Charleston, South Carolina

Printed in the United States of America

Library of Congress Catalog Card Number: 2005921823

For all general information contact Arcadia Publishing at:
Telephone 843-853-2070
Fax 843-853-0044
E-mail sales@arcadiapublishing.com
For customer service and orders:
Toll-Free 1-888-313-2665

Visit us on the Internet at www.arcadiapublishing.com

CONTENTS

ACKNOWLEDGMENTS

The authors dedicate this book to the late W.C. Dugan, former editor of the *Lewis County Herald*, who was most instrumental in collecting and saving many of the photographs included in this book.

We are grateful to the Vanceburg Depot Museum and a number of people who shared their photographs: Bob Brown, Dennis Brown, Nancy Donaldson Kollin, William Florence, Fanny May, Shirley Miller, George M. Plummer, Joni Pugh, Helen L. Smith, Lois Taylor, Janie Nute-Thomas, Merrill Osborne, Chris Ash, Pauline Applegate, Robert Brewer, Betty Ruggles, Orville Chatman, Betty Call Lewis, Hildreth Polston, Doris Mae Thomas Callihan, Fonda Griffith, Ben Pugh, James "Bubbles" Switzer, and Helen Liles Lewis.

INTRODUCTION

Lewis County is one of Kentucky's largest counties in terms of land mass and has the longest boundary with the Ohio River. The area comprising the county was taken from Mason County by an act of the Kentucky Legislature in December 1806, and its first court meeting was held at the home of Oke Hendrickson at Poplar Flat early in the year 1807. The village of Clarksburg was designated as the county seat in 1809 and was eventually moved to Vanceburg in 1863–1864.

What was Vanceburg like in 1797, when it was chosen as the location for a town? In all likelihood, it was a heavily forested area where very little of the original timber had ever been touched by an ax. There was no town or village as such, but there may have been two or three log cabins somewhere within the 55-acre section that was the original layout of the town.

No doubt there were people in small boats going in and out of the mouth of Salt Lick Creek, where there was considerable activity at the salt wells located between Vanceburg and Clarksburg. There was probably the smell of wood smoke in the air because of the constant fires, where kettles of salt water were boiled day and night. There were many flatboats, loaded with settlers and their possessions, passing downriver on their way to settlements like Limestone (now Maysville) further downstream.

All in all, it was still a wilderness that had not been exploited by man.

The heavily forested hills of the county have some of the best oak hardwoods in the United States. Throughout the county's history, the forests have been the mainstay for laborers and their income, always producing vast amounts of lumber, barrel staves, tanbark, railroad ties, firewood, and numerous wood products.

The county is well watered by several streams, the most notable of them being Kinniconick Creek, well known for its fishing and camping attractions. Other major streams are Salt Lick Creek, Cabin Creek, Indian Creek, the North Fork of Licking River, Montgomery Creek, and Quick's Run. The Ohio River, which serves as the county's northern boundary, originally contained four interesting islands (now only three); one group, known as the Three Islands, was a major landmark for early settlers making their way downstream.

The site where Vanceburg now stands began to draw attention when the salt-making operations, known as the Ohio Salt Works, opened in 1794, and the first wells were dug by Moses Baird, Joseph C. Vance, and John Heath. Soon afterwards, there followed numerous other persons who were interested in the salt-making industry.

Baird and Vance saw the advantage of laying out a town and selling lots; thus, on June 30, 1797, they purchased a 55-acre tract from Alexander Keith Marshall out of his 200-acre patent and shortly afterwards drew up the plat, recorded in Mason County. The town was named for Vance rather than Baird because there was already a Bardstown, which would be much confused with a Bairdstown.

Unfortunately, it was later found that Marshall did not have clear title from the Virginia Land Office for the patent on the land. This created many headaches for Baird and Vance, who had to deal with the people who had purchased lots in "their town." Baird lived across the river on his farm near Sandy Springs, and finally Vance left the area and moved to Urbana, Ohio, where he died.

Who were some of the first European people ever to walk across the land where Vanceburg now stands? Some of the earliest explorers of the Ohio River Valley indicate that the Native Americans knew of the salt licks behind Vanceburg, and they came to hunt deer, buffalo, and other animals that came there to lick salt. Perhaps the Shawnees, who had settlements near the mouth of the Scioto River in both Ohio and Kentucky, were frequent visitors at the site. The French fur traders who spent time at Shanoah (a Shawnee town) were probably the next people to visit this place after the Shawnees shared their information with them. An old newspaper article, published in 1881, says that the French came to Vanceburg as early as 1762 and made salt.

Many of the old maps that were drawn up by both the French and English explorers showed the location of Salt Lick Creek, one of them as early as 1744. It was noted on many subsequent maps as a place where salt was made.

It was in July 1766 that Capt. Harry Gordon, a British explorer, came down the river and stopped at this place. Captain Gordon, in his journal, described the site of Vanceburg as a "pretty cove at the end of a stony shore." No doubt it was a peaceful, forested cove and was an ideal place to camp for a while. In Captain Gordon's company were several Native American guides who killed 15 or 16 buffaloes for the men. It is hard for us to picture buffalo being that plentiful and to realize that they roamed and grazed peacefully where this town now stands. An old buffalo path (later Indian War Road) led up Salt Lick Creek to the interior of the state.

Vanceburg grew slowly, partly because of the land disputes mentioned earlier, and partly because Clarksburg was chosen as the county seat. Many of the persons who bought lots in the town farmed them, and the town served mainly as a landing place for persons coming to the salt works or going to Clarksburg on business. It was sometime in the 1830s that people began to build permanent structures in the town. Its first "boom" did not come until the county seat was moved to Vanceburg

In its earlier days, there were two locations that served as focal points. The first was the tavern and boat landing of Rowland T. Parker at the foot of Court Street, and the second was the Carr Tavern and boat landing at the foot of Main Street, where the Veterans Memorial Park now exists.

The original plan of the town was small, and since that time, it has certainly outgrown its original boundaries. Originally there was a street along the low mark of the Ohio River, but it has since eroded away, and First Street has now become Front Street. The street now called Front Street extended all the way down the river to Salt Lick Creek, but in 1862, after a season of extremely heavy rains, a huge section of the street, including several buildings, slipped into the river.

The loss of this street and some buildings did not seem to hinder Vanceburg's progress. The steamboat trade was heavy, and many boats that ran between Portsmouth and Cincinnati, Ohio, and further downriver stopped at Vanceburg to do business. In addition to being Vanceburg's primary source of long-distance transportation, the boats delivered produce and picked up farm products, freestone, tanbark, and lumber. The Ohio River was one of the main transportation highways of the country in those early days, and Vanceburg stood on its doorstep. It was easy to travel to Cincinnati, St. Louis, or New Orleans by buying a ticket at the foot of Main Street.

Yet there was to come even further development with the railroad. The surveyors of the Maysville and Big Sandy Railroad began making their surveys for the venture as early as 1852, but the Civil War and engineering problems between South Portsmouth and Trinity delayed its completion until 1888. The railroad displaced some of the streets and homes, as the surveyors brought the railroad right through the middle of the town. It had become so prosperous by 1913 that a second track was laid, displacing even more of the town. The railroad brought an end to the steamboat era.

The AA Highway has now replaced both the river and the railroad in importance, and it has started a trend of centering Vanceburg's future prosperity on the interior of its Kentucky home. Vanceburg is now an easy drive to Cincinnati.

With the recent increase in genealogical research, we are often contacted by former Lewis Countians seeking family information, sharing their own research, and helping identify photographs. We hope that this book will build on that interest.

One

River and Railroad

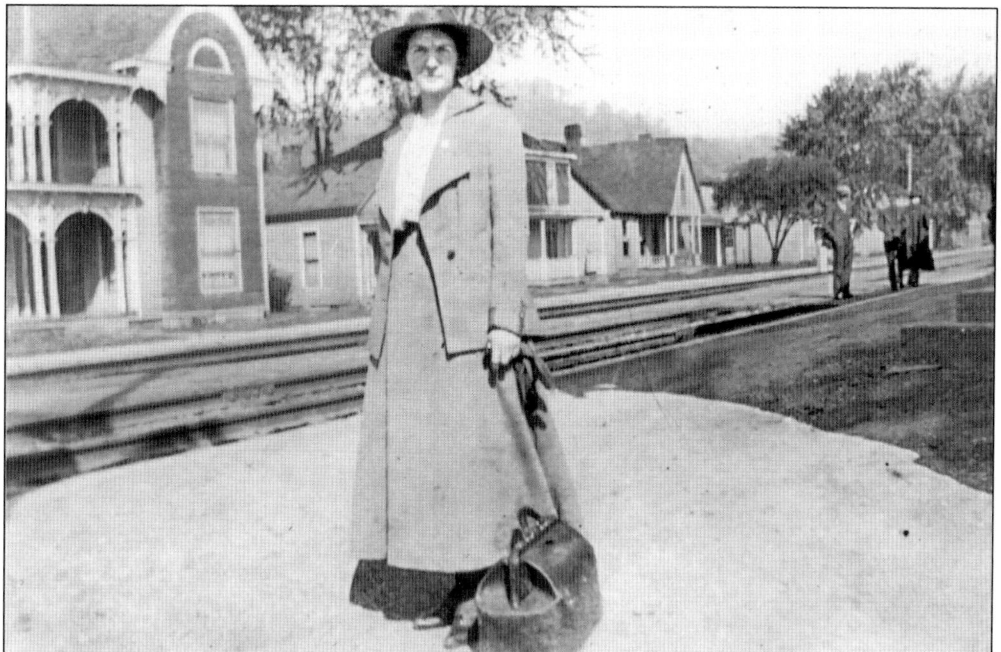

In 1916, Nelle Grant waits for a train to arrive at the Vanceburg Depot to return home after a visit with Lena Wells Lykins.

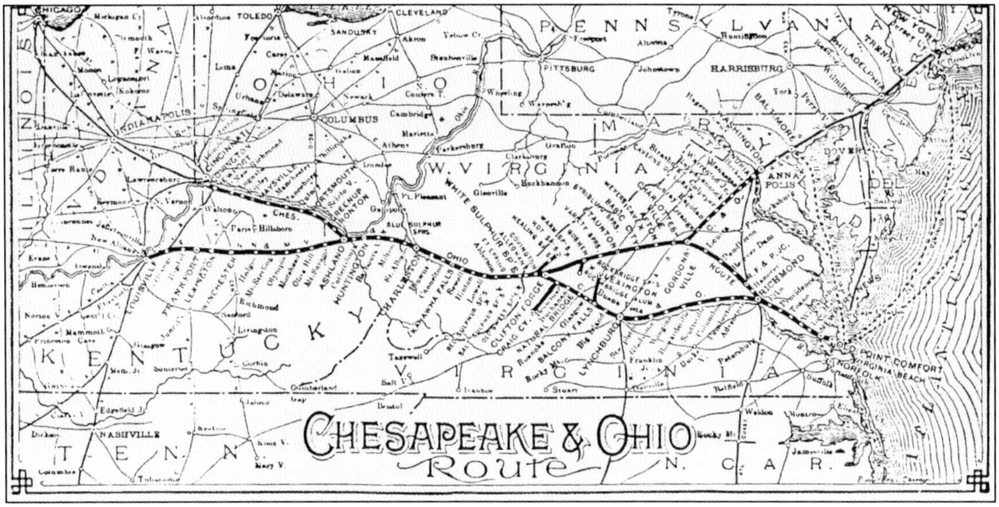

This early map of the Chesapeake & Ohio Railway shows the names of the towns where the trains stopped in the early days of the railroad. The railroad crosses the Ohio River at Cincinnati and goes on to Chicago. It was known as the Maysville and Big Sandy Railroad until Collis P. Huntington bought it and integrated it into the Chesapeake & Ohio.

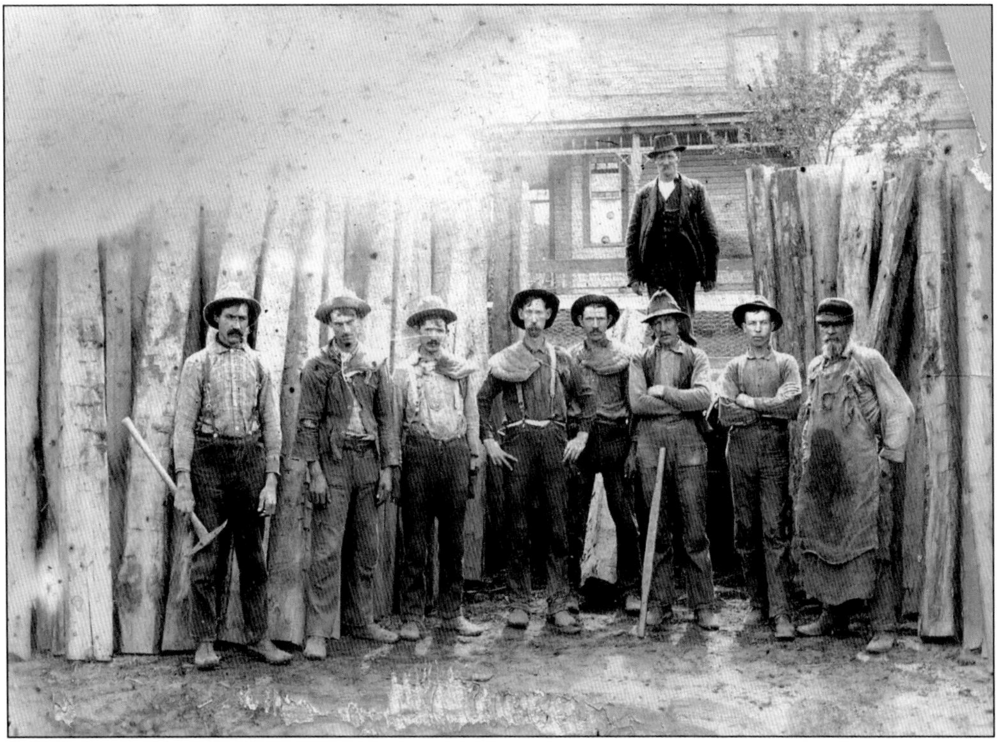

The railroad tie yard was on Third Street in Vanceburg, just east of the Pugh house garage and the lots up to Market Street. A spur of railroad track connected with it. The men, from left to right, are a Mr. Lewis, Mr. Shope, an unidentified man, James "Jim Crow" Qualls, another Mr. Lewis, an unidentified man, Simon Scott, and "Uncle" Charley Plummer. Standing on the side porch of the present-day Denny Lykins house in the background is Jordan Slack, the tie inspector. This photo was taken 1909–1910.

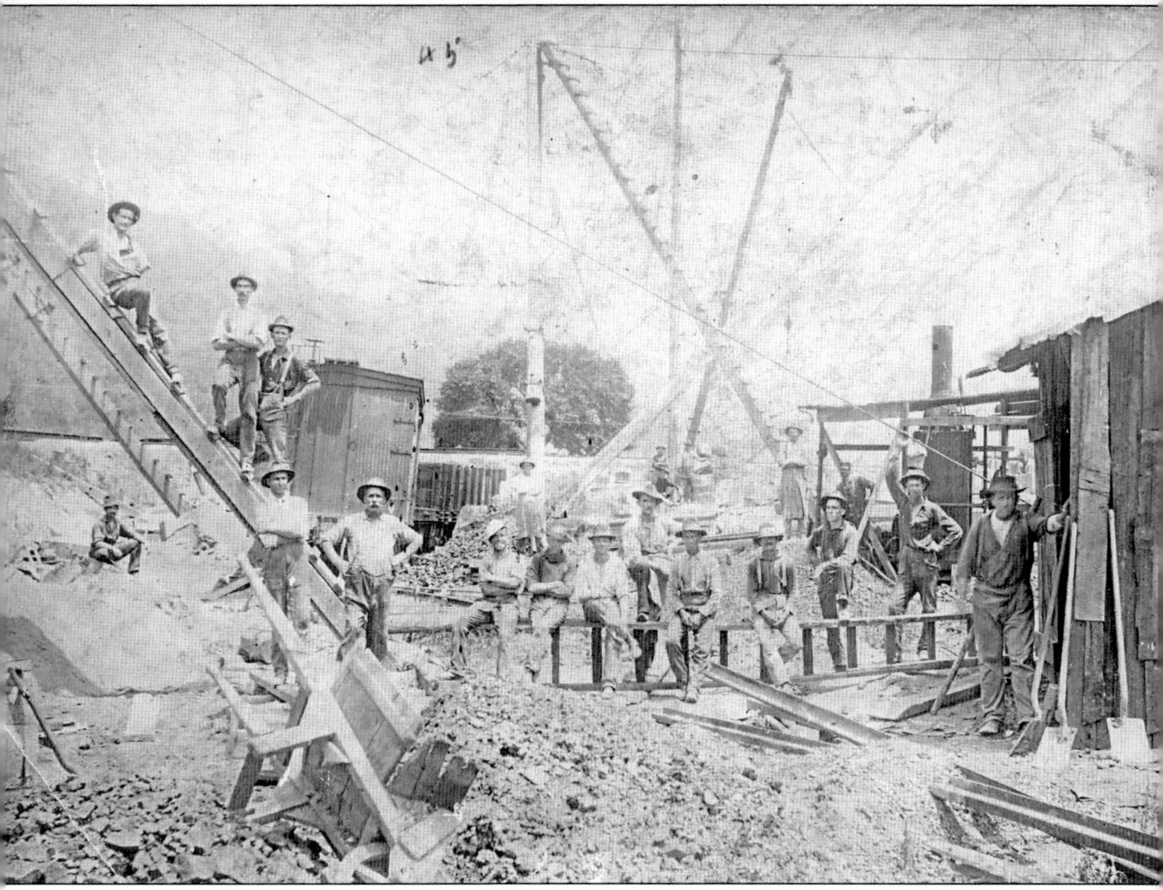

The inscription on the back of the picture says: "Building the C&O Railroad." The date or place the picture was taken is uncertain, but it was most likely taken about 1913, when the second track was added to the railroad.

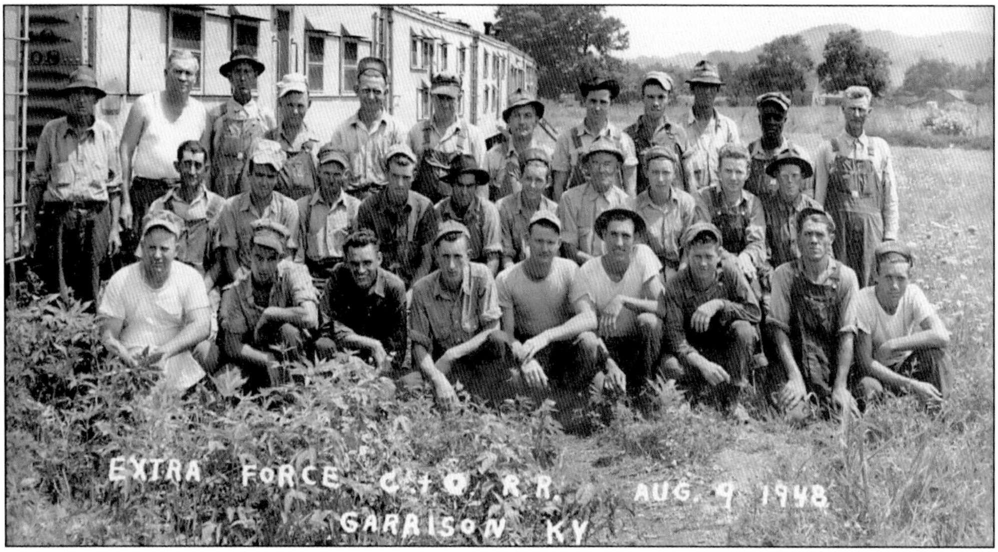

This picture of Extra Force crew of the C&O Railroad was taken August 9, 1948, at Garrison. The men are identified from left to right as follows: (front row) Mr. Trailer (Traylor), cook; Mr. Bays; Mr. Wright; Mr. Howard; Winford Dyer; James Caseman; Esham Collins; Bill Pollitt; and Buster Goldenburg; (middle row) John Conley; Mr. Combs; Mr. Craig; Luther Parson; Jackie Riffe; Paul Cooper; Bob Thomas; John Howard; Rev. Bruce Lunsford; and Jess Jarrells; (back row) Orville McGlothlin; Grover Porter; Delbert Brown, sub-boss; Mr. Jones; Ernest Setters; George Hickle; Buck Baldwin; Brit Ratcliff; Sam Pollitt; Milt Abrams; Richard Robertson; and Goebel Bradford, boss.

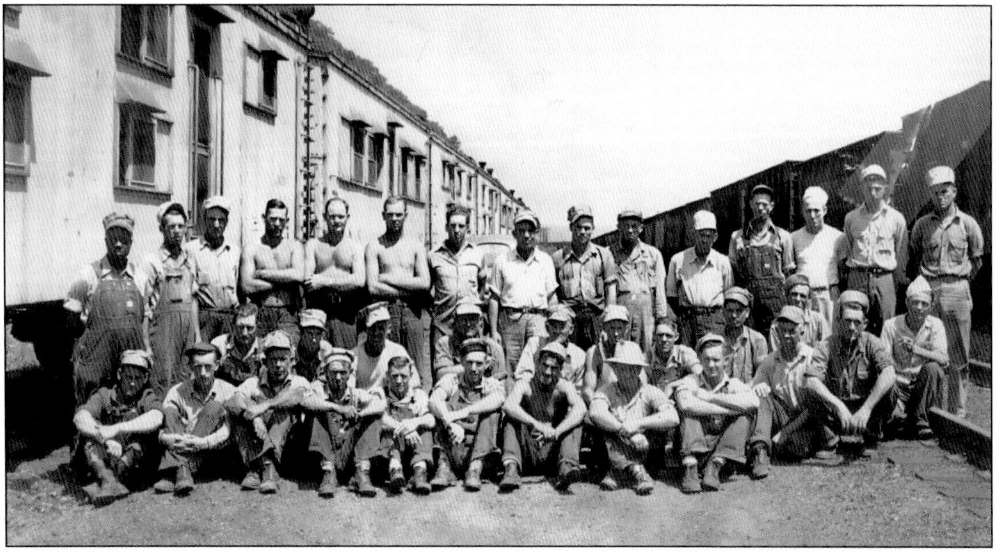

This scene of C&O Railroad workers was at an unknown location (probably Limeville, in Greenup County) about 1948 or 1949. Several of the men are not identified. All of the men from Lewis County are in the front row. Pictured from left to right are (front row) two unidentified men, Curtis McCleese, unidentified, Ike Potter, Tony Christy, George Hickle, unidentified, "Jum" Burriss, unidentified, and Charley Cassidy; (back row) Richard Robinson, four unidentified men, Winford Dyer, six unidentified men, Charley Heater, unidentified, and Bill Bivens.

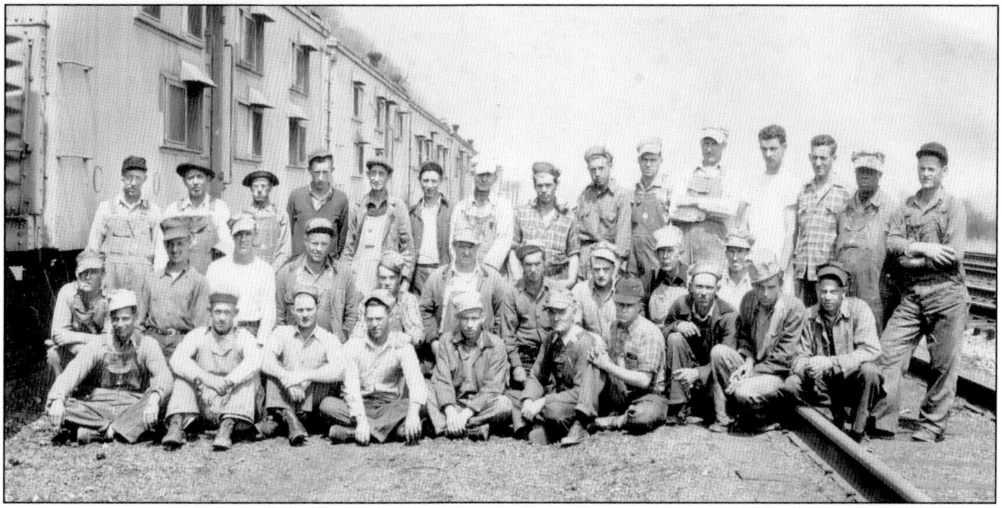

These men, mostly from Lewis County, were the section crew on the C&O Railroad on April 11, 1949. They are, from left to right, (front row) unidentified, Russell Bivens, Winford Dyer, unidentified, Mr. Harr, Bob Thomas, Sam Christy, Roy Clark, Ronald Rigsby, and George Nelson; (middle row) "Wildhog" Craycraft, Vernon Craycraft, Raymond Traylor, Glen Osborne, Tony Christy, George Hickle, Jackie Riffe, Ora Faulkner, Curt McCleese, and Homer McCarty; (back row) Roy Pollitt, Earl Stapleton (boss), Jesse Jarrells, Russell Howard, John Conley, Johnnie Howard, Ernest Setters, Harry Cooper, Buster Goldenburg, Russell Bayless, Earl Lewis, Joe Bays, Willard Hughes, Richard Robertson, and Esham Collins.

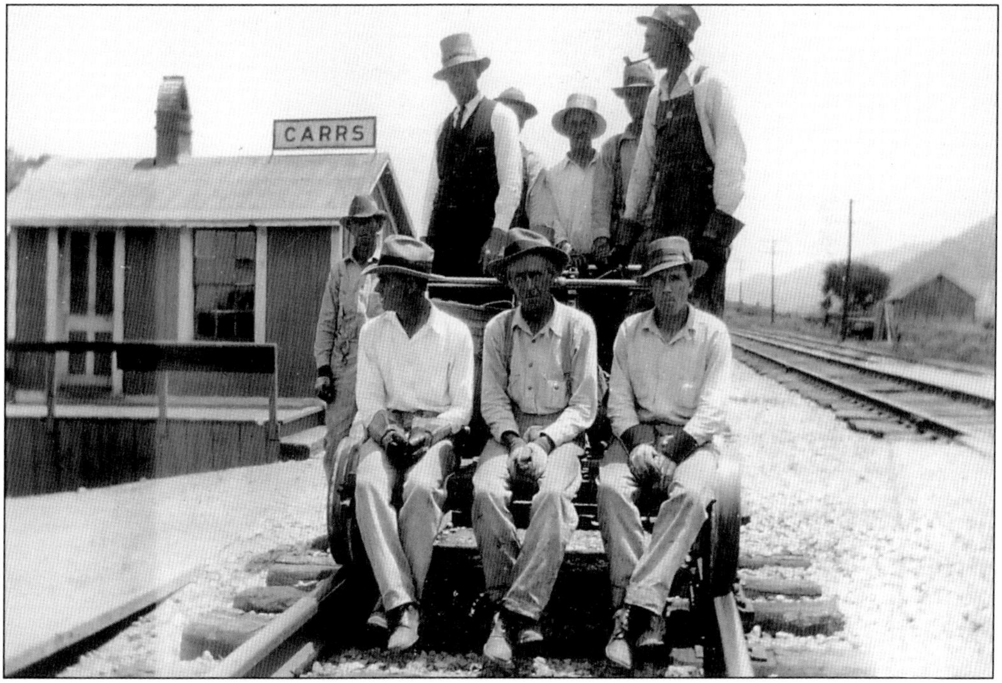

Railroad workers at Carrs Depot, which faced the road that came up from Route 8, are pictured. From left to right are (front row) probably Bob Thomas, unidentified, and Clarence Doyle; (back row) Clarence Voiers, three unidentified men behind him, and probably Jack Stout on the right.

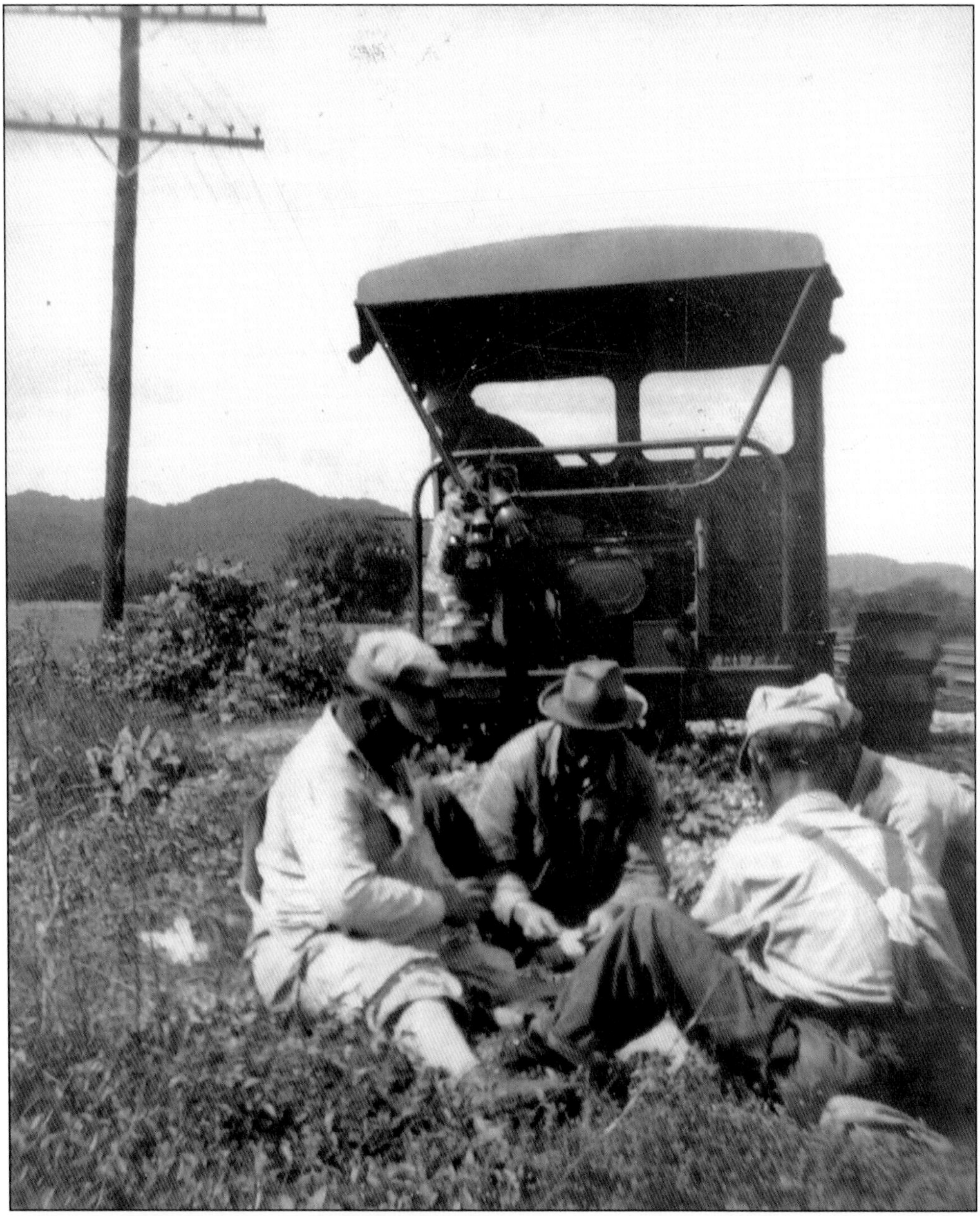

Railroad workers in 1949 have lunch at the crossing at Sam Bierley's farm at Carrs. Pictured, from left to right, are Bill Clark, Burt Matisse (Montieth?), Bill Johnson, and Earl Kennedy, with Maurice McCann in the railroad car.

This rare picture, taken about 1901, shows the Kinniconick & Freestone locomotive as it is proceeding up the Lewis County side of the railroad at Deep Cut, ready to enter Carter County. The rail line ran from Garrison to Gesling and operated for 50 years. The rail bed is now the bed of the Trace Creek and Ruggles Road.

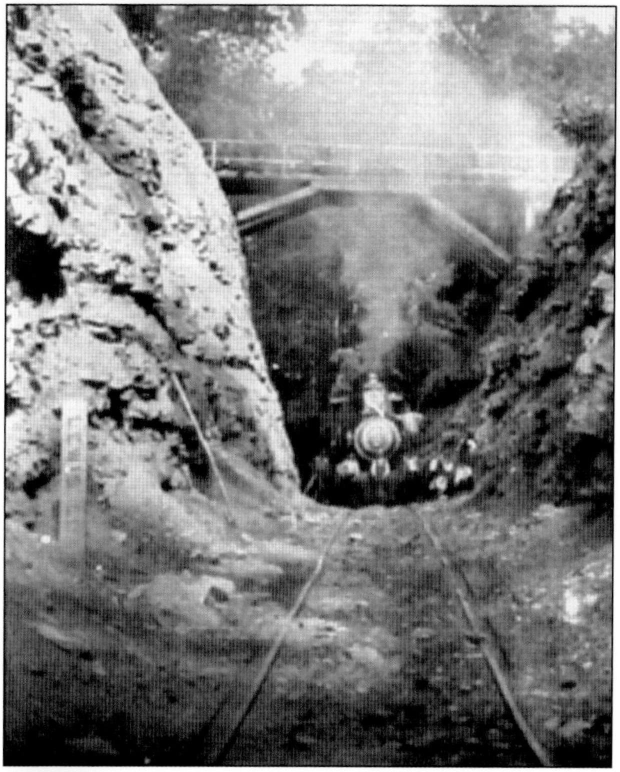

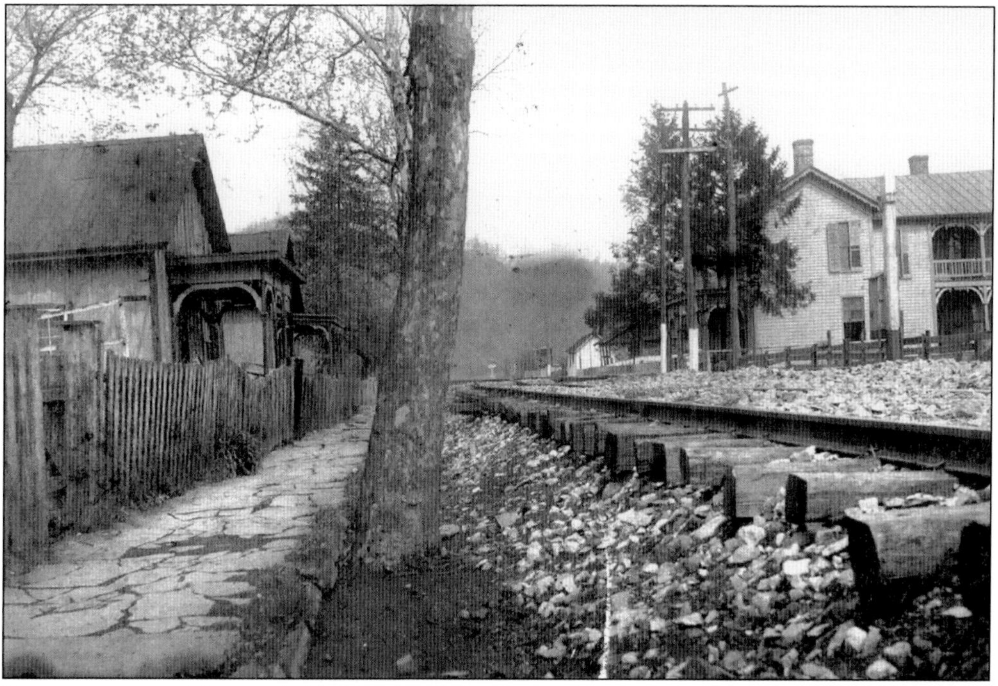

Here is a view of the newly built railroad (single track) in Vanceburg looking west from the depot, probably in the 1890s. The large house seems to be on the site of the present feed mill on Rowley Avenue.

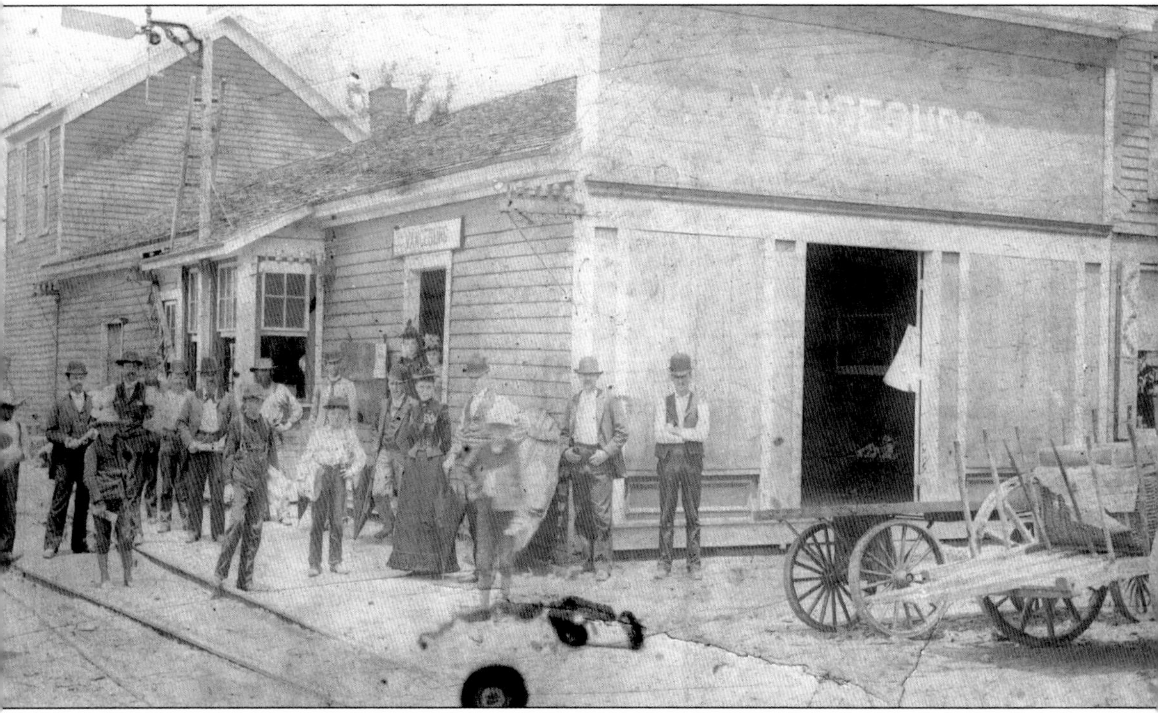

This was Vanceburg's first C&O depot sometime in the early 1890s. Every person in the picture is wearing a hat. The lot was once the site of Lyman B. Baird's Hardware Store, which burned in the 1880s.

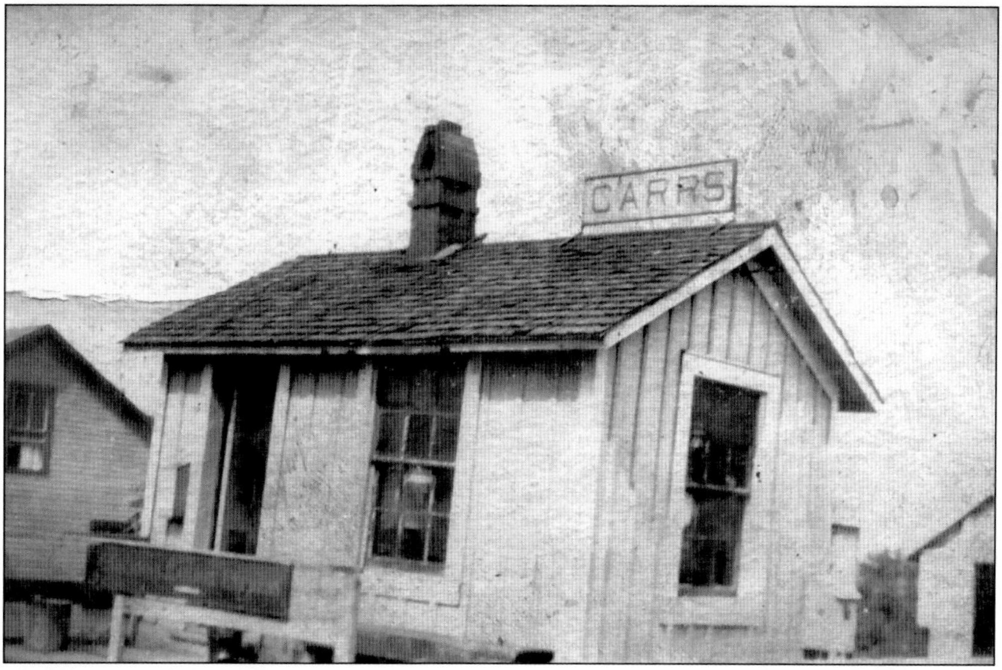

This picture of the C&O depot at Carrs was taken in the early 1930s. The little depot served the small community that grew up around it. Most of the early small village depots were similar structures.

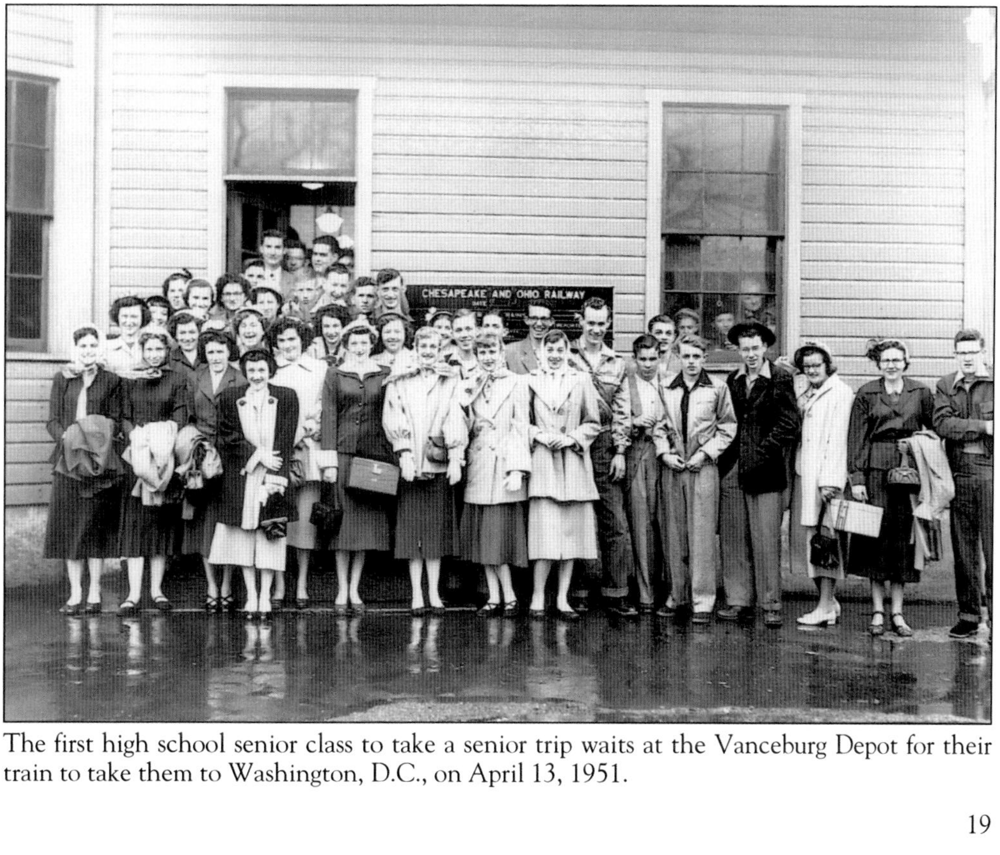

The first high school senior class to take a senior trip waits at the Vanceburg Depot for their train to take them to Washington, D.C., on April 13, 1951.

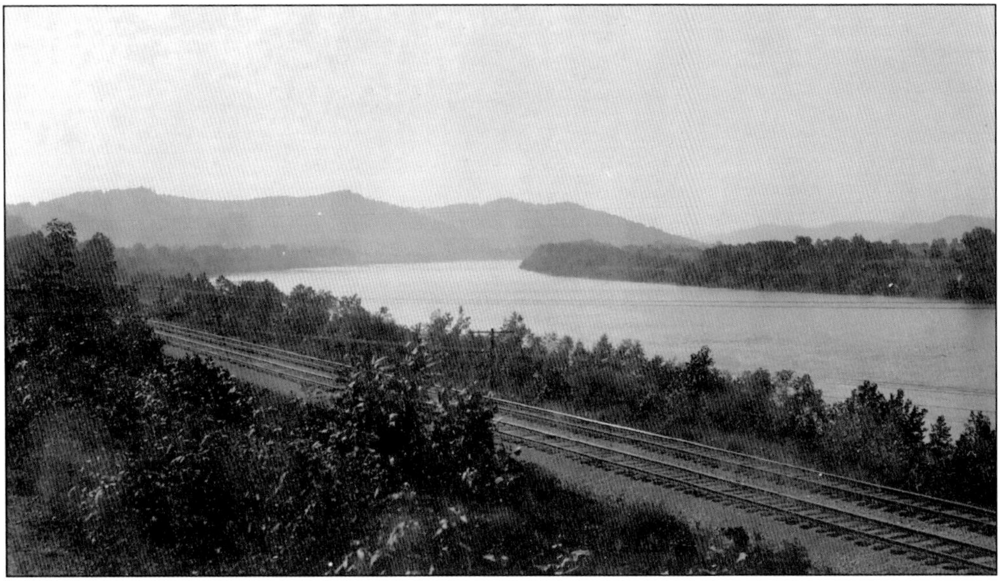

This is the lower curve of the six-mile bend at Vanceburg. The town of Rome, Ohio, is just a short distance below this bend.

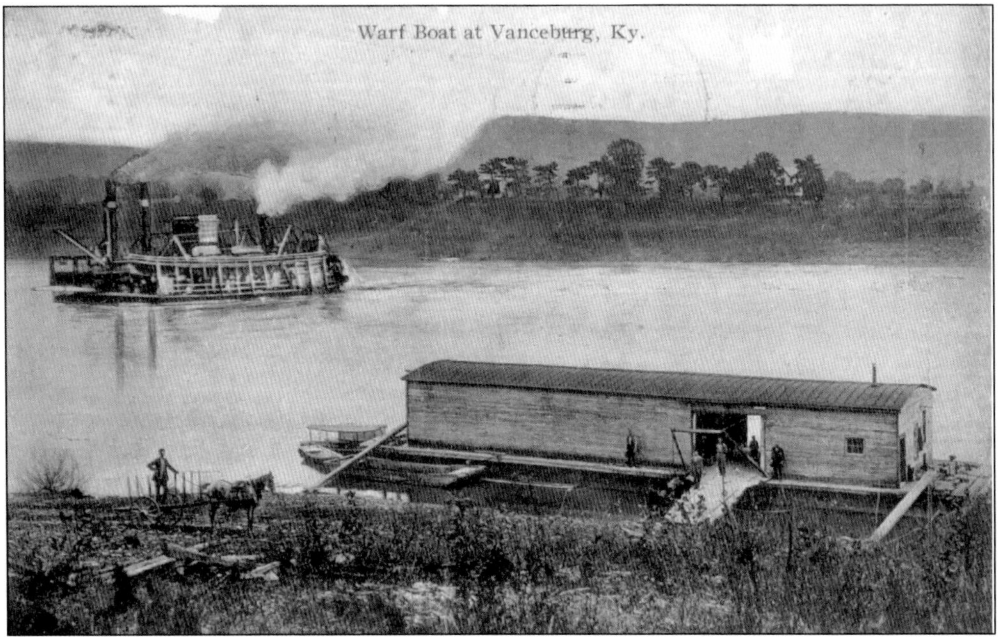

This wharfboat resting at the foot of Main Street in Vanceburg was an important part of commerce in the river days. Cargo was stored here until owners came to take it home.

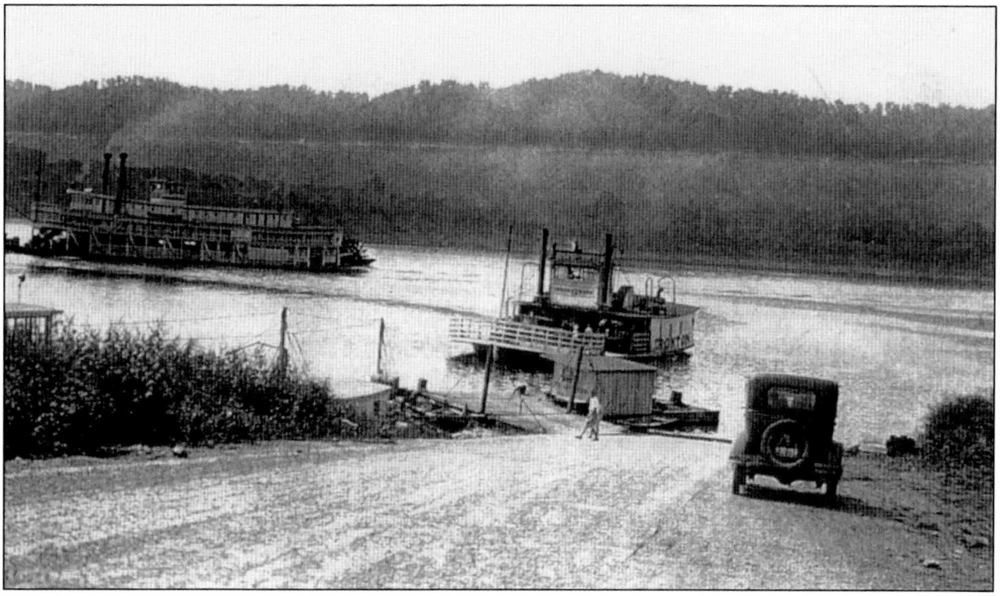

This ferry boat is landing while the steamboat *Ironton* floats in the background. Note the old car waiting to board the ferry.

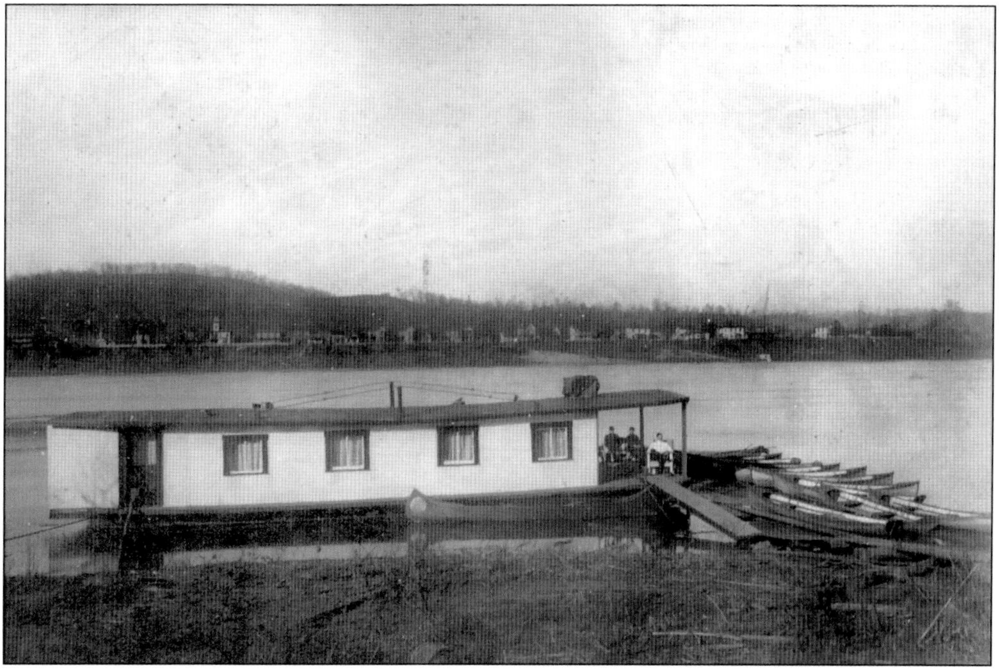

Several people enjoy a day on a houseboat/wharfboat. The Ohio River has long been a popular recreation destination for Lewis Countians.

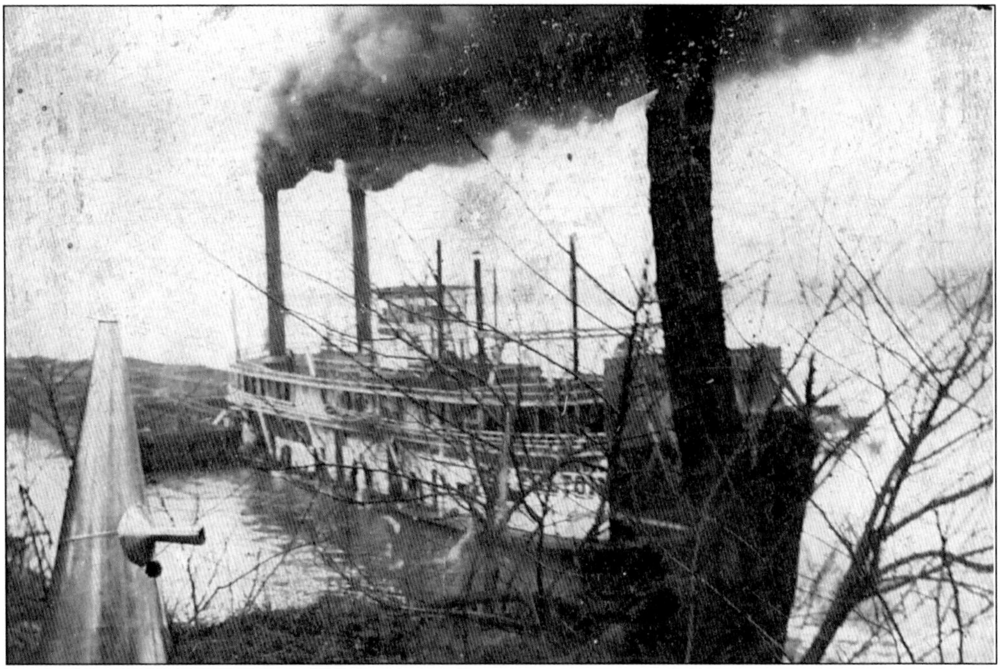

This tugboat, whose name and location are unknown, was typical of the early tugboats that passed by Vanceburg in the 1890s. The metal stand at left may be a riverboat signal.

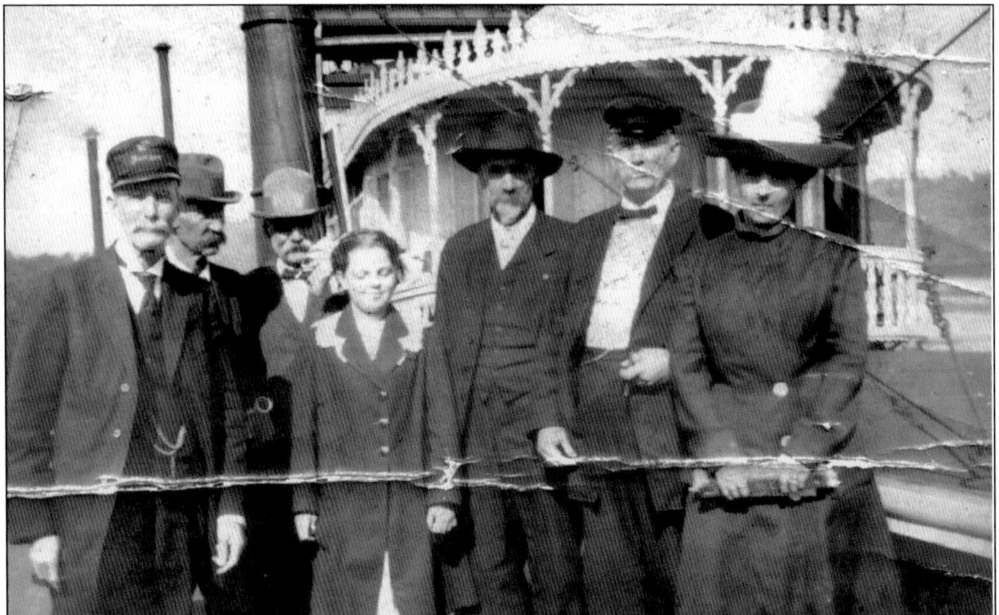

A group of people pose on the deck of a steamboat around the turn of the century. The only one identified is Alexander Bertram (1845–1917) in the back with the Stetson hat. He was born in Scotland and came to the United States about 1850 with his parents, Alexander (1803–1872) and Helen (1806–1876). He was the father of Helen Darlington Bertram Willim (1878–1951) and George Thomas Bertram (1876–1927).

Two

Early Businesses

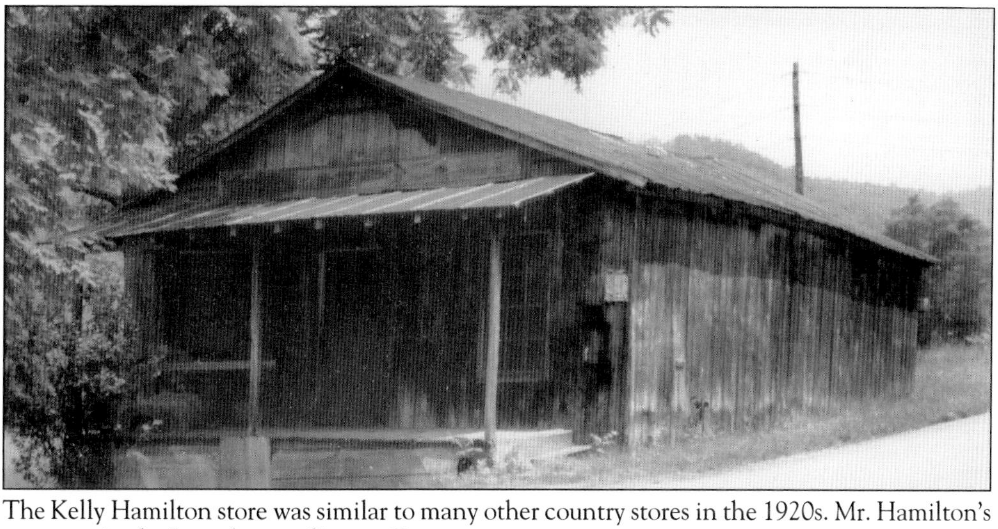

The Kelly Hamilton store was similar to many other country stores in the 1920s. Mr. Hamilton's store was in the Laurel area of Lewis County.

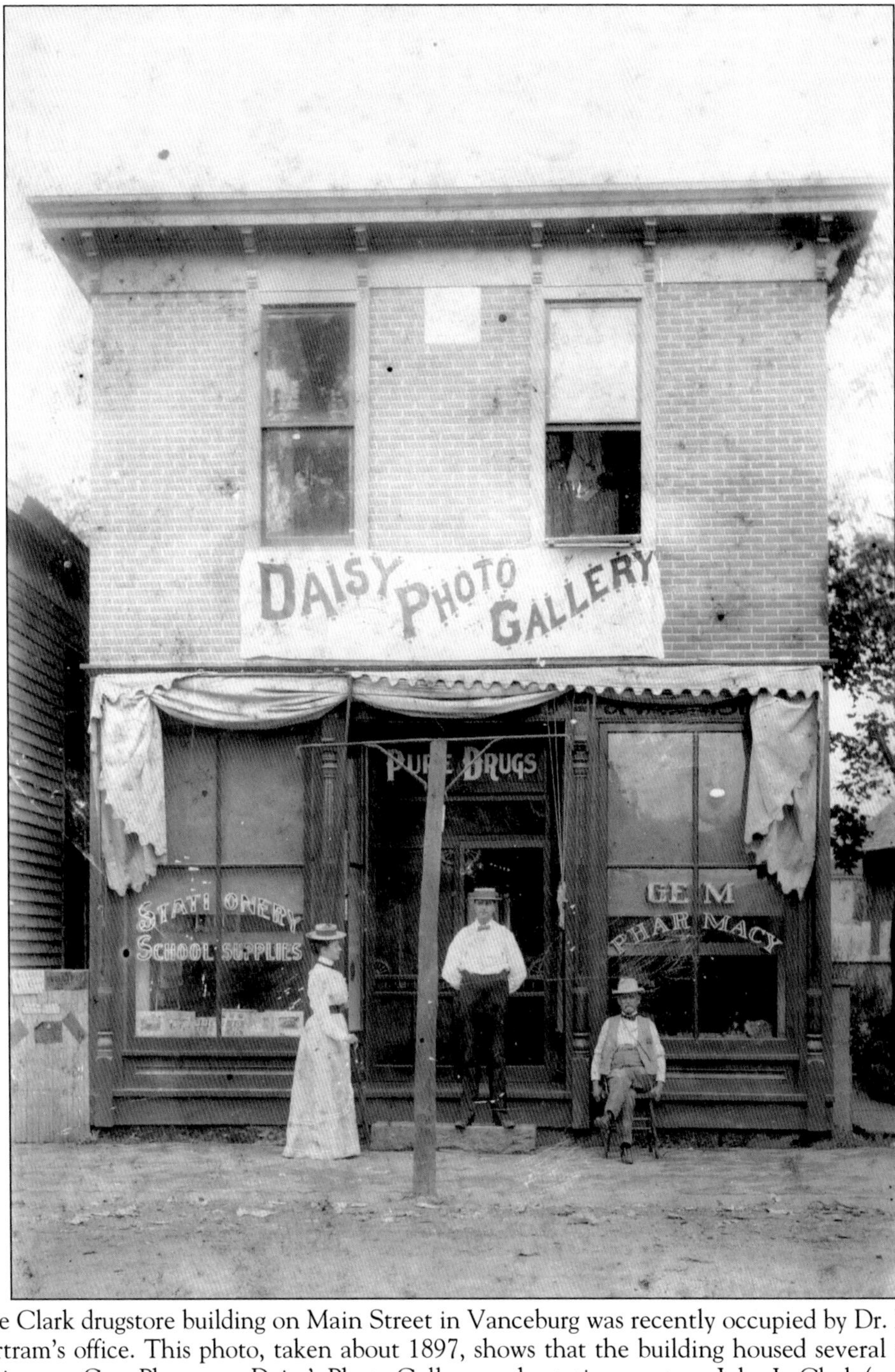

The Clark drugstore building on Main Street in Vanceburg was recently occupied by Dr. Mike Bertram's office. This photo, taken about 1897, shows that the building housed several small businesses: Gem Pharmacy, Daisy's Photo Gallery, and a stationery store. John L. Clark (center) was the proprietor of the drug store until his death on June 30, 1902. On his right is his wife, Clara "Kitten" Carter Clark. Seated is William Birely, operator of the old Vanceburg Mill. Reflections of people on the other side of the street can be seen in the left upstairs window. It is believed the plaque in the upstairs wall was of the Order of United American Mechanics (OUAM), now placed at the Depot Museum.

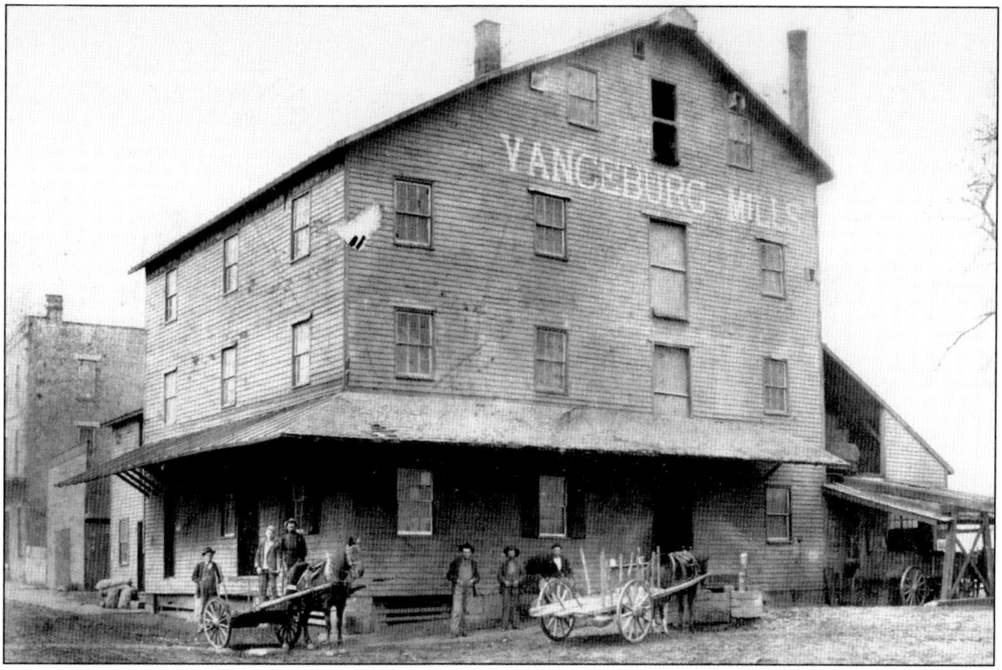

The Vanceburg Mill was built by William C. Halbert around the time of the Civil War. After the war, he sold it to William C. Birely, who operated it until his death. This picture was taken some time in the 1890s, before the third floor was removed. It stood until the 1980s. Part of Vanceburg's Veterans Memorial Park is laid out on the spot where this mill stood.

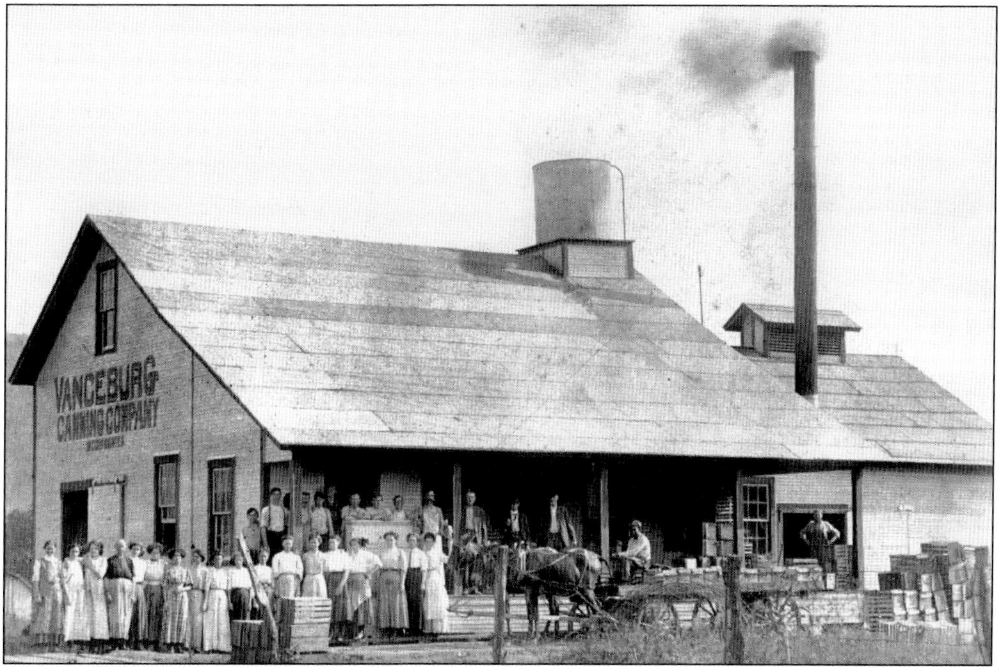

The Vanceburg Canning Factory was built in 1911 and stood west of the River Road Bridge. Several small houses stand on the site now. It "folded up" after a few years. Miss Lelia Stout, the only one identified, is third from the right in the row of women.

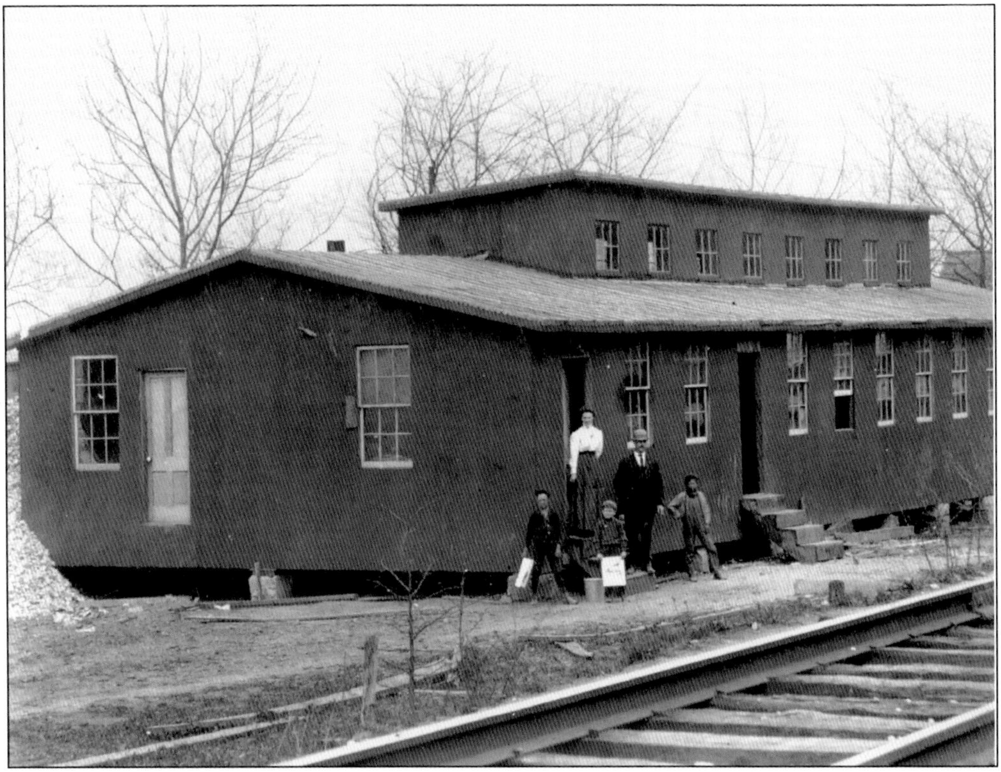

This old button factory, pictured about 1911, stood in the east end of Vanceburg between the railroad and the river. Some of the mussel shells used for cutting out buttons can be seen in the background.

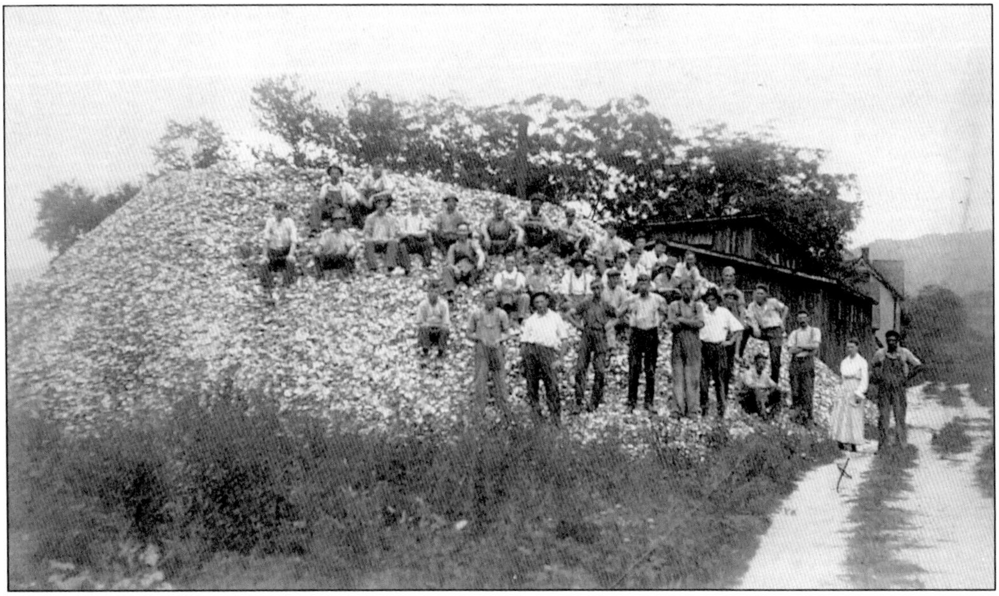

The Vanceburg Button Factory (about 1911) can be seen behind this mountain of mussel shells, from which buttons were cut. The building sat between the railroad and the river. None of the workers are identified except Exie Marshall, standing at the bottom second from the right.

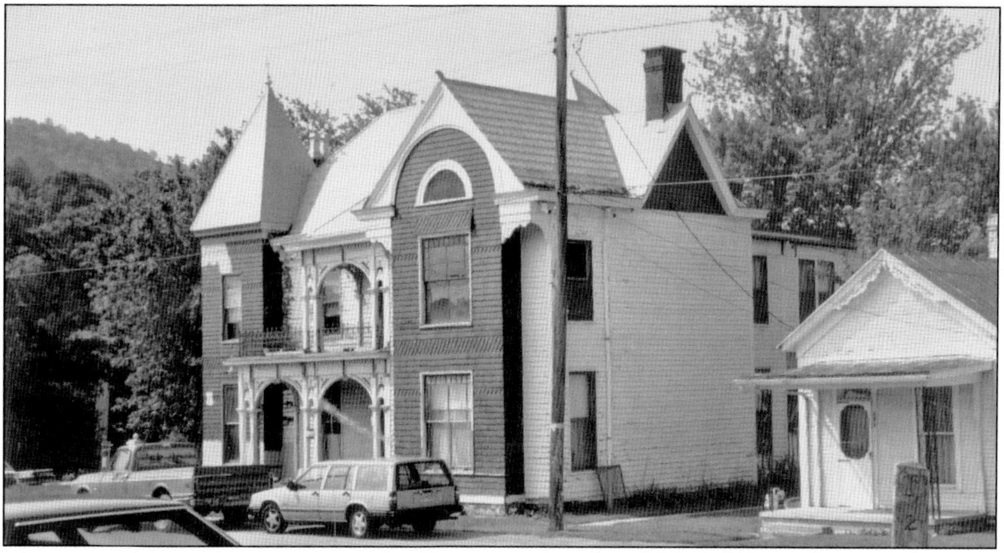

This view of the Commercial Hotel was taken around 1990. The hotel was formerly the home of Judge George Morgan Thomas and is now being restored to its original condition.

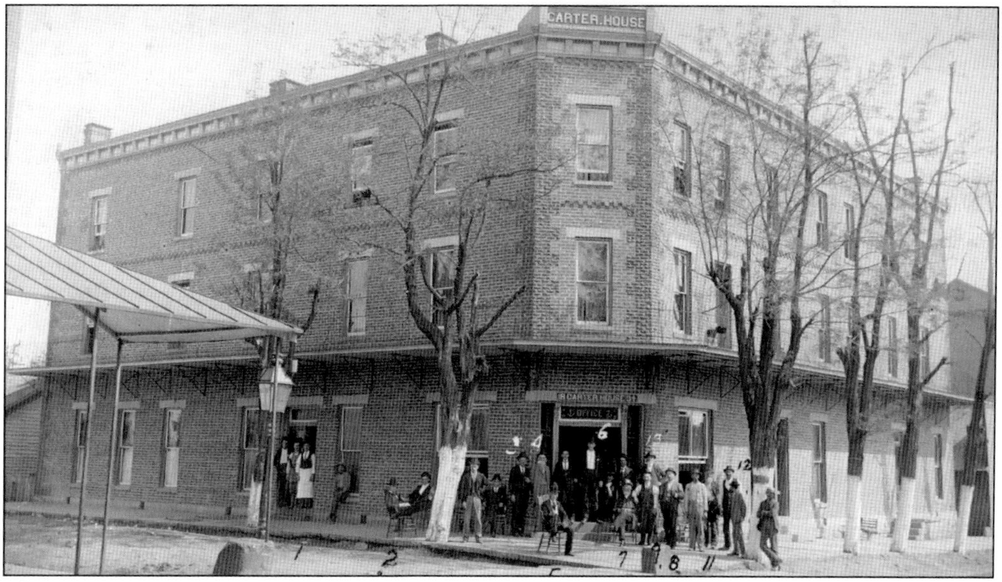

The New Carter House Hotel, on the northwest corner of Main and Second Streets, was built shortly after the old Carter House burned in 1893. The stone above the front door says, "Carter House, 1894." It was said to be one of the finest hotels along the river at that time. It had wrought-iron balconies and was adorned with Italian marble. Jack Carter took the job as manager in 1897. In 1920, a fire badly damaged the building and, later, the top story was removed. At left is an unusual modern-type awning and light fixture. There is also a step for people getting into carriages. The persons marked with numbers are: 1. Gaines Clayton, the bartender; 2. W.W. Dugan; 3. G.W. Stamper; 4. George M. Thomas; 5. Arthur Ruggles; 6. Dud Rummonds; 7. Lindsay Ruggles; 8. James Gardner; 9. Ben Davis; 10 is omitted; 11. Jim Adams; 12. Enos Hays; and 13. Thomas H. Carter, owner of the hotel. The wheelbarrow (barely visible, even in the original) belonged to Jim Trice, the African-American porter. The building has been remodeled several times and is now vacant.

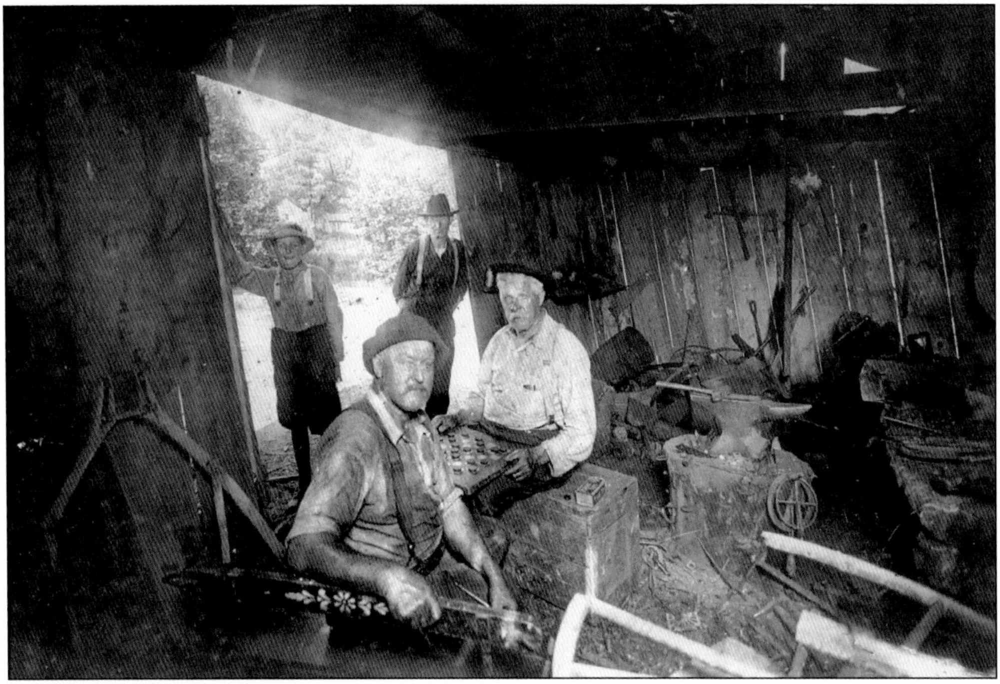

Chapman's Blacksmith Shop was located at Quincy on Briery Creek, behind the Howland (now Parson) home, about 1915. Shown from left to right are (front row) Bud Raike and James Howland playing checkers; (in the doorway) Luke Chapman (1902–1955) and an unidentified man.

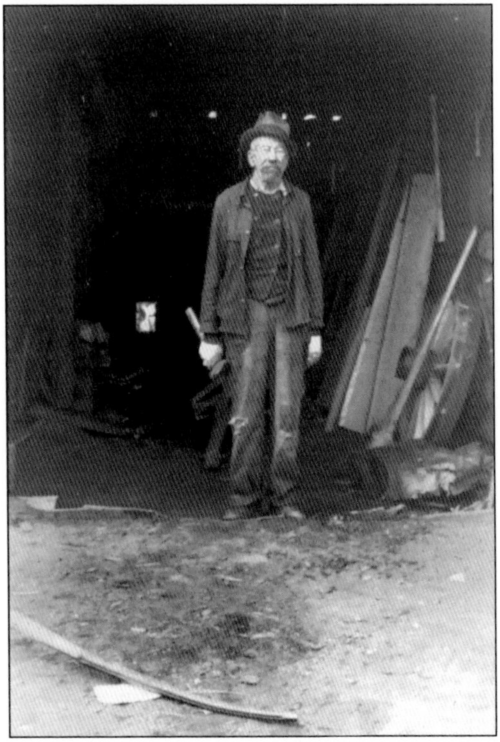

Ralph P. Gulley (1884–1959) was the last blacksmith in Vanceburg. He is shown here in the late 1930s or early 1940s. He was killed by a train in 1959.

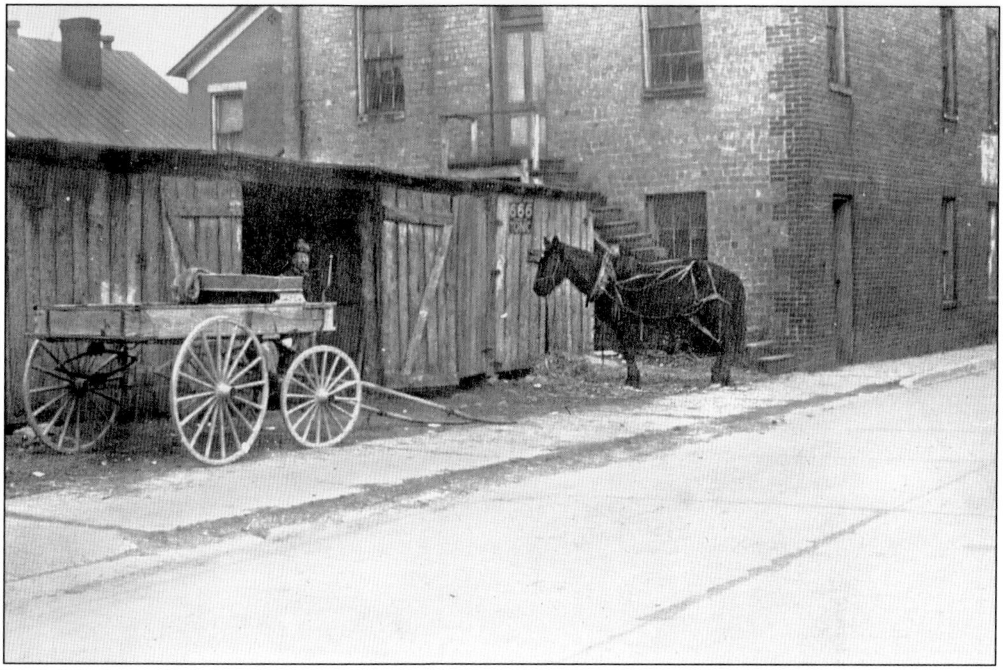

This blacksmith shop was located behind the present Harmany House in Vanceburg, on the spot that was occupied by a garage for many years.

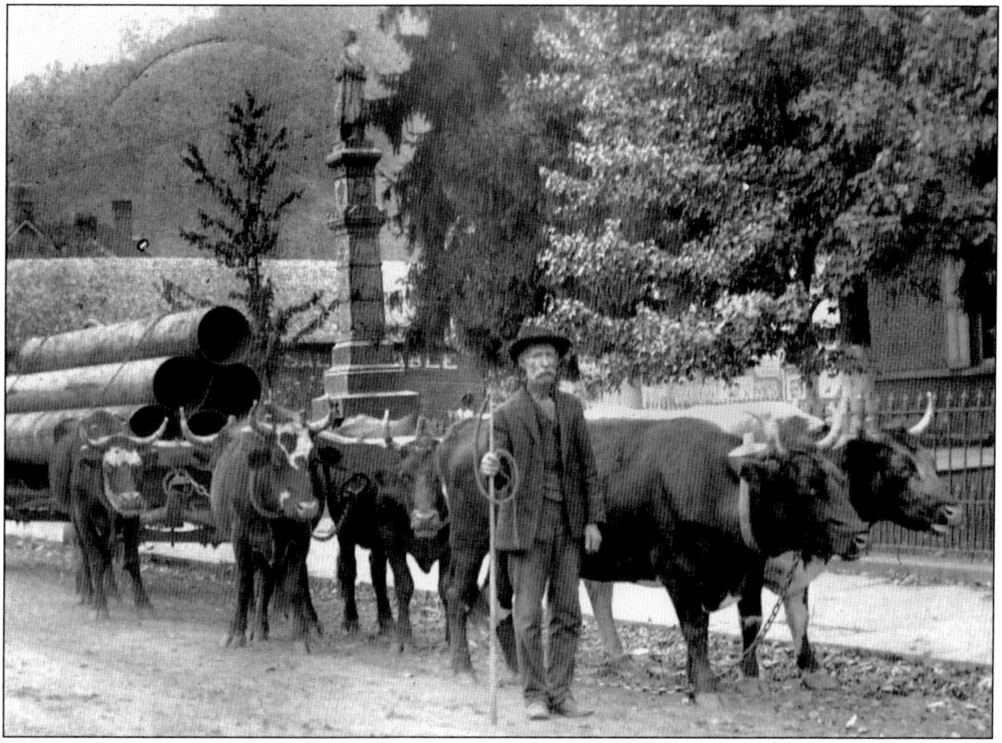

An unidentified man is driving three or four teams of oxen hauling gas lines in front of the old courthouse and the monument about 1907. In the background is the Pollitt Livery Stable.

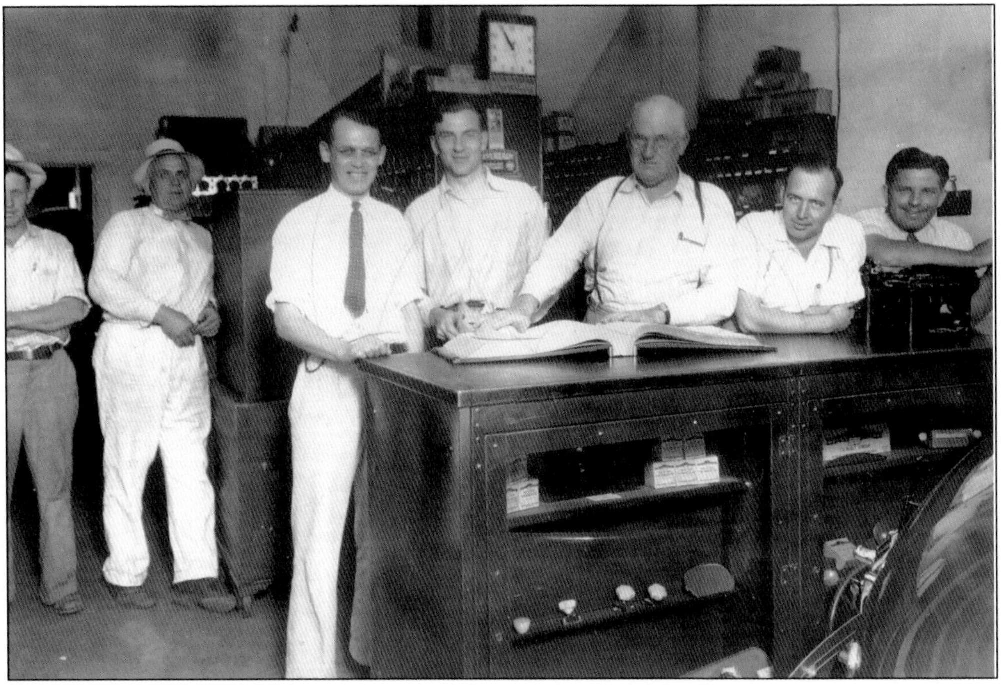

Shown here at the J.F. Bertram Chevrolet dealership in 1939, from left to right, are Winston Lykins, Frank Lykins, Owen Cooper, William Bertram, John F. Bertram Sr., "Bun" Hinton, and George M. Plummer. This was the area's first Chevrolet dealership.

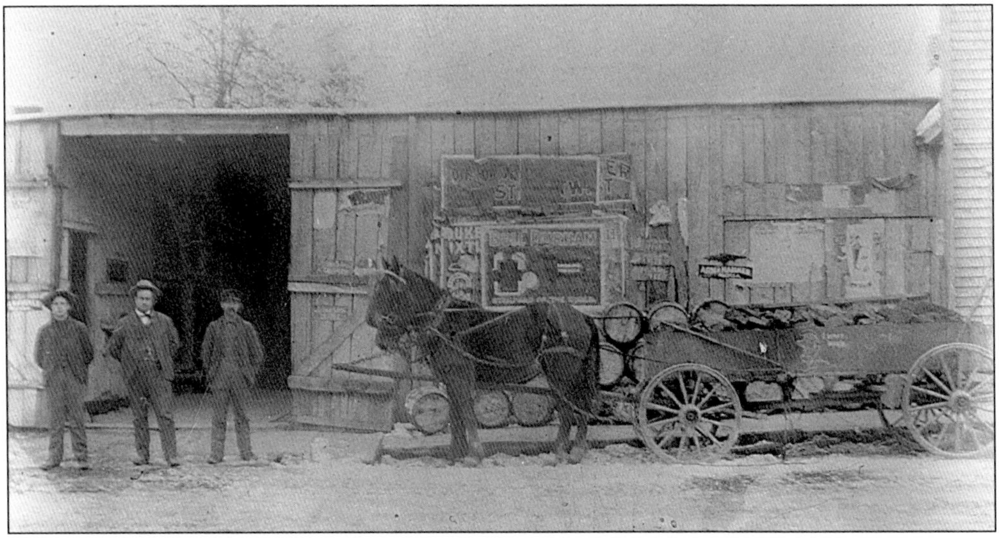

This looks like a livery stable or feed store. The men, from left to right, are W. "Tidy" Staggs, Grant McDaniel, and unidentified. This building stood on the northwest corner of Market and Third Street. It is reminiscent of Chris Caines's advertisement for delivery of coal and salt: "There's coal and salt to be had at the river, And a galloping mule that's glad to deliver, An excellent mule that's both willing and able, And would rather haul coal than to stand in the stable." The signs above the horses advertise tobacco: Duke's Mixture and Bull Durham. The little black sign advertises Arm & Hammer Soda. This is now a vacant lot beside the Trace Creek Construction Company.

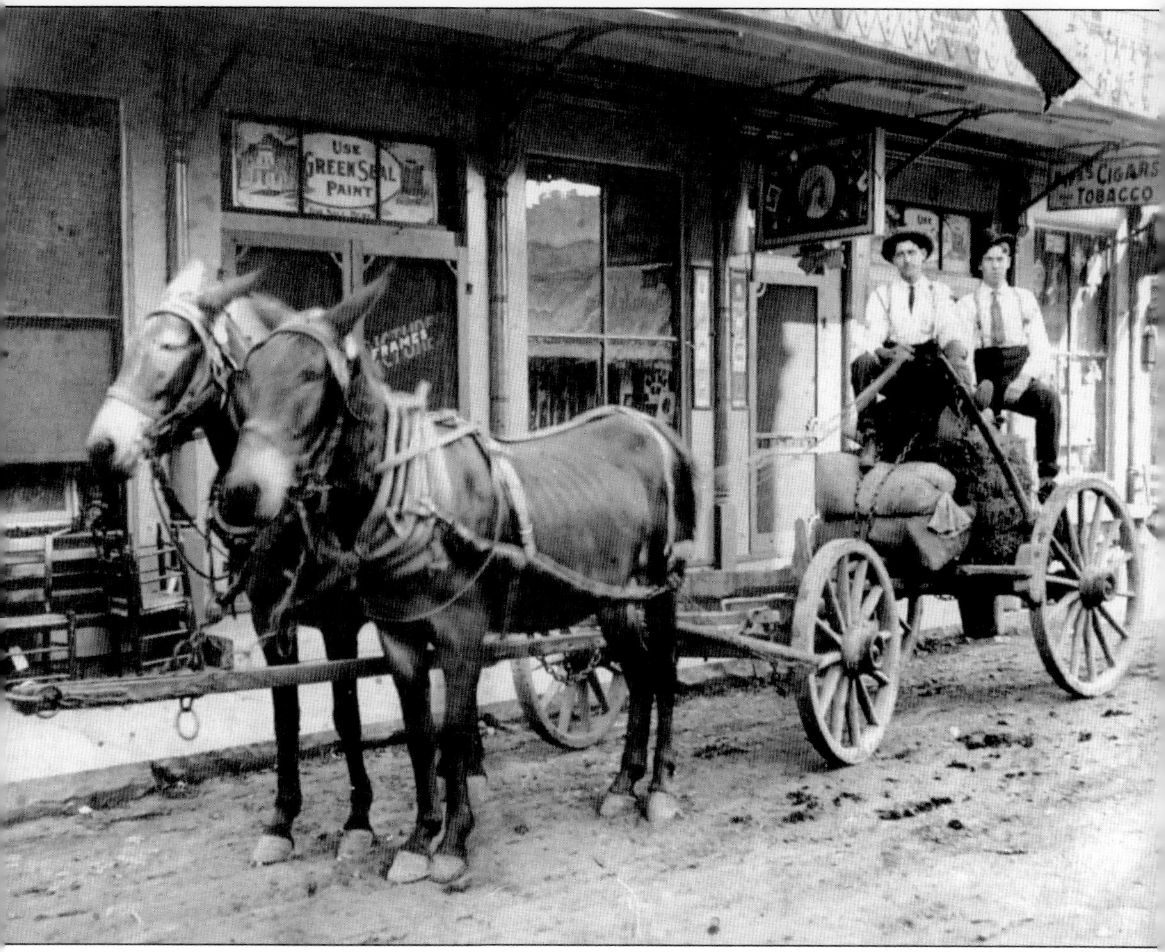

Mr. Stafford (left) and Will Cox (right) are the two young gentlemen riding in their horse-drawn wagon on Second Street. Merchant advertisements include Green Seal paints, picture frames, pipes, cigars, and tobacco.

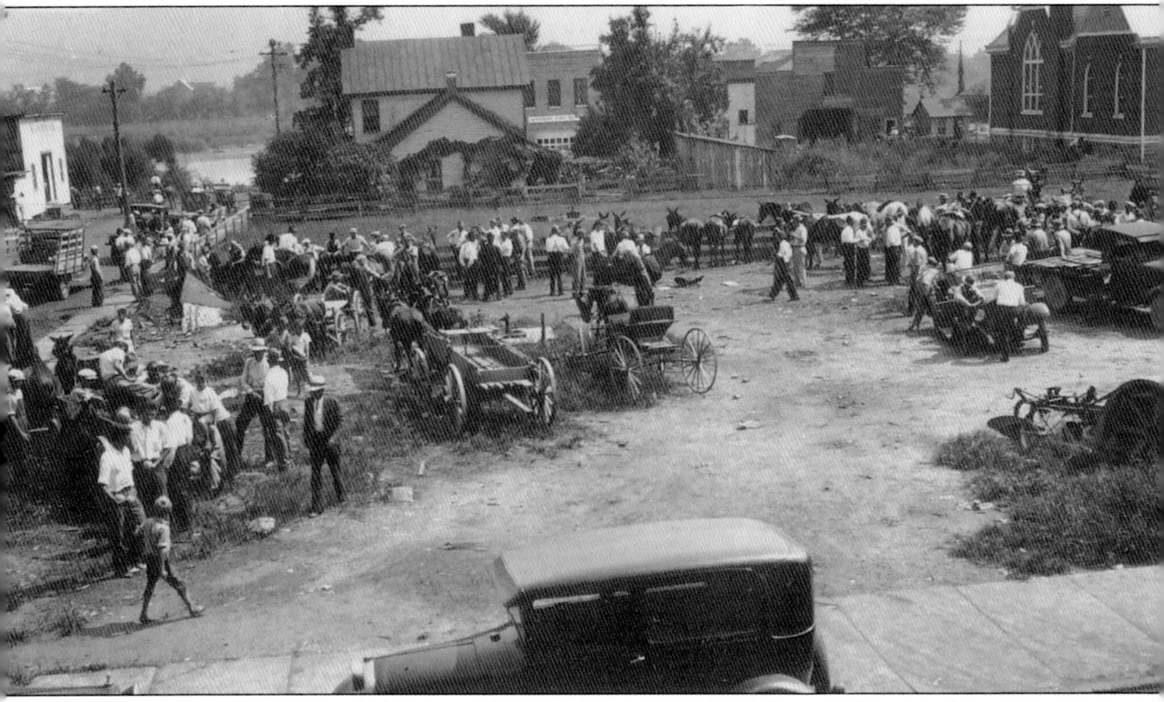

This scene of a stock sale day was taken on the north side of Second Street in Vanceburg in 1934. The old mill can be seen at left, and the Kimble-Jarrells home and the Christian church can be seen in the background. The photographer was standing on the lot where the St. Charles Hotel burned in March 1926, before construction started on the Holder-Lykins Law Offices and the Professional Care Pharmacy.

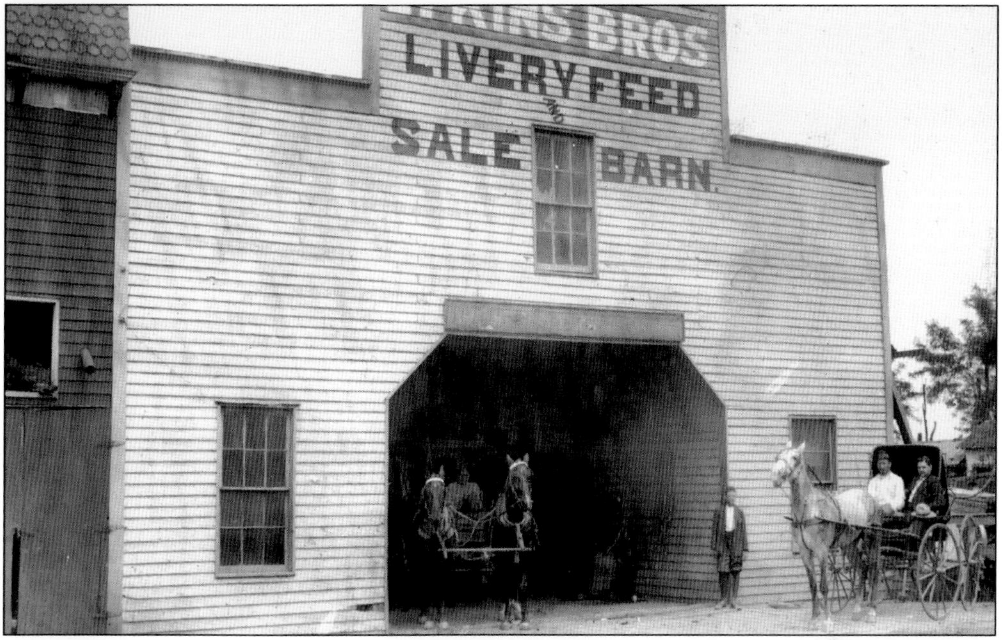

The Lykins Brothers Feed Store was the livery feed and sale barn operated by the Lykins brothers—Frank, Jesse, and Bruce—at Petersville.

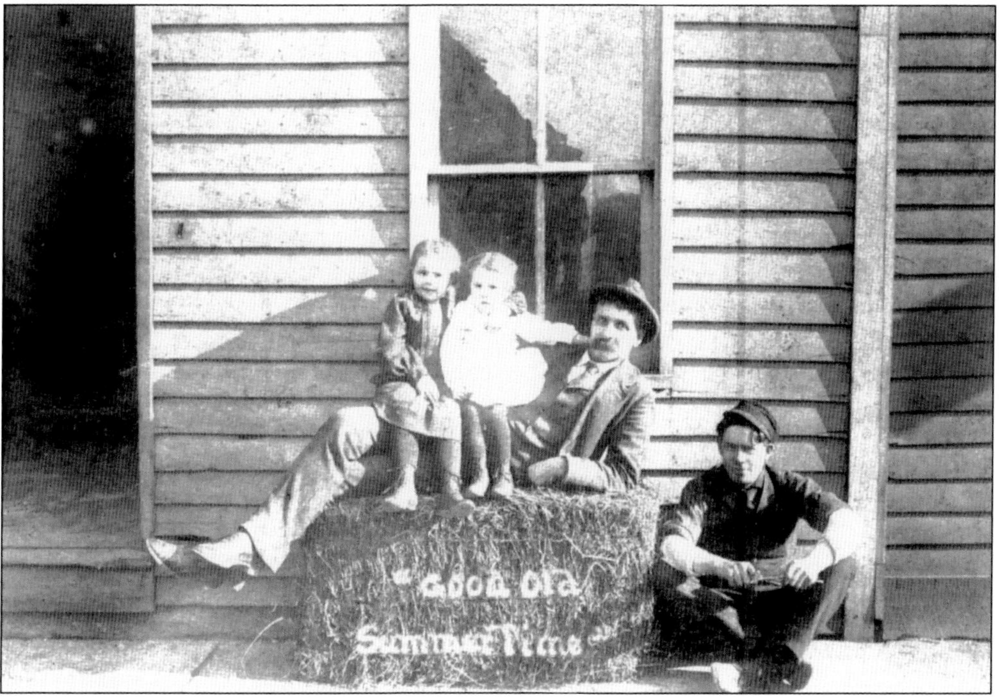

This was taken in front of the "Doc" Shumate Feed Store on Market Street, opposite the current Trace Creek Construction Company building, about 1905. The two girls, Ramona and Lois Mathewson, are standing in front of D.B. Shumate. Will C. Cox is seated at the right of the bale of hay. The building later became the I.W. and C.A. Staggs Feed Store and was still standing in 1975. It is now the parking lot of the Vanceburg Baptist Church on Market Street.

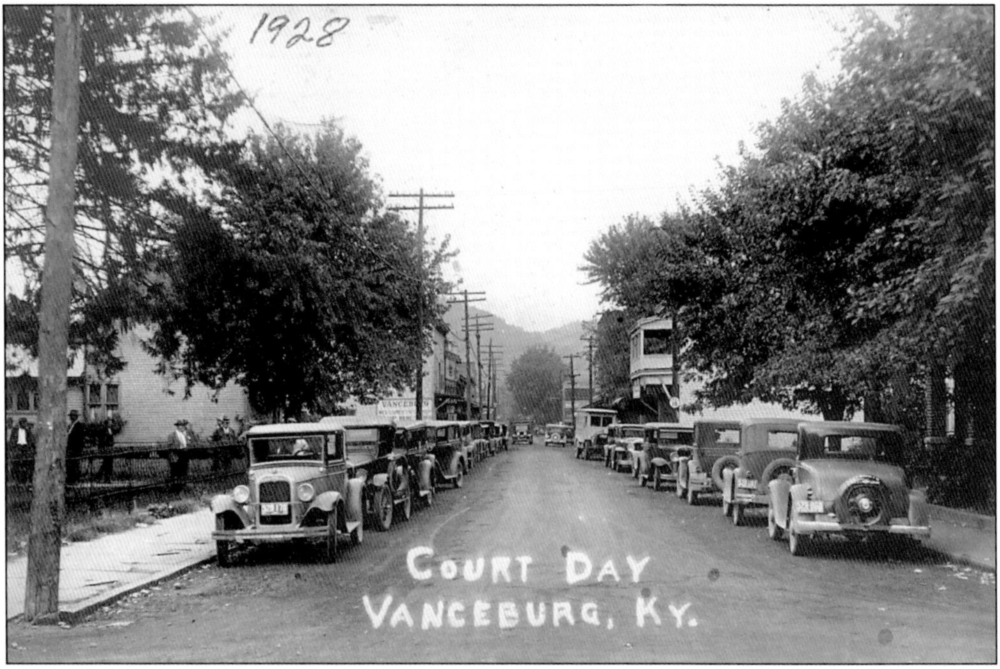

Vanceburg's streets filled for a court day in 1928. Court days were important social events, with people traveling many miles to take part in the sales surrounding the courthouse.

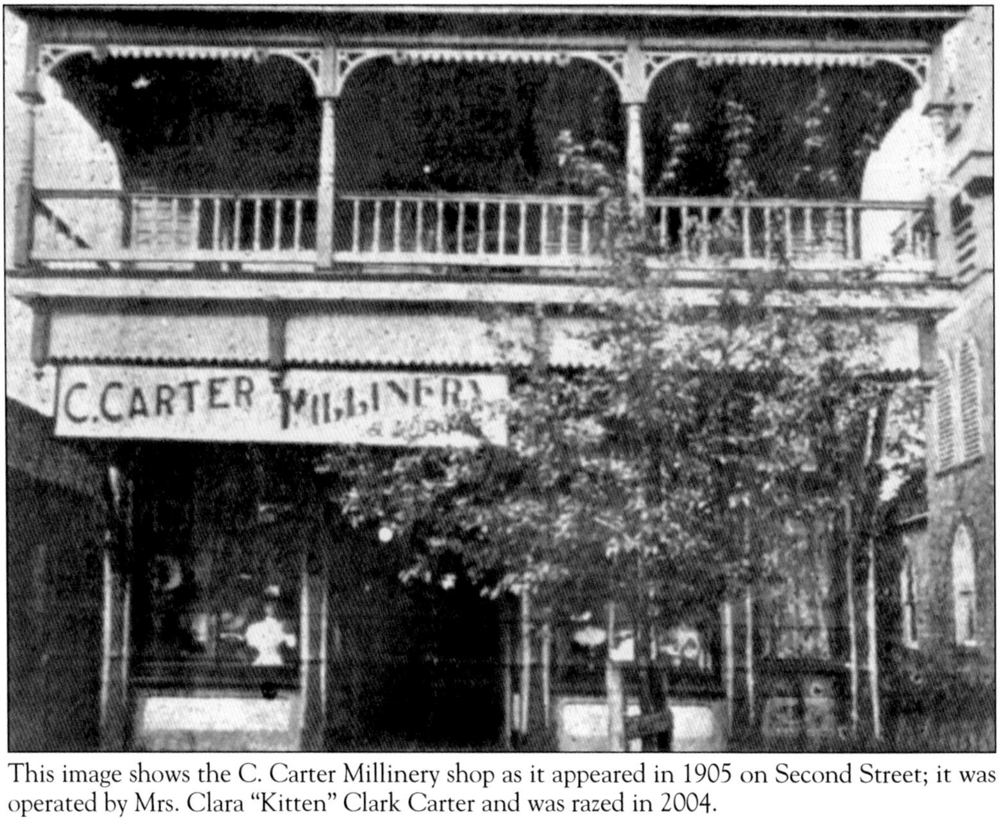

This image shows the C. Carter Millinery shop as it appeared in 1905 on Second Street; it was operated by Mrs. Clara "Kitten" Clark Carter and was razed in 2004.

William A. Voiers Sr. built this shoe store in 1876. The Masonic Lodge is housed upstairs. This building was damaged badly by a great fire on the night of December 22–23, 1913, and was rebuilt in 1914.

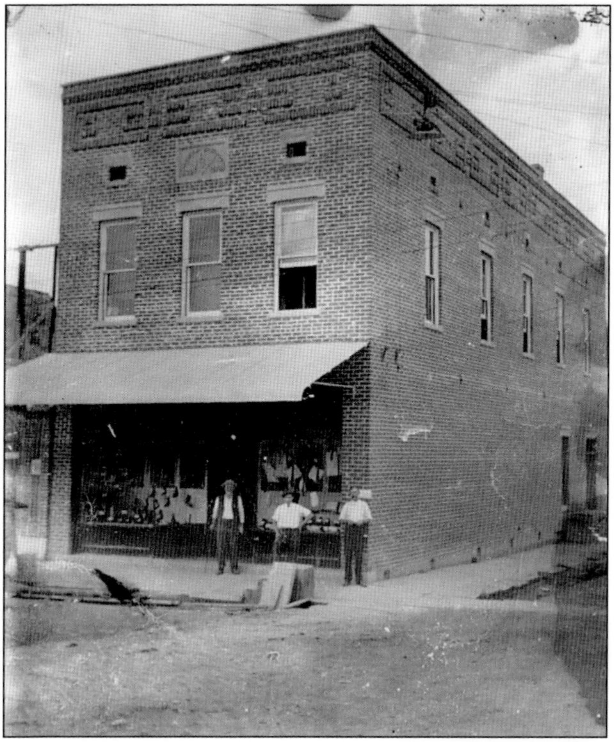

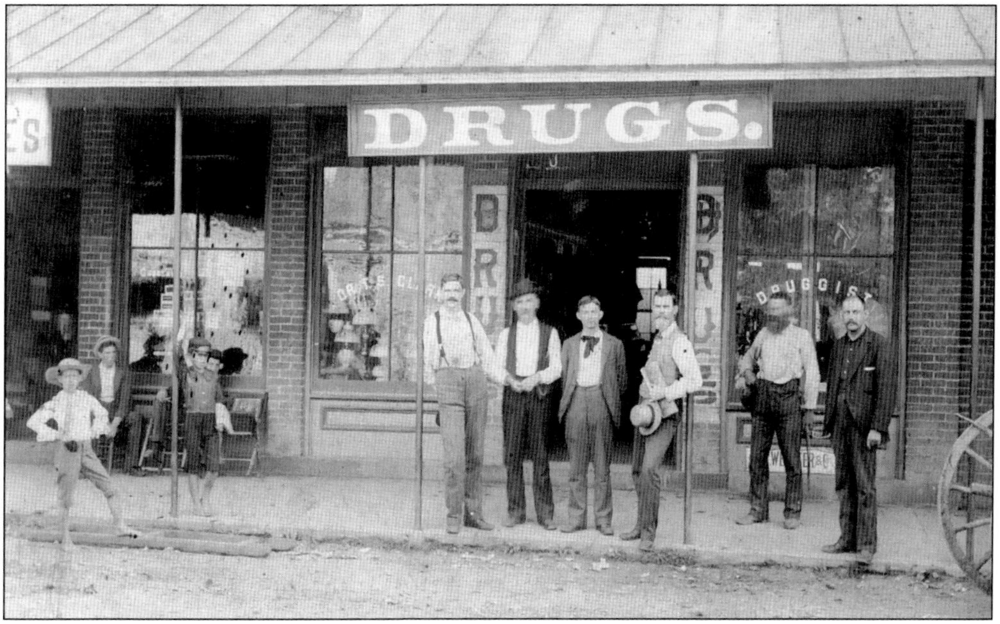

This is the drug store of Dr. T.S. Clark and John L. Clark in 1893, when it was in the upper half of the present-day Ron's IGA in Vanceburg. Shown here, from left to right, are four unidentified boys, John L. Clark, Joe E. Pugh, Ed Pugh, an unidentified man with hat in hand, an unidentified man standing by window, and Ernest C. Applegate. J.W. Cox's Groceries can be seen at left, and at right is a portion of W.A. Voiers's Shoe Store, all of which burned on the night of December 22–23, 1913, and was rebuilt the next year.

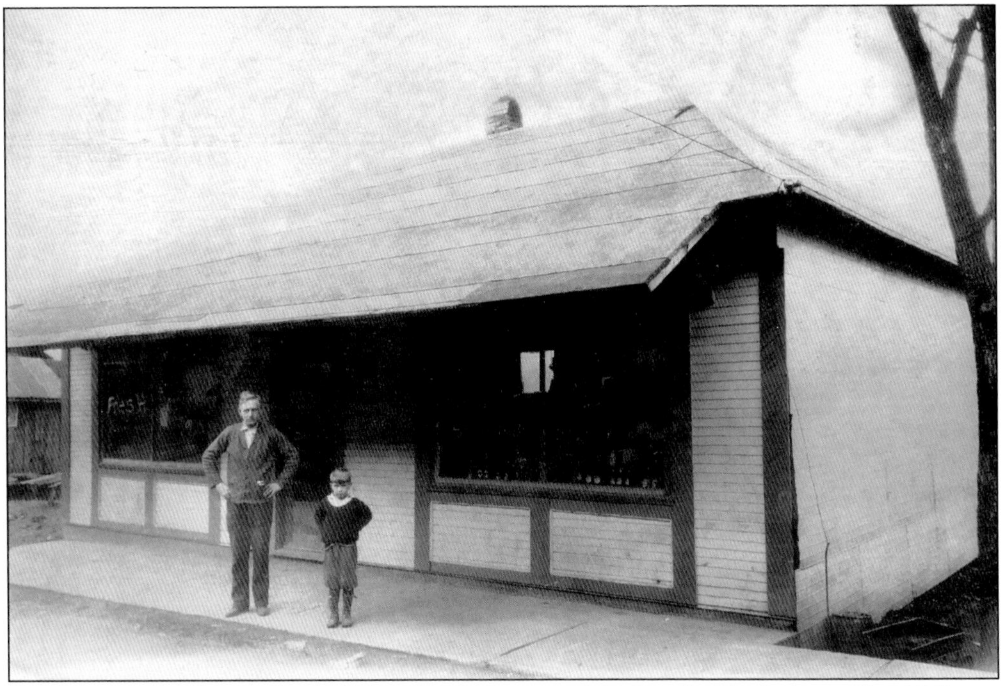

The Plummer Grocery is shown here around 1929, set in the small triangle formed by old Route 10 and the railroad. Later, to the left, the Gooch family built a small brick grocery store. Shown here are Oscar M. Plummer and his son, Luther K.

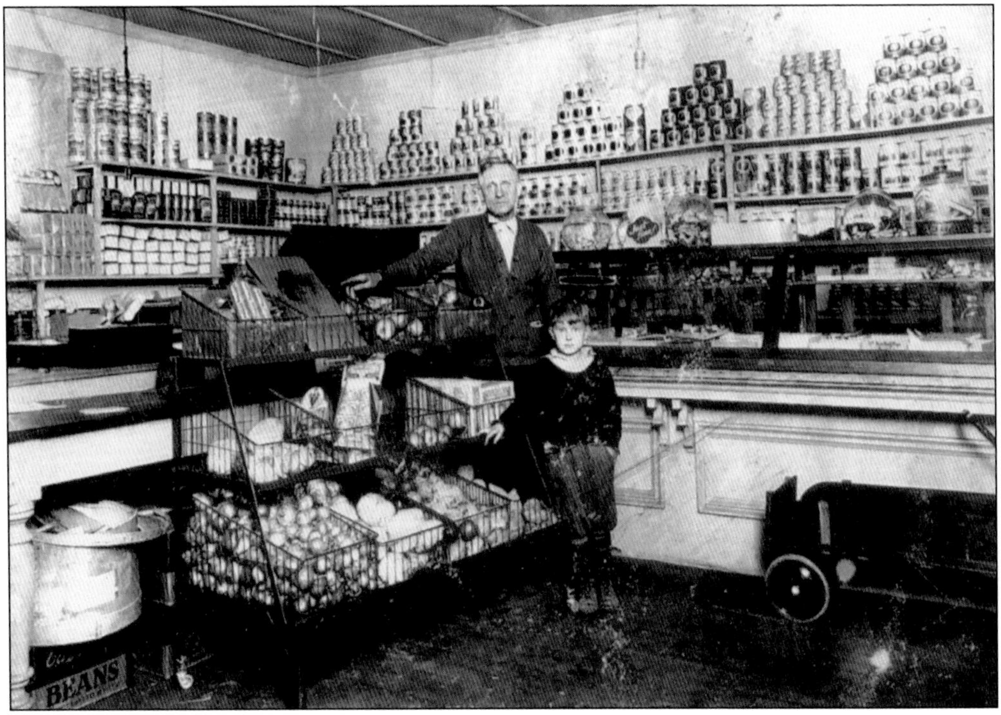

Oscar M. Plummer Sr. and his son, Luther K. Plummer (born 1923), are inside their grocery store on East Second Street in Vanceburg about 1929.

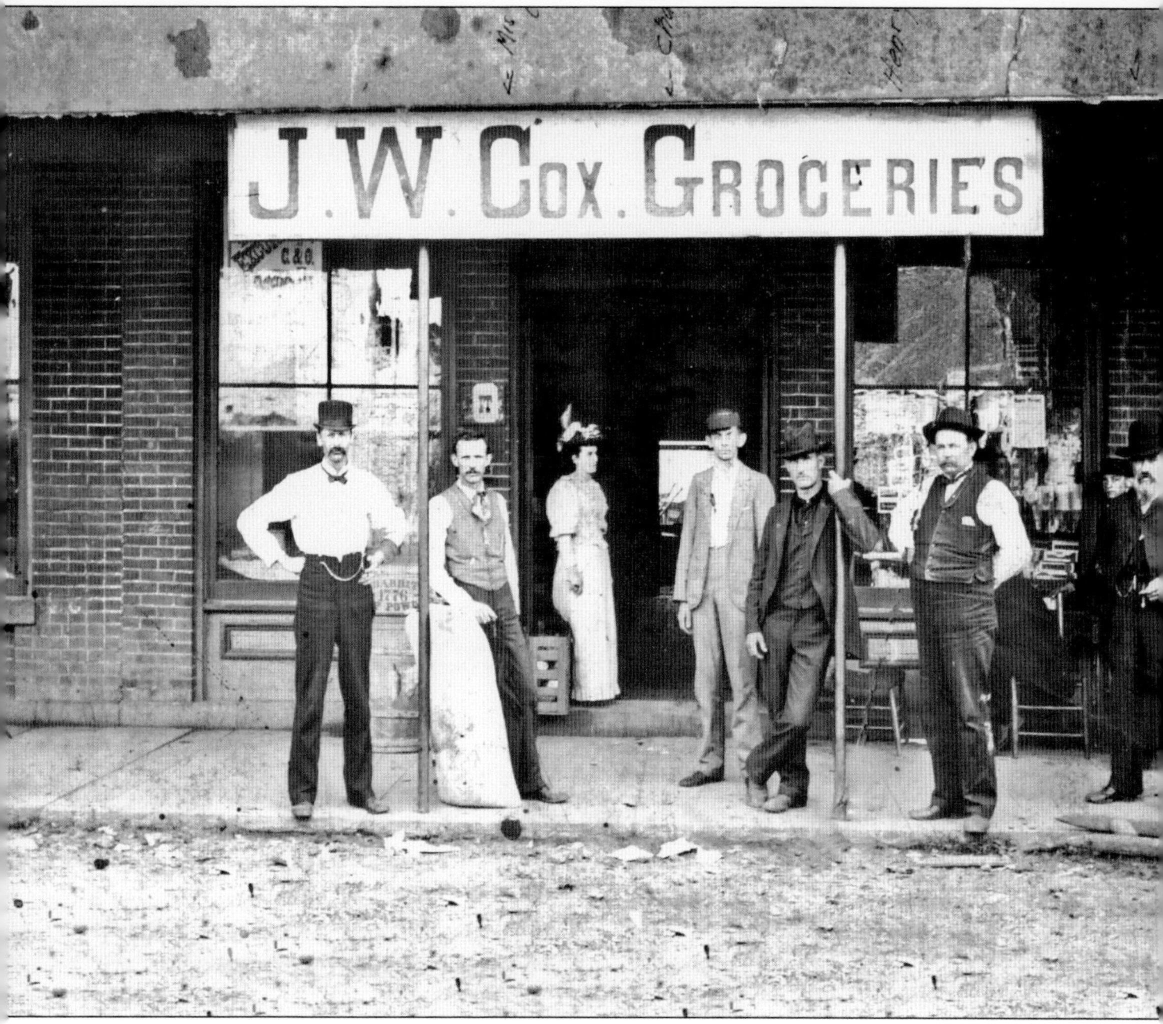

J.W. "Skinny" Cox's Grocery on Second Street in Vanceburg (now the site of Ron's IGA) burned on the night of December 22–23, 1913. Shown here, from left to right, are J.W. "Skinny" Cox, Sam Bruce, Mrs. Josephine Bruce, Charles Hammond, unidentified, Henry McElhaney, and Dr. William H. Campbell. The boy behind Dr. Campbell is unidentified.

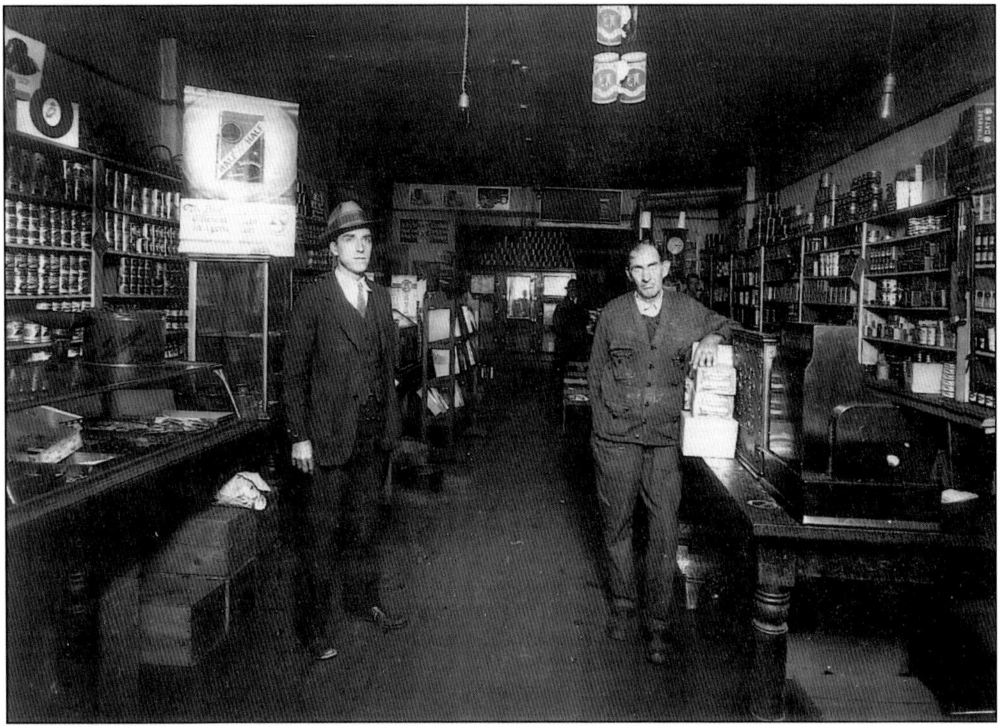

This is an inside view of the Adams & Ruark Grocery Store in the early 1900s.

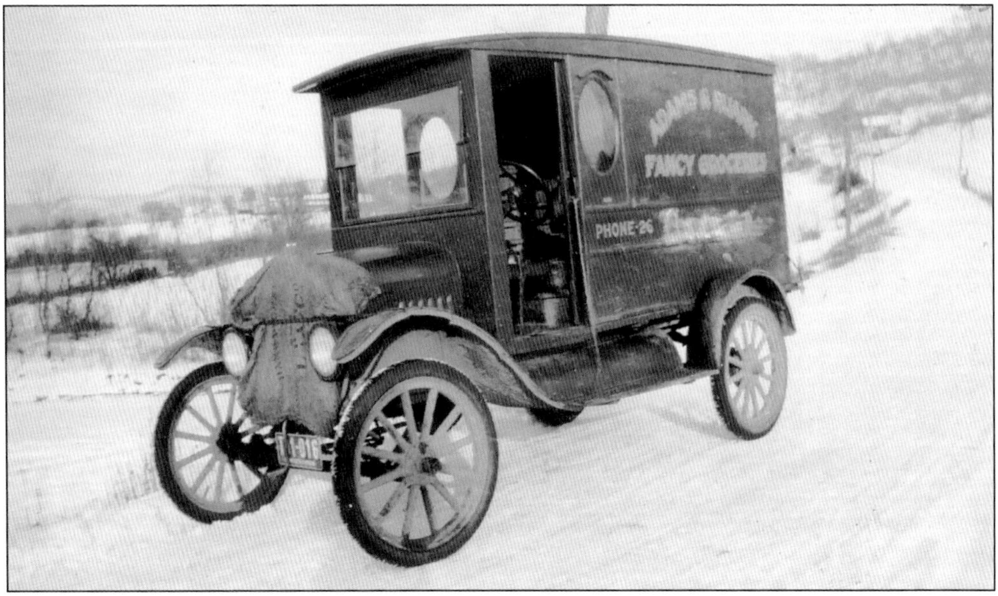

D.L. Lykins drove this Adams & Ruark Grocery delivery truck in 1926. Notice the two-digit phone number and the radiator "coat" on the hood.

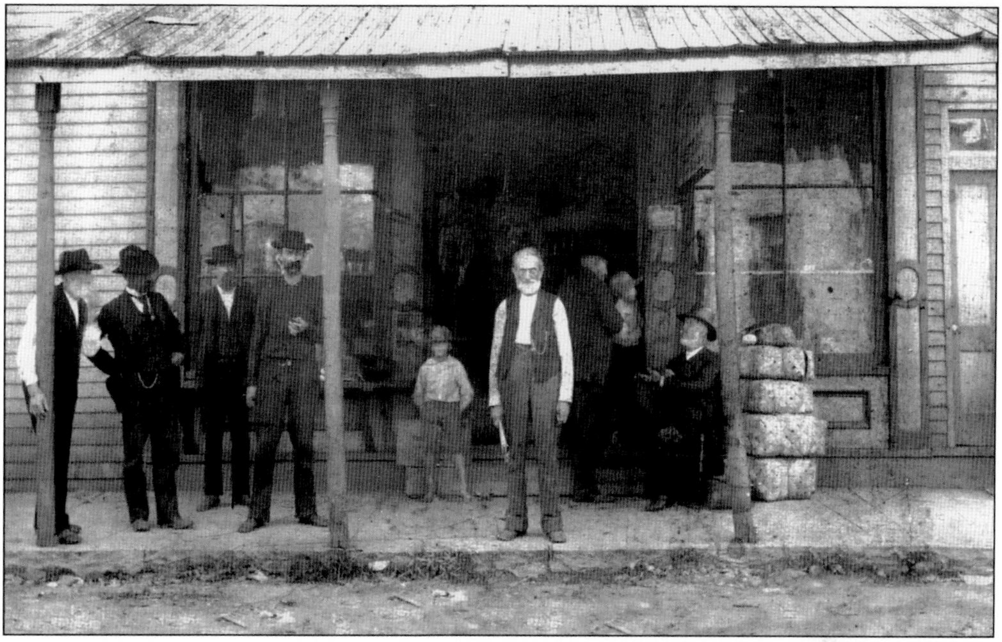

The Barber Grocery store was located on Second Street in Vanceburg, on the present site of the Justice Center. The gentleman in front with a white beard is the owner, Dr. R.G. Barber, a Civil War veteran. Fourth from the left is Tom Wilson, and the gentleman seated at the far right is Lindsay Ruggles.

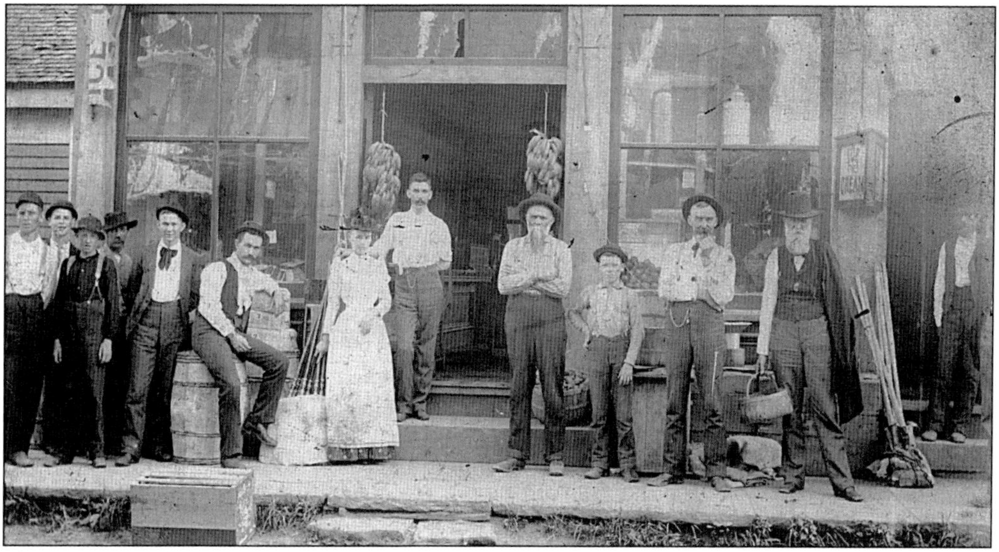

The L.M. Stricklett Store stood where the present-day Kegley Furniture Store is located on Second Street in Vanceburg. The picture was taken some time before 1899, probably in the late 1890s. From left to right are two unidentified young men; Jim Carroll with the black shirt and white suspenders; an unidentified man behind Carroll; Ed Pugh with the flowing black tie; Mason "Mace" Parker sitting on the barrel; Maggie Fryer Stricklett, wife of owner Lewis M. Stricklett, who is standing on the step; William "Bill" Plummer beneath the bananas; Garland Ruark; Joe E. Pugh with the watch chain; and Judge J.R. Garland, the man with the basket and beard, who died in 1899. The man at the far right standing in the shadows is unidentified.

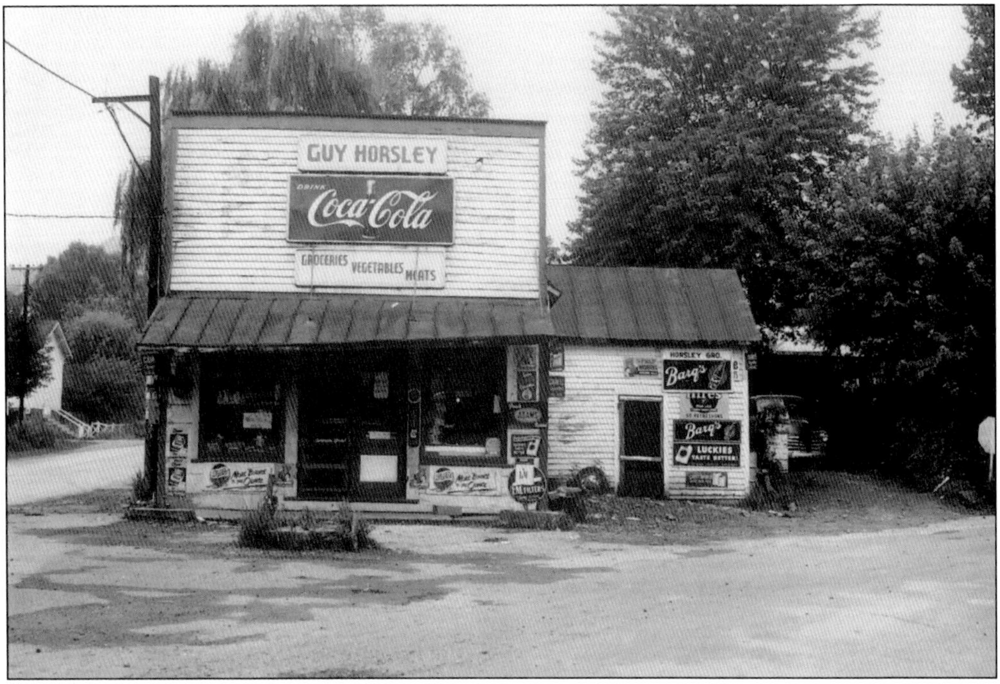

Guy Horsley's old grocery store at the forks of Lexington Avenue and Shelton Drive in Vanceburg, shown here probably in the late 1950s, was typical of many small general stores.

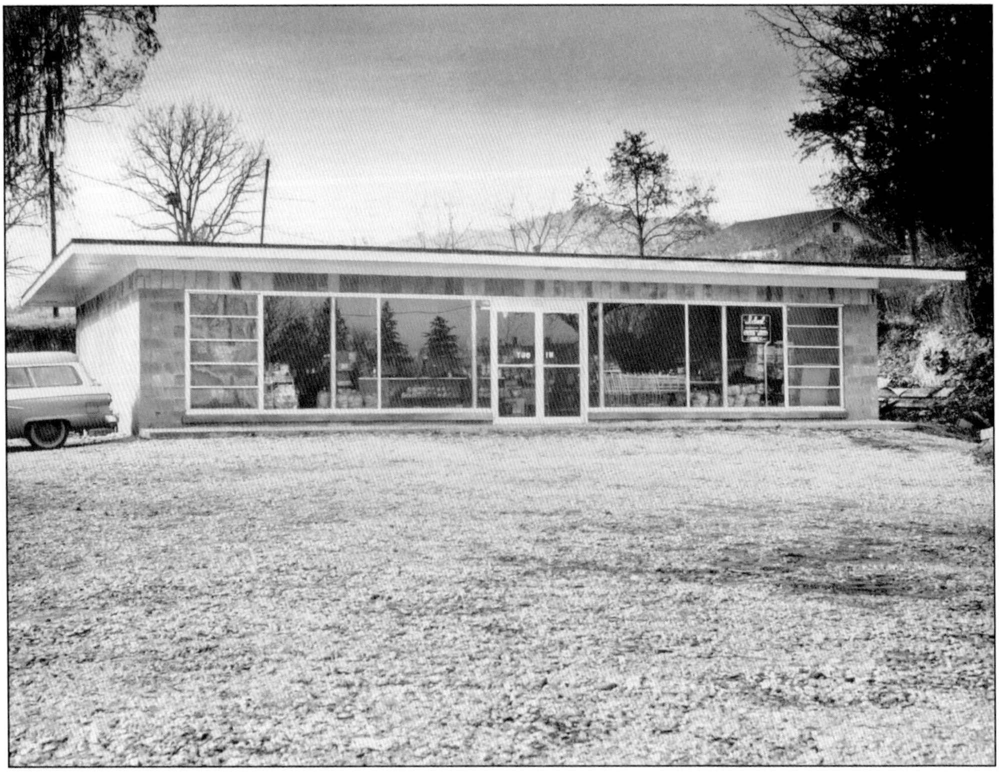

The new Horsley Grocery was built in the 1960s. Over the years, it has housed several businesses.

Three

Houses and Other Structures

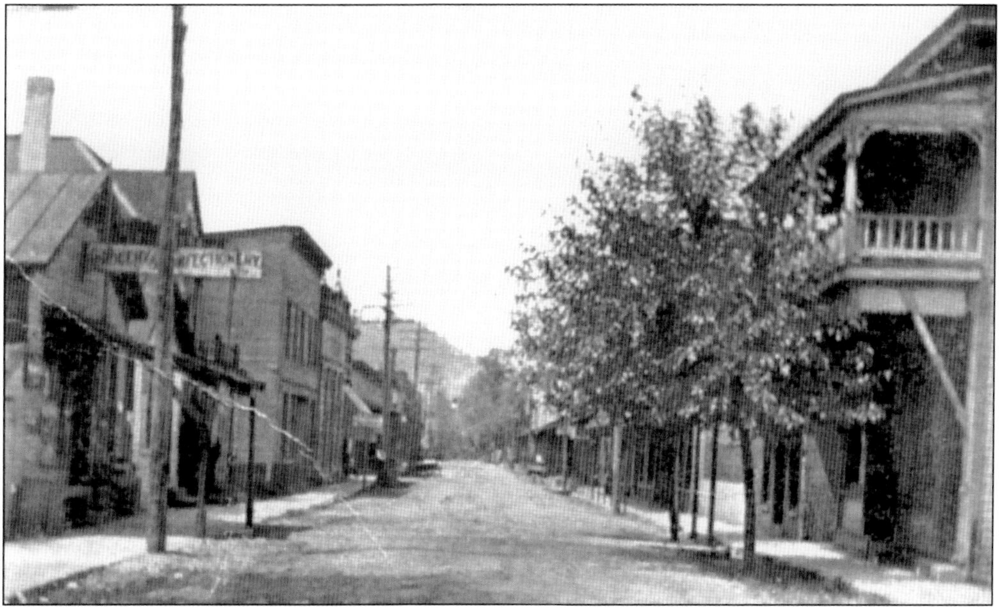

This 1910 view of Second Street looking west shows an unpaved street, and most of the buildings appear to be of wood construction. At the near right is C. Carter's Millinery Store, which was torn down in 2004, and on the left is a sign for Dr. R.G. Barber's groceries and a confectionery. Also on the left, after the tall building, one can see the newly erected Deposit Bank.

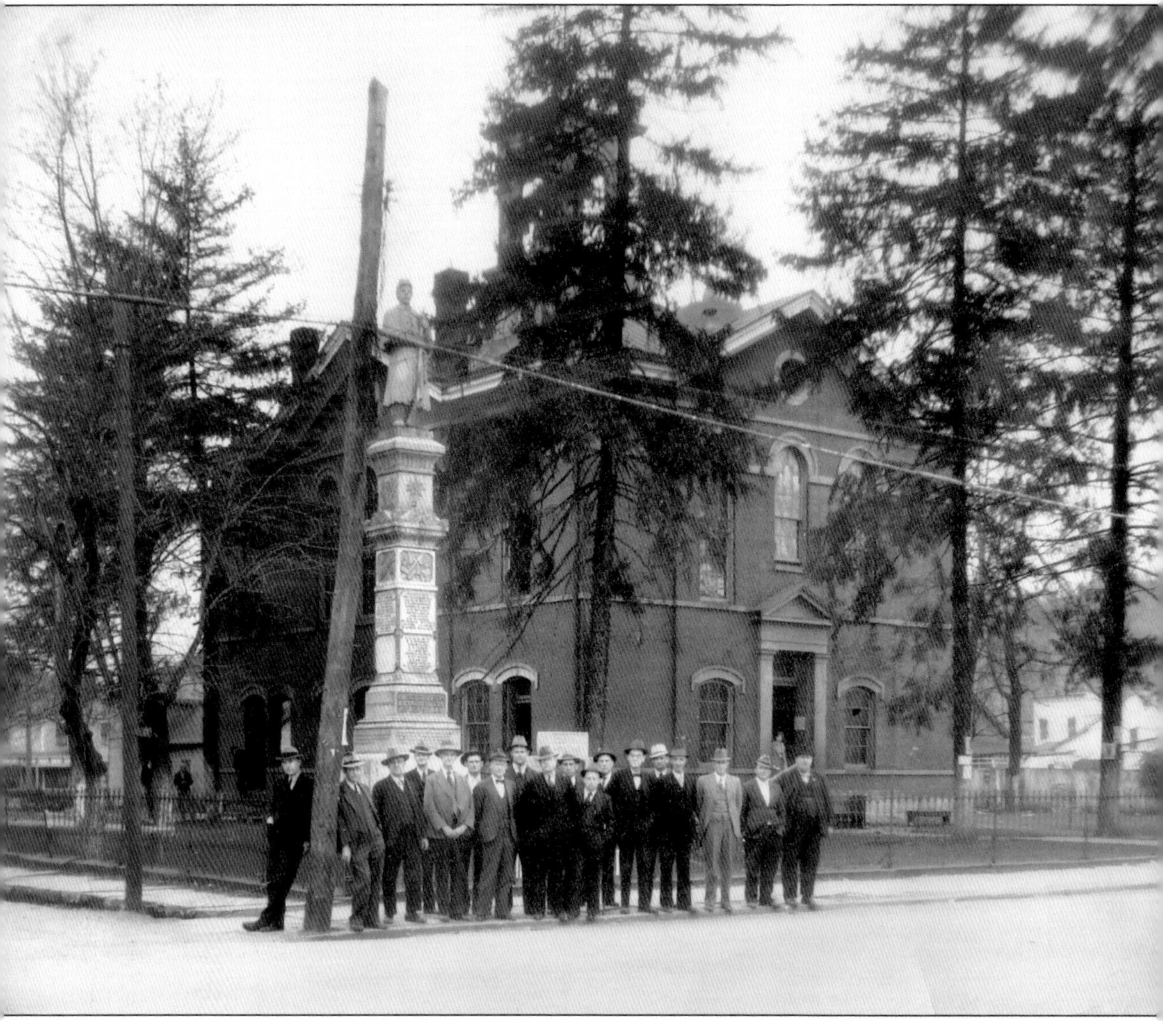

This is the old courthouse as it appeared in 1937 or 1938, before its demolition. The men standing on the corner by the Union Civil War monument include Charles Riedinger and Judge Harvey Parker (center of picture), Delbert Ash behind Judge Parker, and Pat Tannian to the right of the pole. The building was heavily damaged by the 1937 flood and a new one was built in 1938–1939.

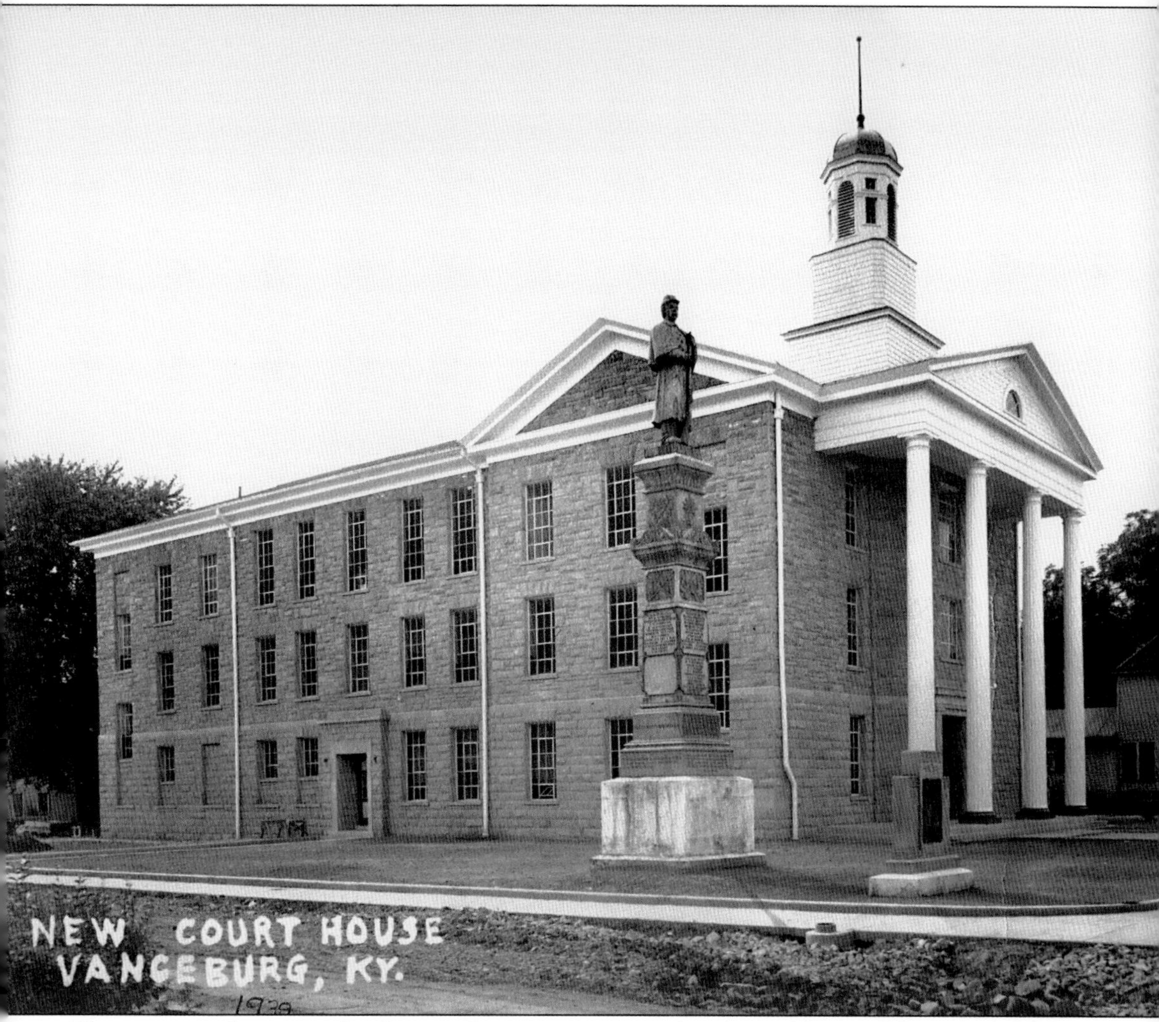

This new courthouse, made of native freestone, was completed in 1939. Its predecessor, a brick building, was badly damaged by the 1937 flood.

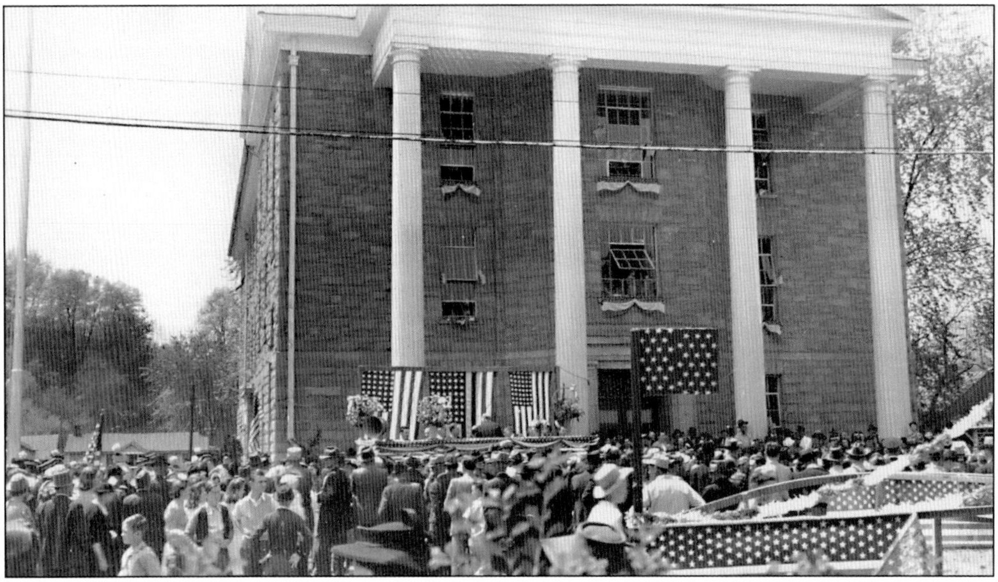

Dedication services for Vanceburg's new courthouse were held in the summer of 1939. It replaced the old brick courthouse, which was ruined by the 1937 flood of the Ohio River.

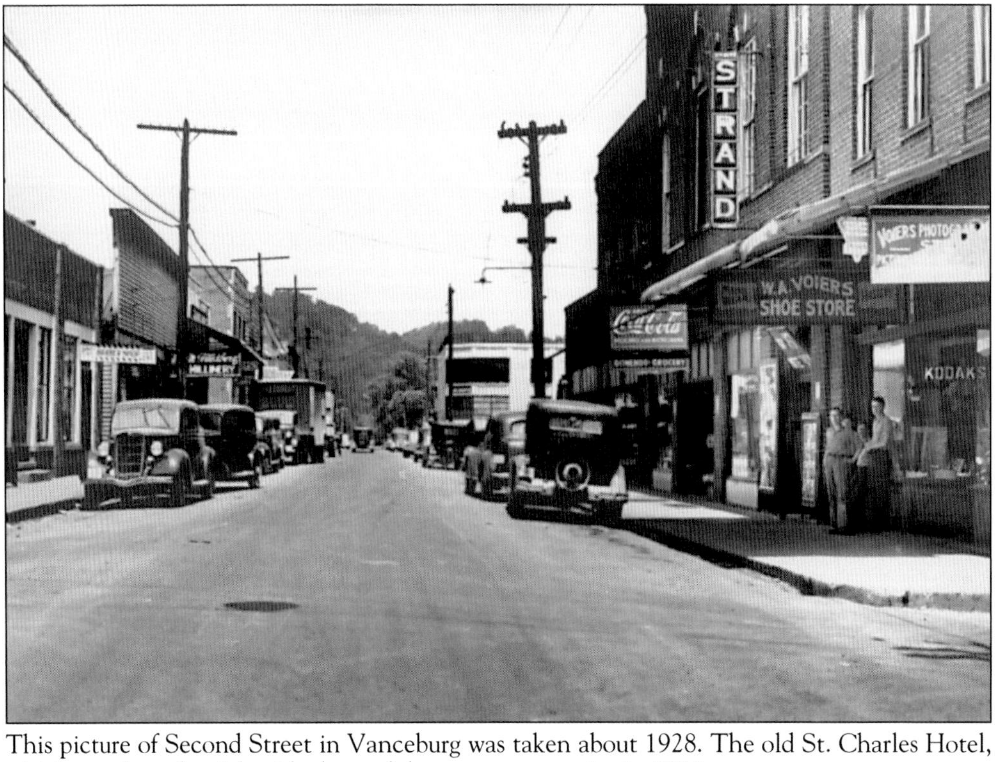

This picture of Second Street in Vanceburg was taken about 1928. The old St. Charles Hotel, which stood on the right side, burned down two years prior in 1926.

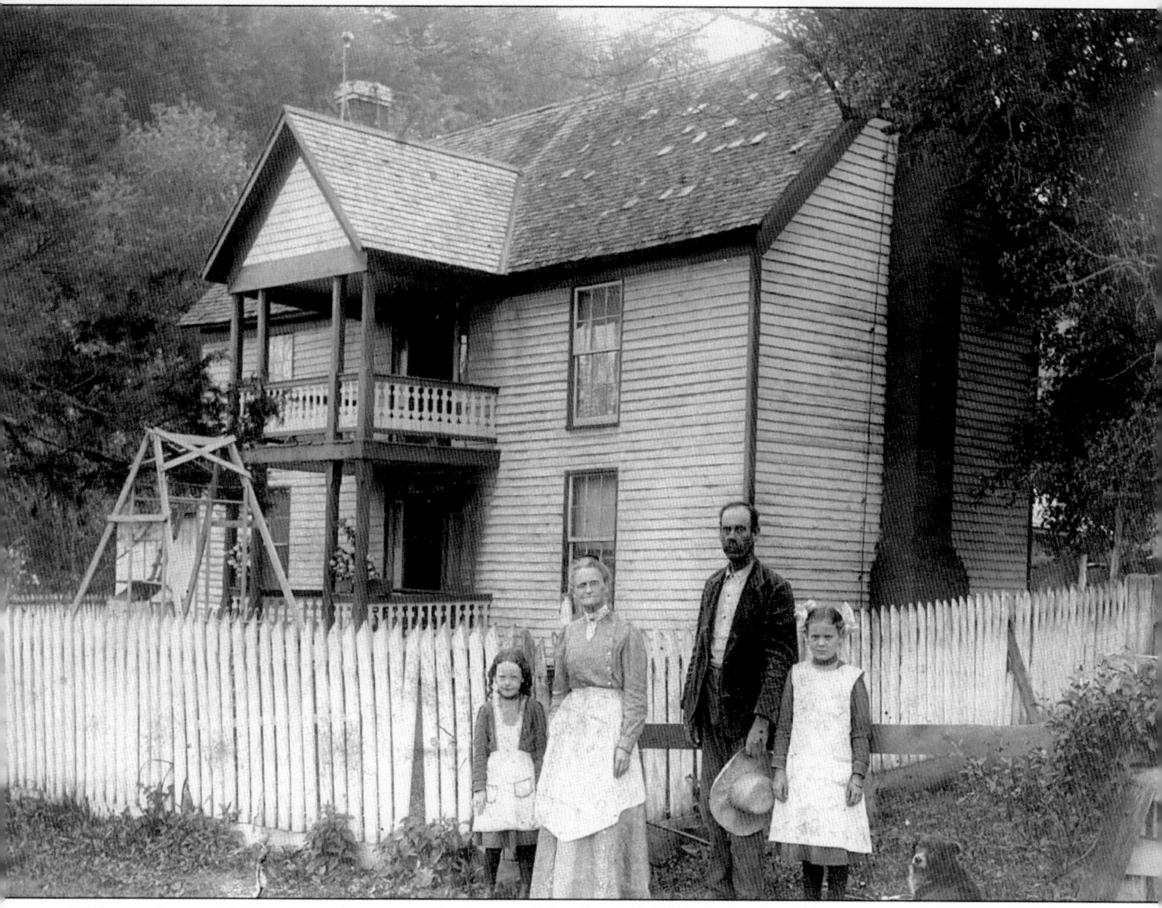

Taken about 1910, this photograph shows Charles McEldowney and his wife, Rose, standing in the front yard of their home with two of their children, Alice (Taylor) and Nancy (Austin). The house, still standing near the McEldowney Cemetery and owned by descendants, has the unique feature of the upstairs porch, common to several old homes in Lewis County. Mrs. McEldowney, it is said, insisted on having a white picket fence around the yard to keep out the chickens.

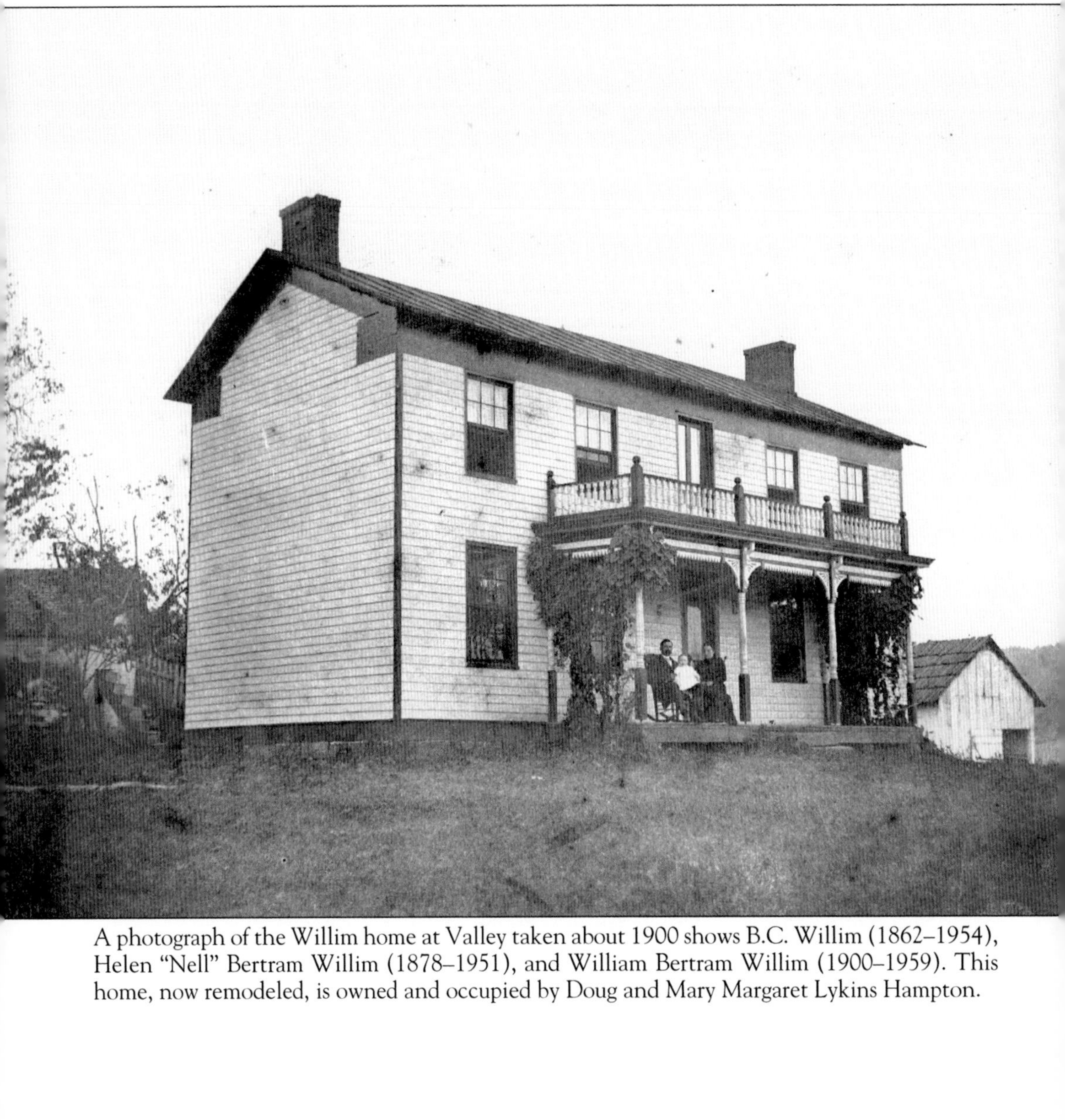

A photograph of the Willim home at Valley taken about 1900 shows B.C. Willim (1862–1954), Helen "Nell" Bertram Willim (1878–1951), and William Bertram Willim (1900–1959). This home, now remodeled, is owned and occupied by Doug and Mary Margaret Lykins Hampton.

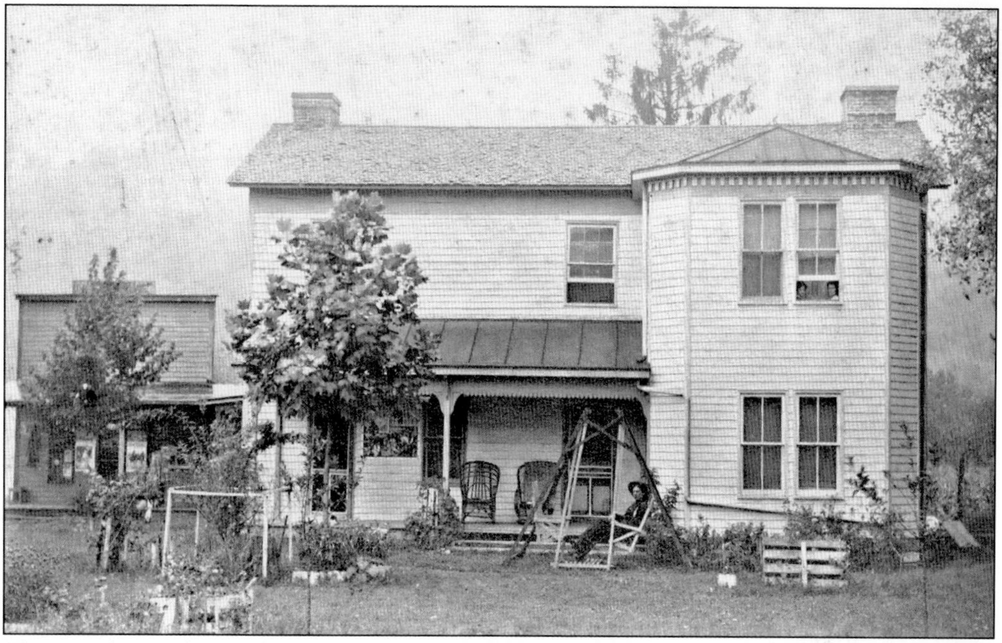

This was the residence of Mr. and Mrs. J.E. Hackworth at Heselton (Glen Springs), September 21, 1908. Interesting features are the two children in the upstairs window, the swing set, and the old building that looks like a country store.

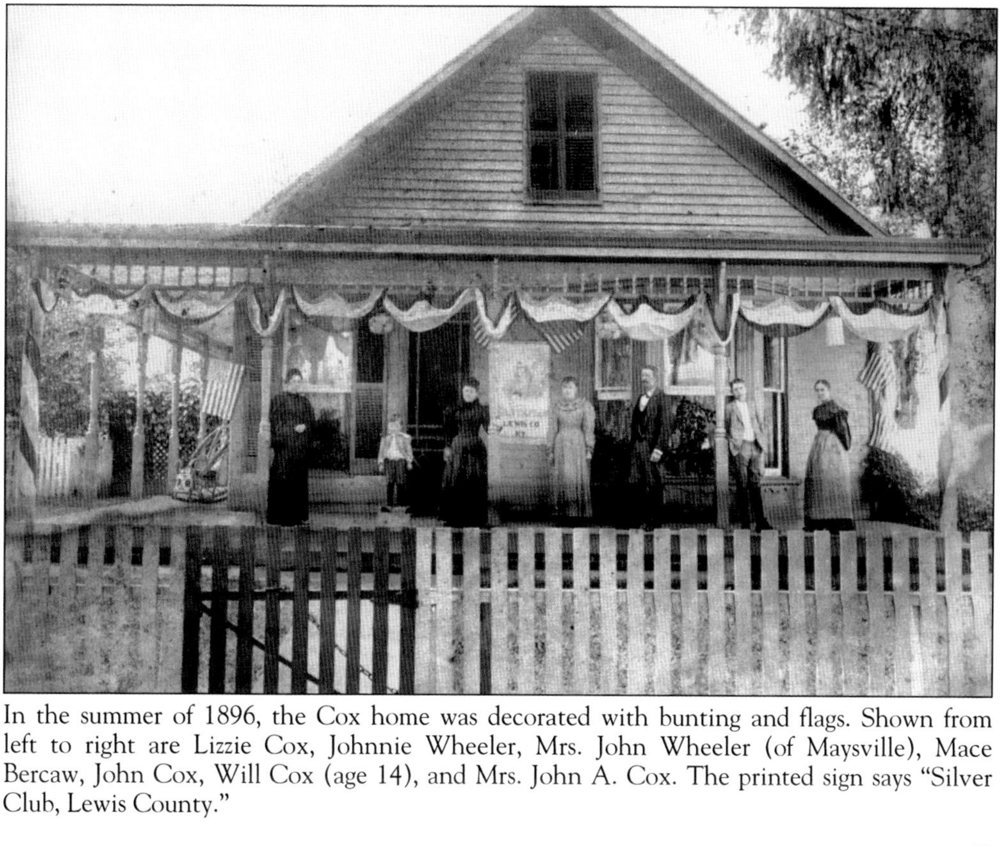

In the summer of 1896, the Cox home was decorated with bunting and flags. Shown from left to right are Lizzie Cox, Johnnie Wheeler, Mrs. John Wheeler (of Maysville), Mace Bercaw, John Cox, Will Cox (age 14), and Mrs. John A. Cox. The printed sign says "Silver Club, Lewis County."

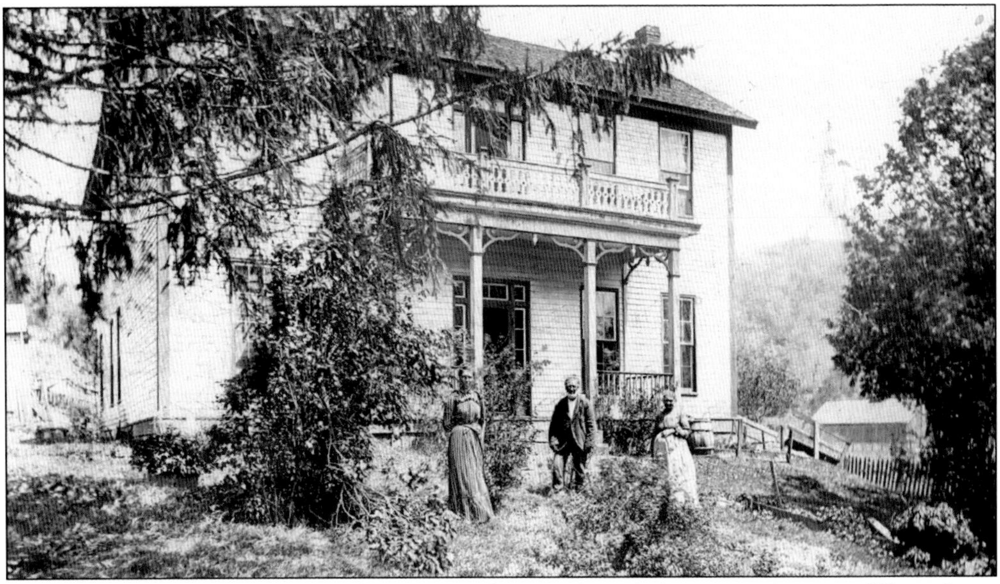

The elegant Grandison home stood on Route 9 (AA Highway) about six miles west of Vanceburg. At the location now are a trailer and a highway marker incorrectly labeled Grannison Branch. Isabella Bertram Grandison (1836–1923) and John Grandison (1820–1909) lived there in the late 1800s with their four sons and two daughters: Jack of Indiana, Henry of Wisconsin, Pete, James and Kate of Portsmouth, Ohio, and Sue at home. It is believed that Jack was an ancestor of Jane Pauley, of NBC fame, and that she gave one of her twins the middle name of Grandison. Pictured are Susan Grandison, John Grandison, and Isabella Bertram Grandison. The house burned on February 22 (year unknown).

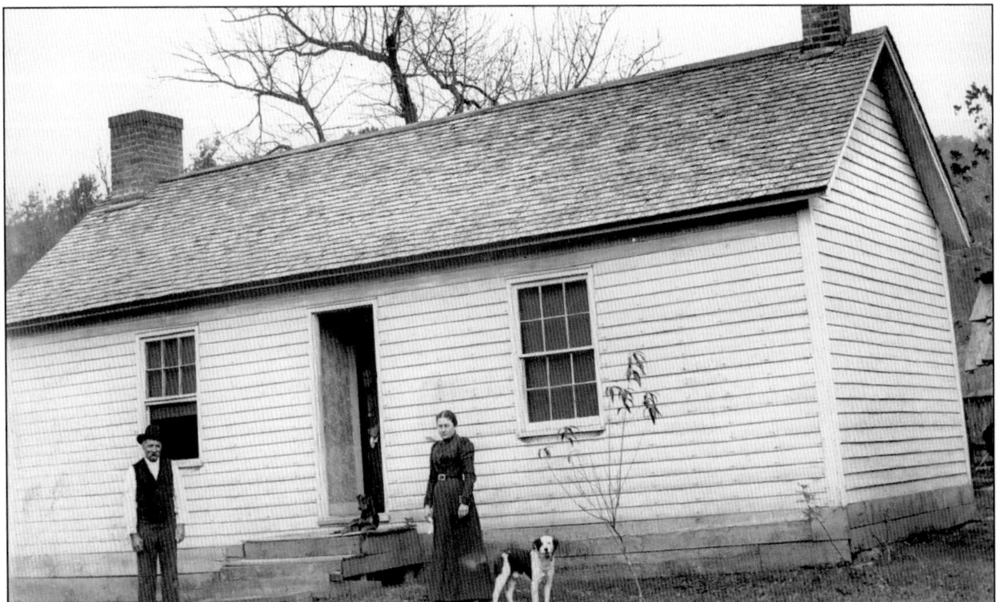

Shown here at the Bertram home at Liberty Grove are Alexander Bertram and his daughter, Helen Bertram Willim, before 1900. The person standing inside the doorway holding a handkerchief is unidentified.

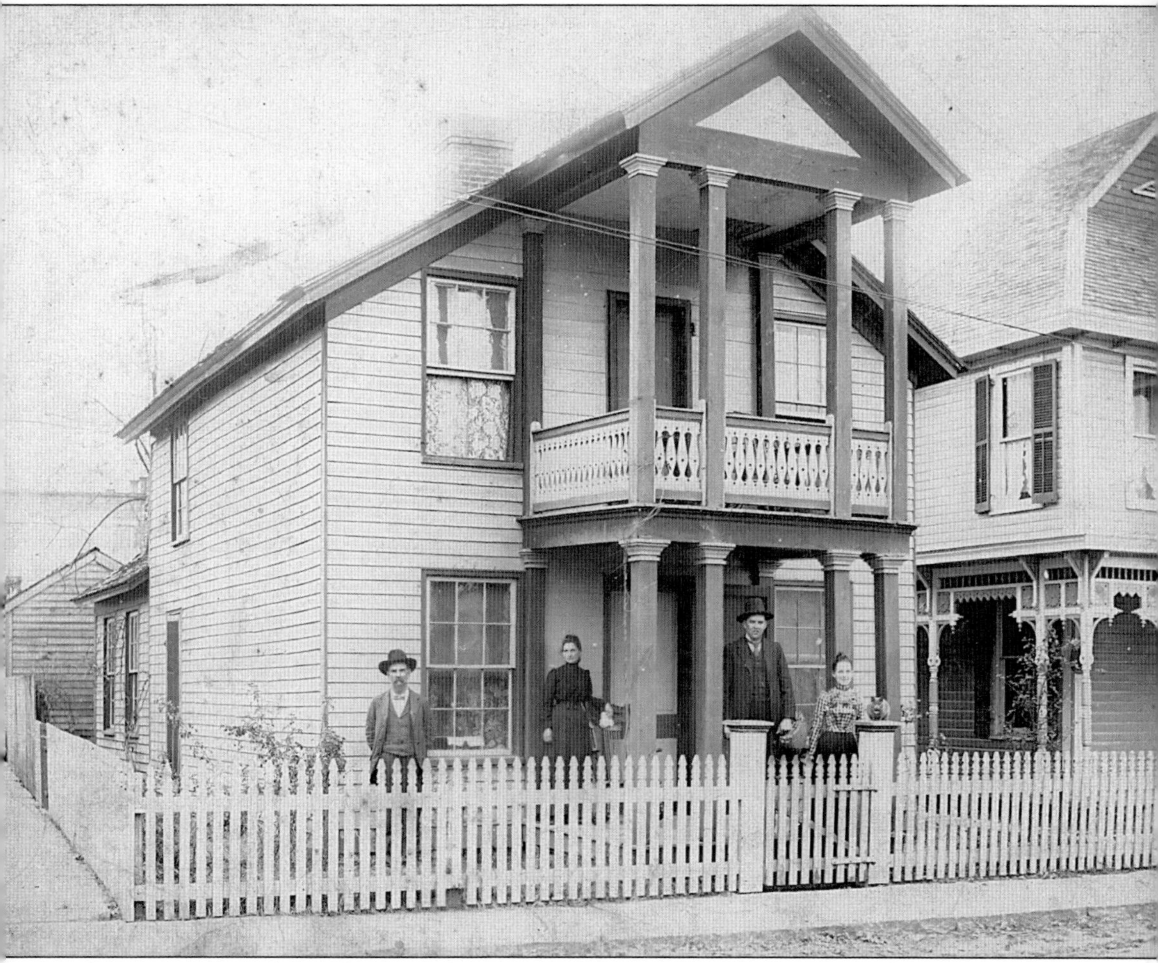

This 1900 image shows the Jones house, set on the corner of Front and Market Streets in Vanceburg. The roof of the porch at one time extended across Front Street to the Beverly House Saloon on the north side of the street. The law at that time made it necessary that any saloon be under the same roof as a regular hotel or tavern. The law was circumvented by building this roof-bridge across the street. Traffic passed under the bridge. The Beverly House burned down in 1867, but the house and hotel parts were untouched by the flames. The house was razed about 1908–1909. The lot is now the east lawn of the Vanceburg Christian Church parsonage, which can be seen at the extreme right. The persons shown here, from left to right, are Rufus Jones; his wife, Sallie Voiers Jones; George Willim; and the Jones' daughter, Emma (Mrs. George T. Willim). There is a cat on the railing by Emma. The house on the right was formerly owned and occupied by Mary and Santiago Voiers.

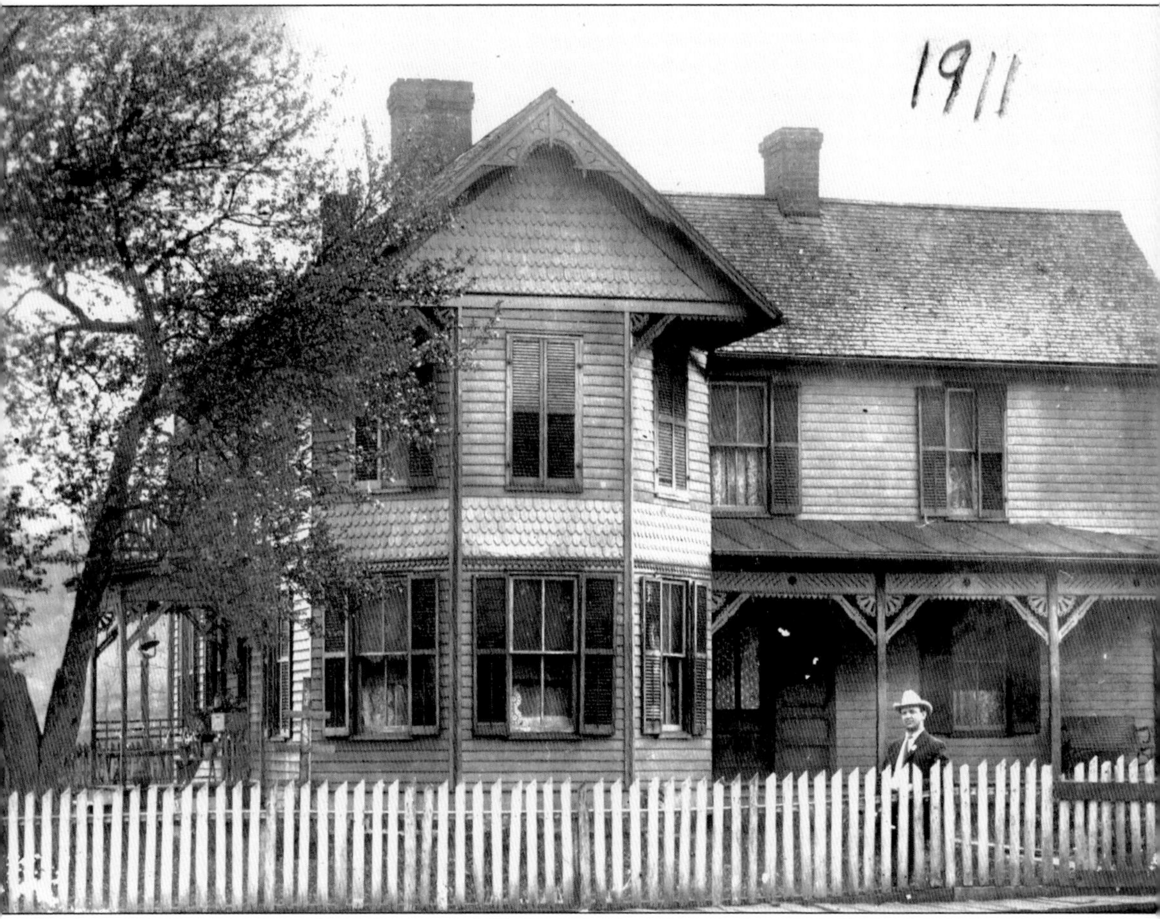

This is a 1911 view of the Dial D. and Elizabeth Lykins home at Petersville. Jesse Lykins, brother to Frank, Lena Wells, and Denny Lykins, is standing by the fence.

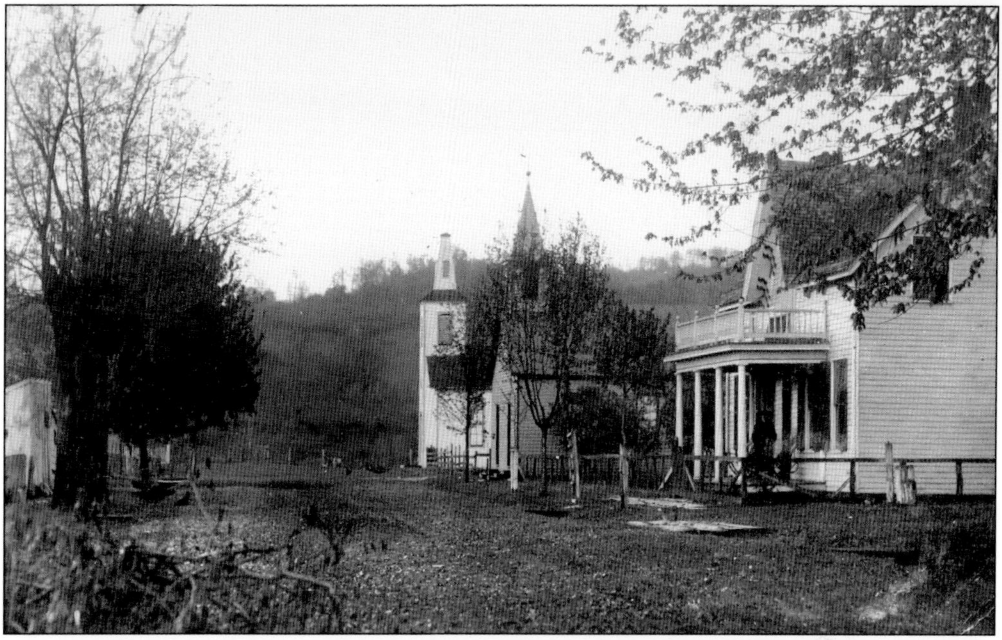

Concord's Main Street is seen here as it appeared in 1910. The house in the foreground and the last church in the background are still standing.

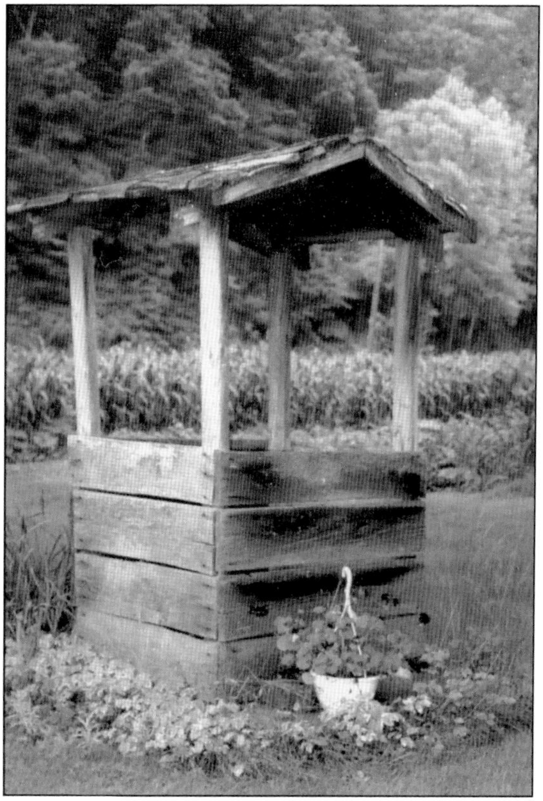

This type of old well that required someone to pull in a bucket of water is becoming rare. The wells were usually hand dug and lined with native stone.

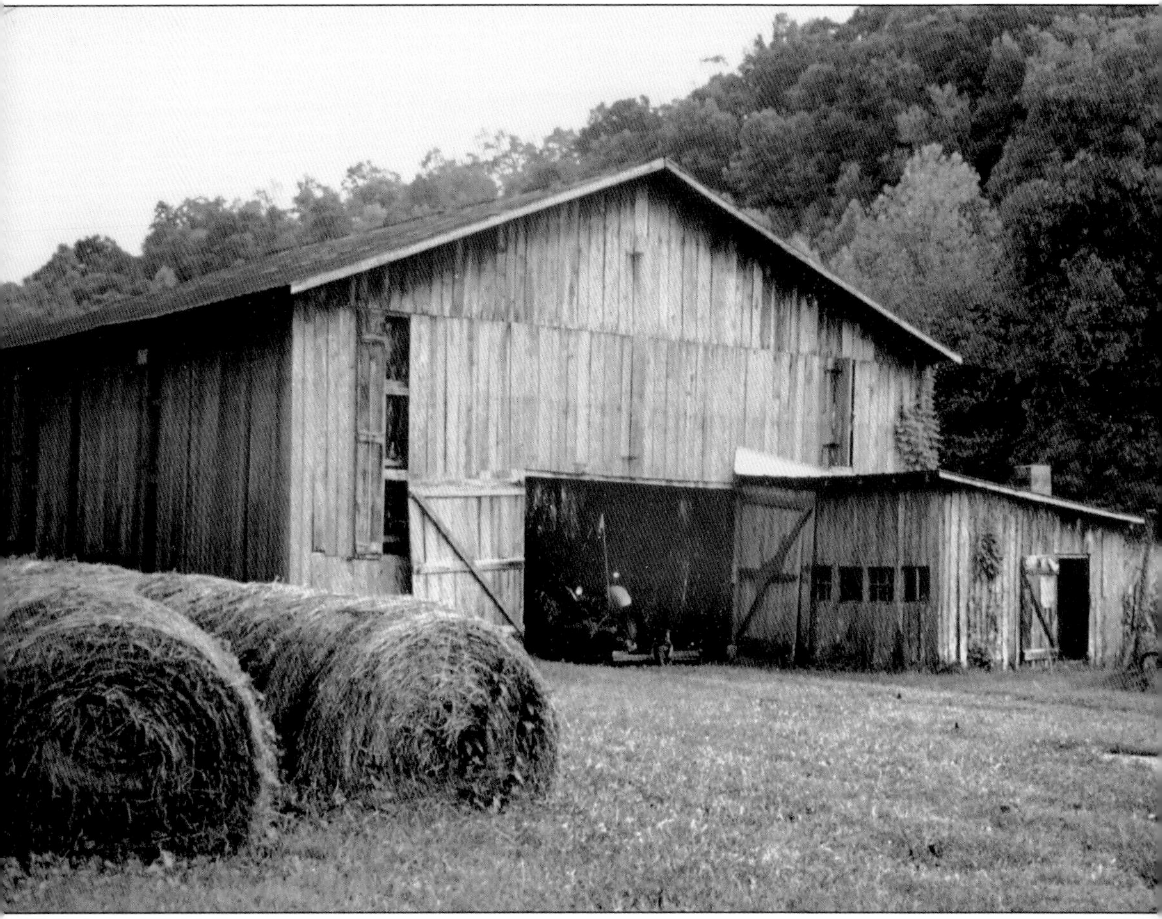

This tobacco barn is typical of the thousands of barns once used to house tobacco, a crop that is now being phased out.

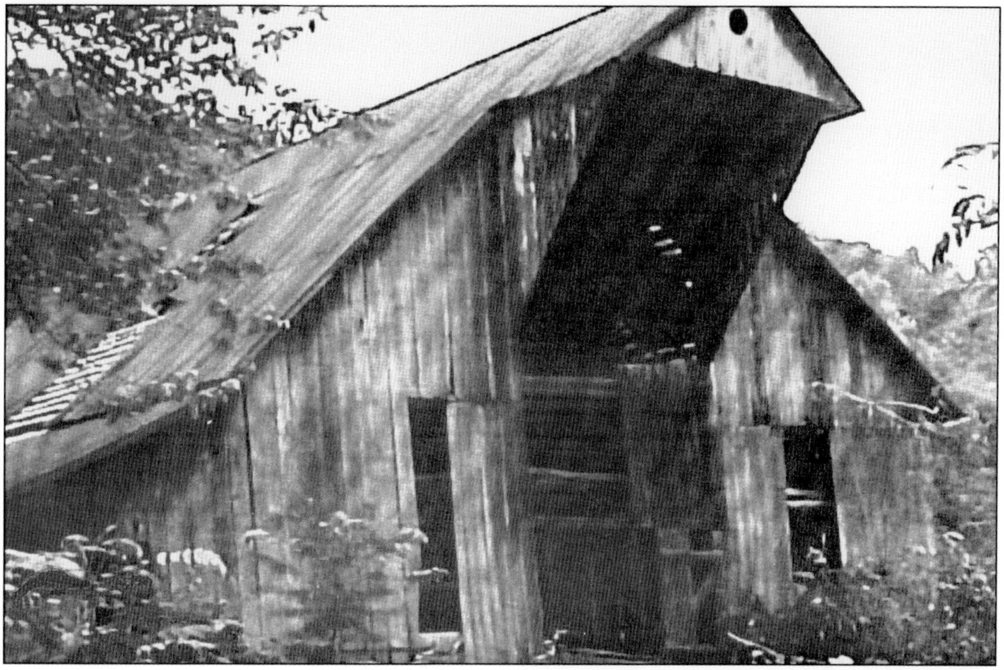

This old barn at Thor on Scott's Branch was once owned by the W.T. Cooper family. The overhanging roof is an unusual barn structure. The building fell down in a storm a few months after this picture was taken.

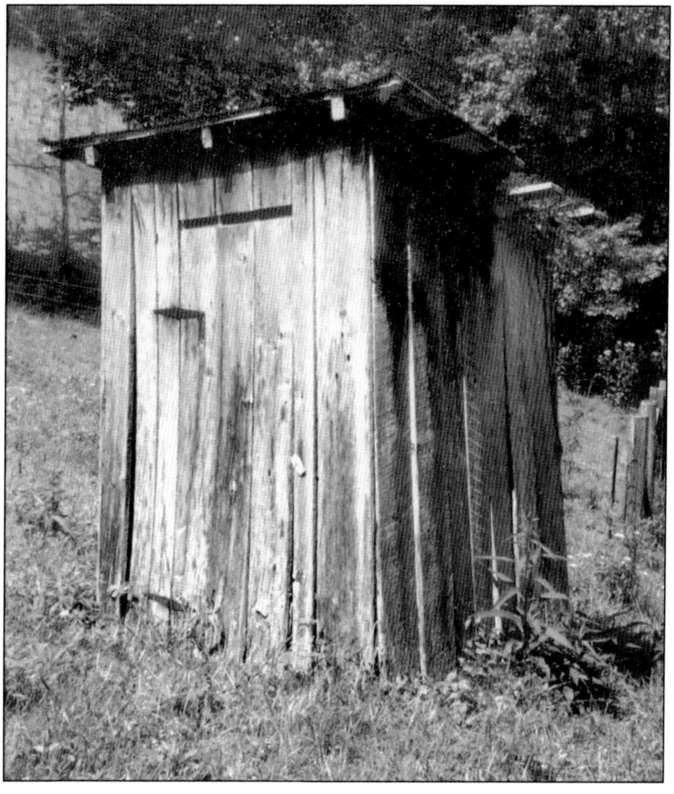

It's a Kentucky icon. In earlier days every home had an outdoor toilet. This one has seen its better days.

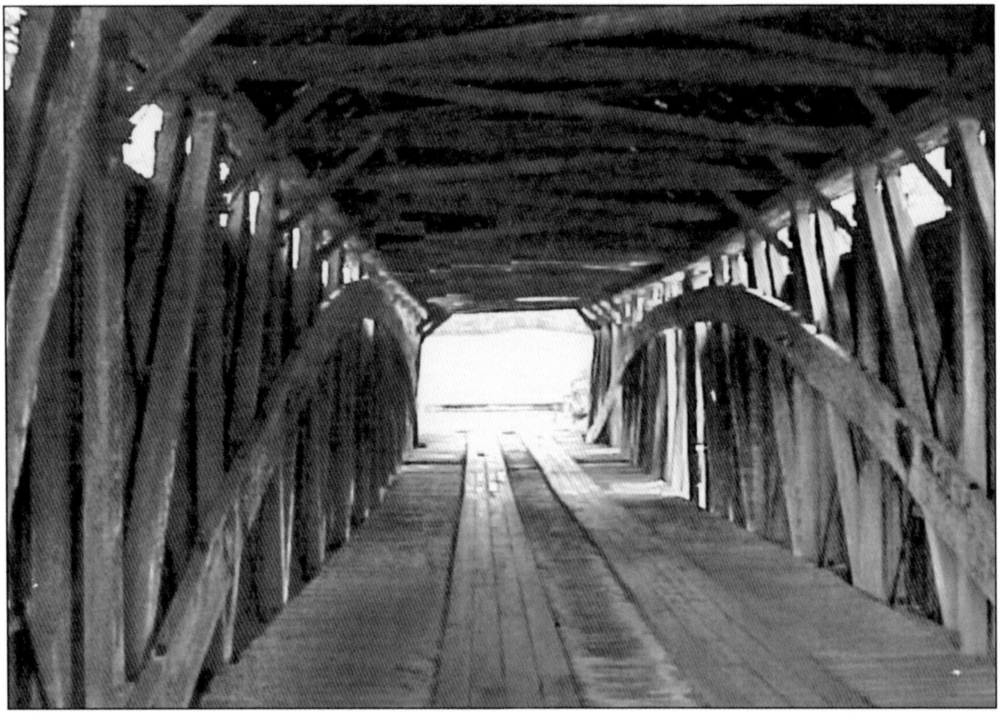

This is the inside structural work (trusswork) of the covered bridge on Cabin Creek. This bridge, built in 1875 by William Henderson, is one of only 13 covered bridges in Kentucky still intact. It is now closed to transportation.

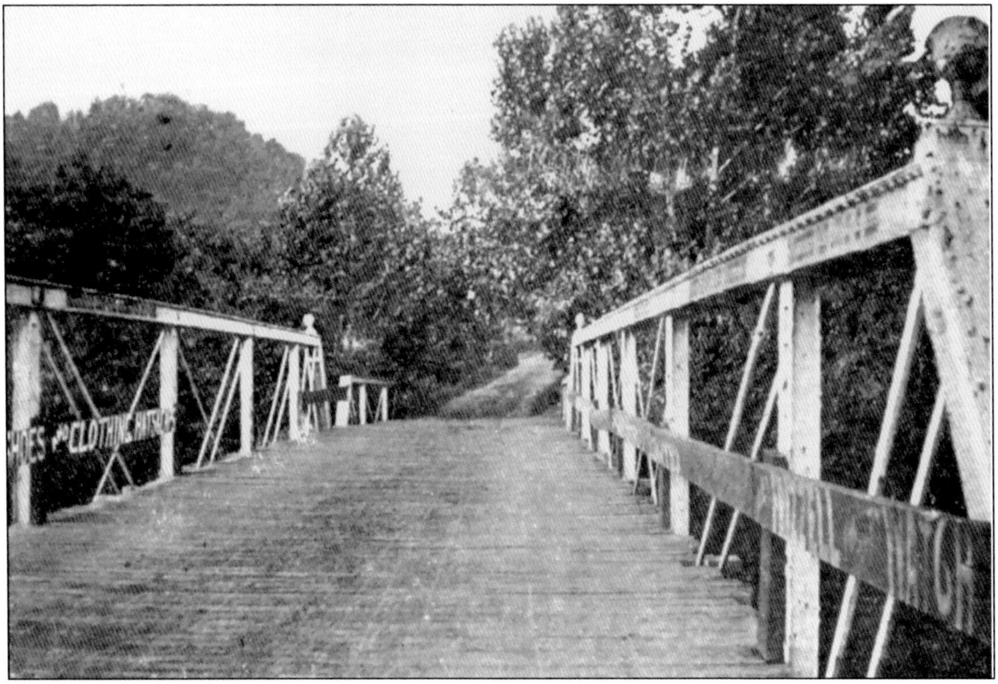

Salt Lick Bridge, also known as River Road Bridge, is shown in 1906. This bridge is still standing but is closed to vehicle traffic. The sign on the left advertises clothing.

Four

The Great Outdoors

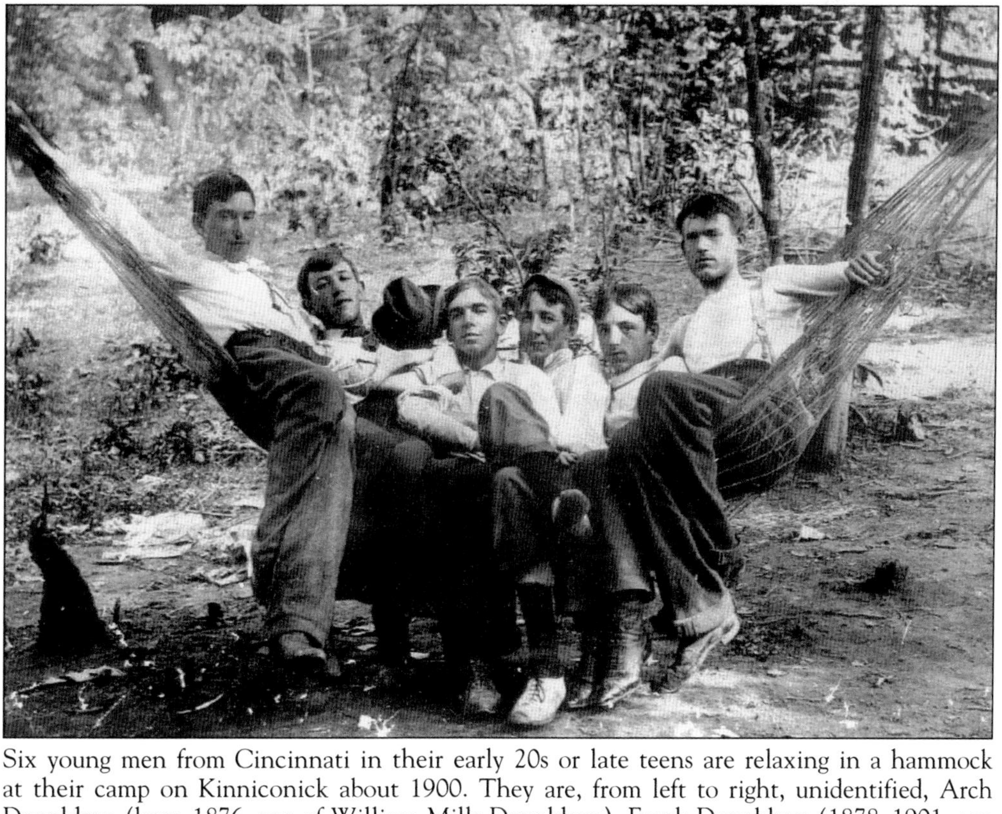

Six young men from Cincinnati in their early 20s or late teens are relaxing in a hammock at their camp on Kinniconick about 1900. They are, from left to right, unidentified, Arch Donaldson (born 1876, son of William Mills Donaldson), Frank Donaldson (1878–1901, son of William Mills Donaldson), Bob Carrel, unidentified, and Charles H. Longley (a professional photographer and son-in-law of William Mills Donaldson). The Donaldsons are descended from Ann Donaldson, of Perth, Scotland, and Cincinnati, who died of cholera at Esculapia Springs in 1850.

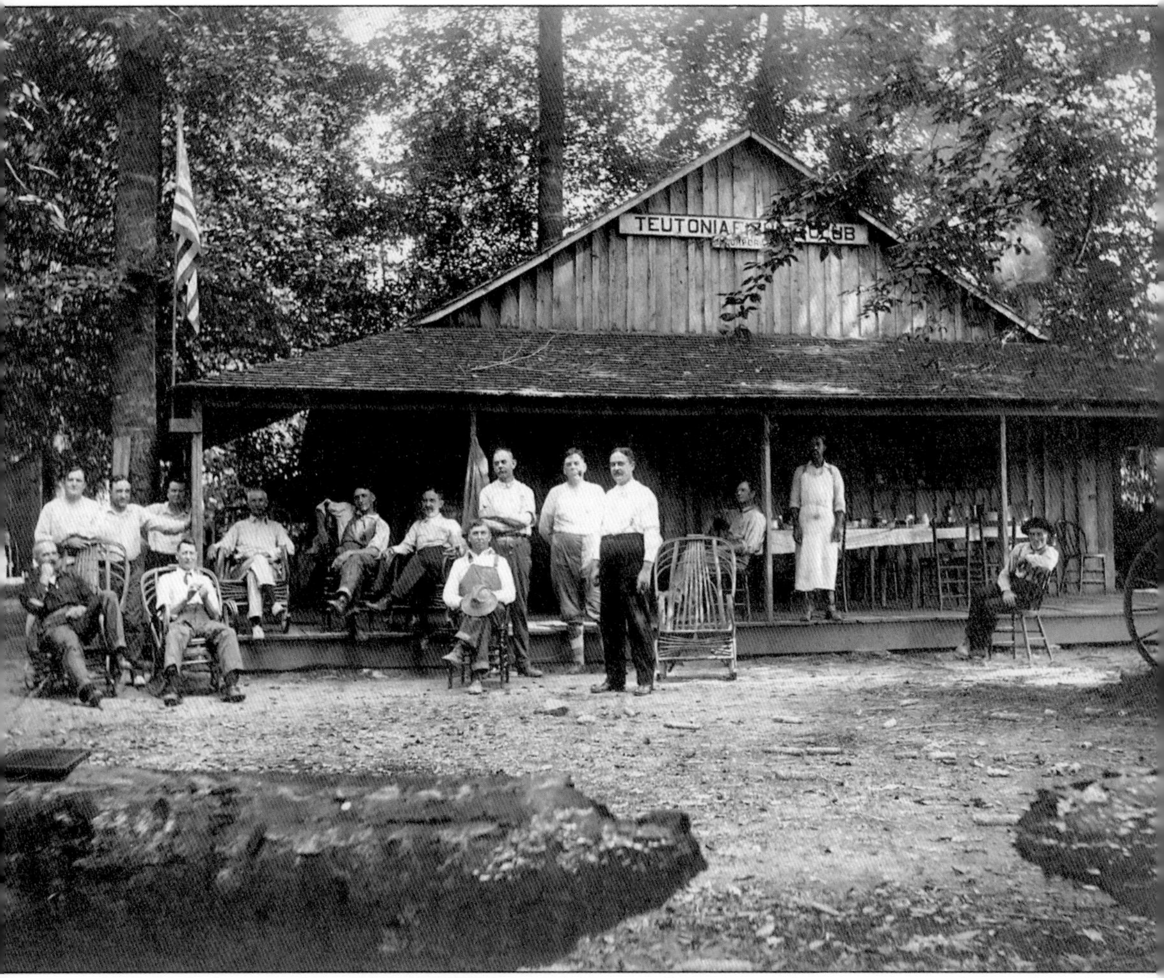

This photograph of the Teutonia Fishing Club was taken September 20, 1914. The cook and "food manager," John Morgan, is dressed in a white outfit standing by the table on the porch. The wagon at right was used to bring in supplies from town.

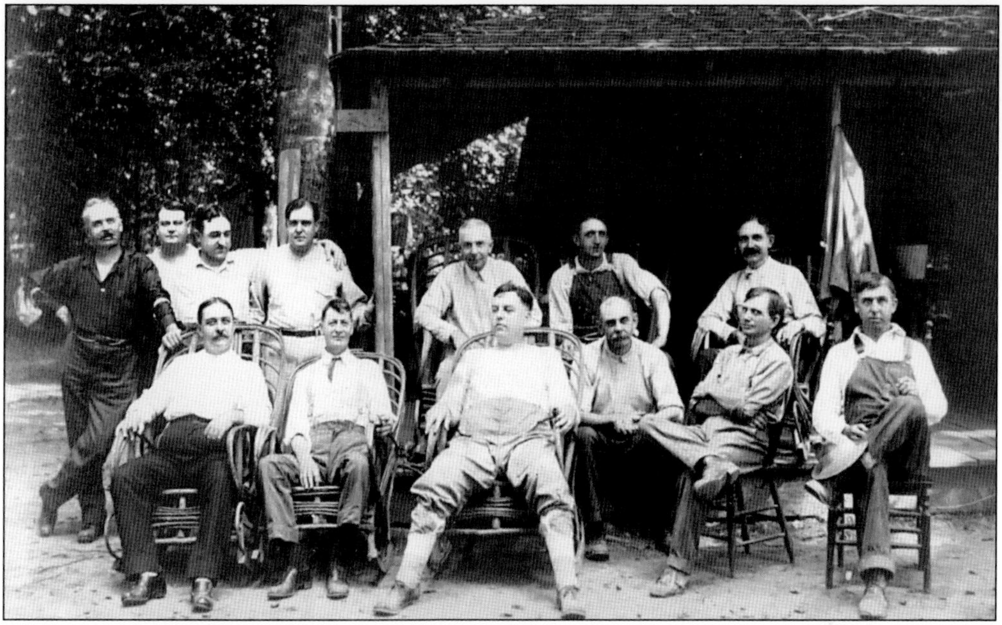

This picture of the private Teutonia Fishing Club on Kinniconick was taken September 20, 1914. From left to right are (front row) James Pugh, J.W. Cox, George T. Willim, Charles Hammond, Fred Young, and John Mason Osborne; (back row) Mr. Anthony, William Gill, Jack Pugh, William Barrett, James Rowley, unidentified, and Henry Lindenburn.

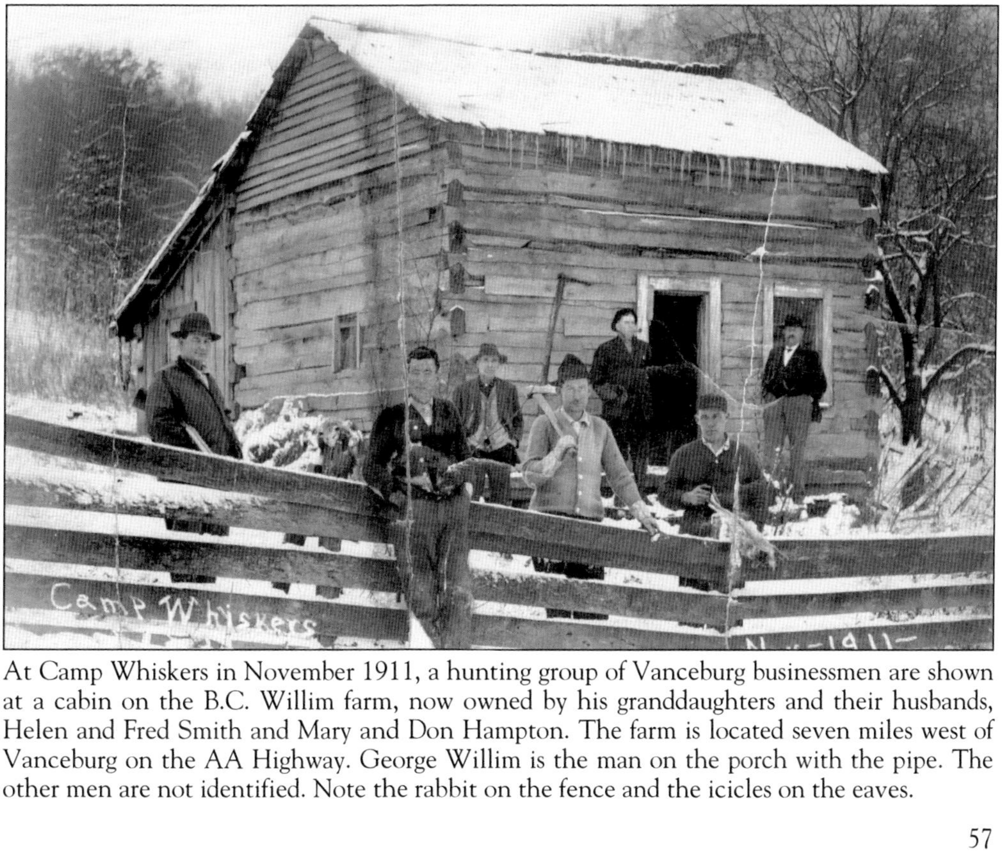

At Camp Whiskers in November 1911, a hunting group of Vanceburg businessmen are shown at a cabin on the B.C. Willim farm, now owned by his granddaughters and their husbands, Helen and Fred Smith and Mary and Don Hampton. The farm is located seven miles west of Vanceburg on the AA Highway. George Willim is the man on the porch with the pipe. The other men are not identified. Note the rabbit on the fence and the icicles on the eaves.

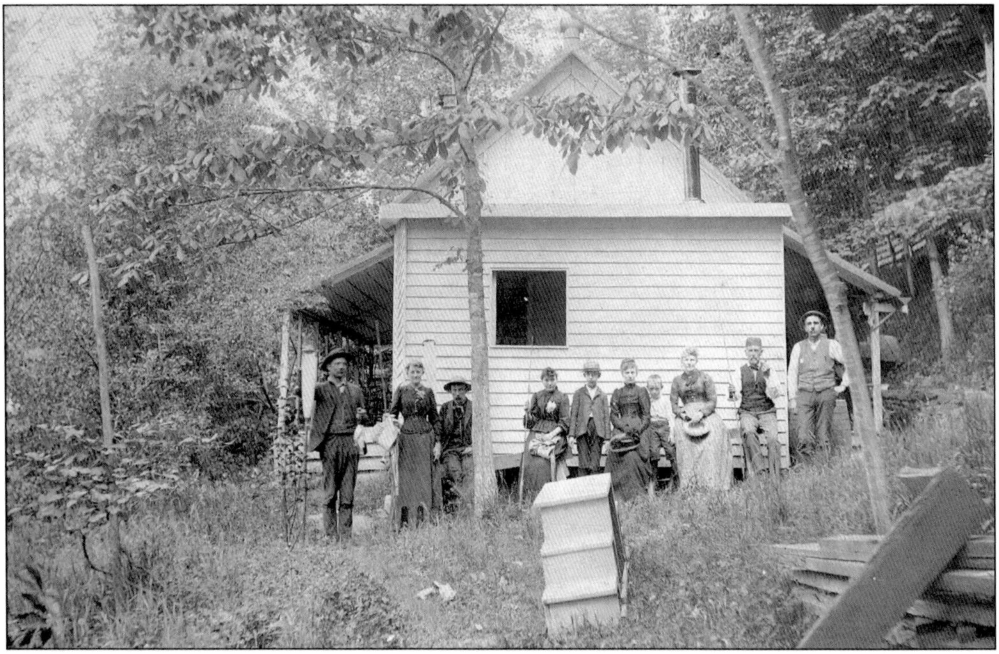

William Birely built this fish camp on Kinniconick Creek near the McEldowney Hotel. The first name is unreadable, but included in the picture are ? Plummer, William Cooper, M.L. Barber, Mrs. A.D. Neal, Mrs. Hamilton, Bertha Neal, and Stella Freeman. The two boys are sons of Mrs. Hamilton. The name Birely was pronounced "barley."

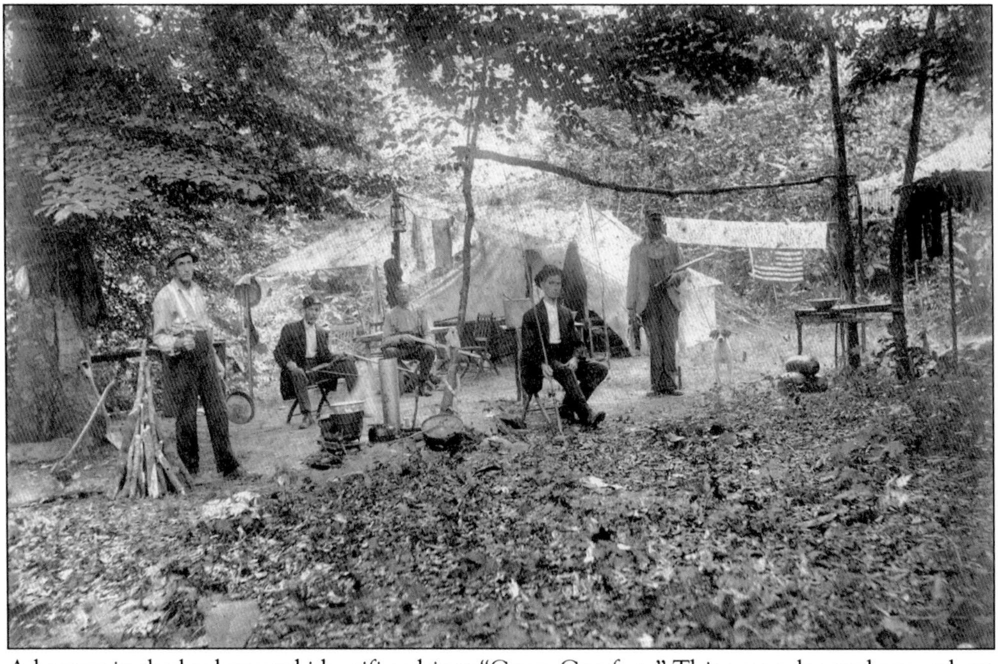

A banner in the background identifies this as "Camp Comfort." This camp, located somewhere on Kinniconick, appears very cozy. If one looks carefully at the picture, many strange and unusual items can be seen. Pictured from left to right are G.P. Adams, L.A. Stricklett, Samuel F. Bruce, J. Martin Donahoo, and A.M. "Cell" Plummer.

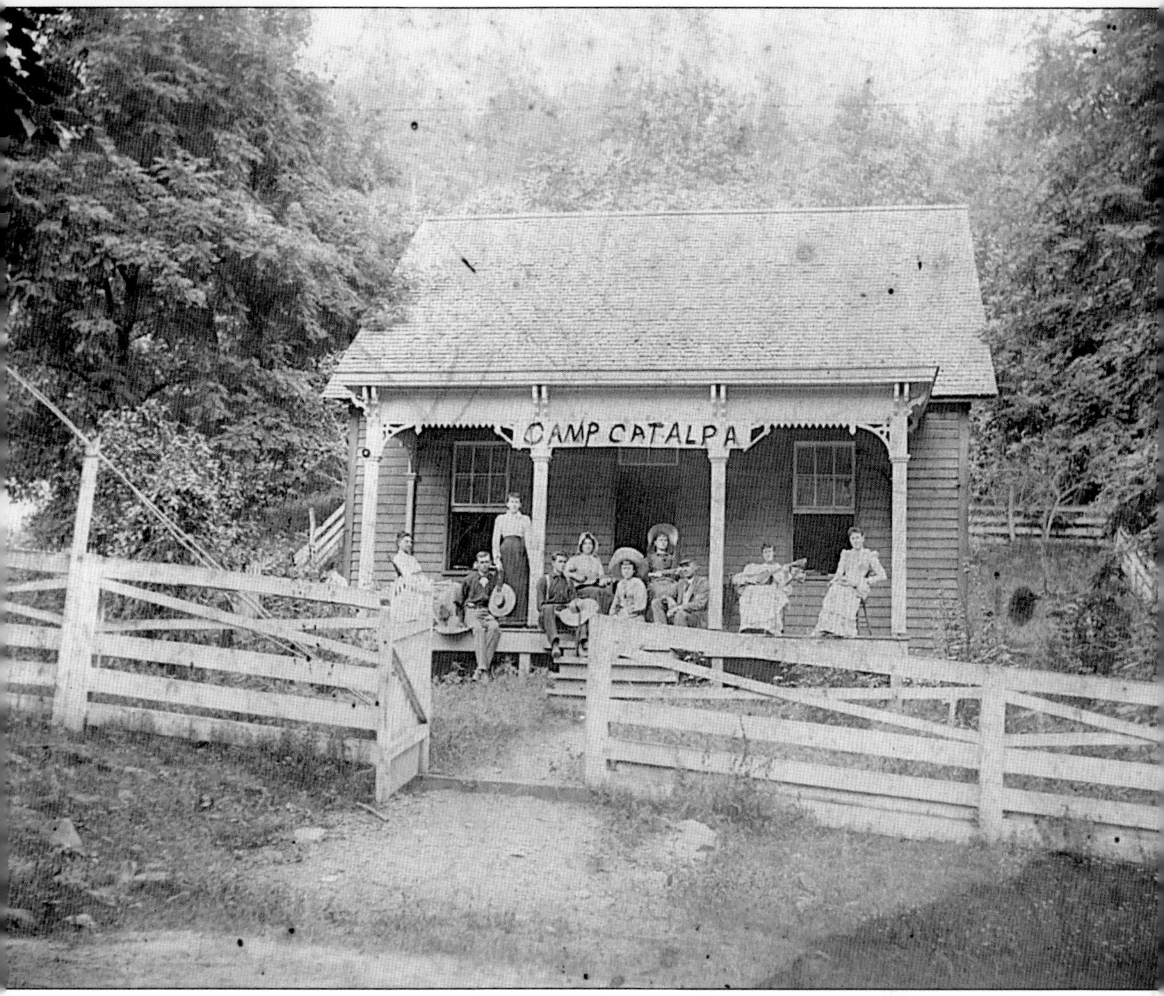

The date and location of this picture of Camp Catalpa are unknown. It appears this was a festive occasion, as several people are holding musical instruments and wearing unusual hats.

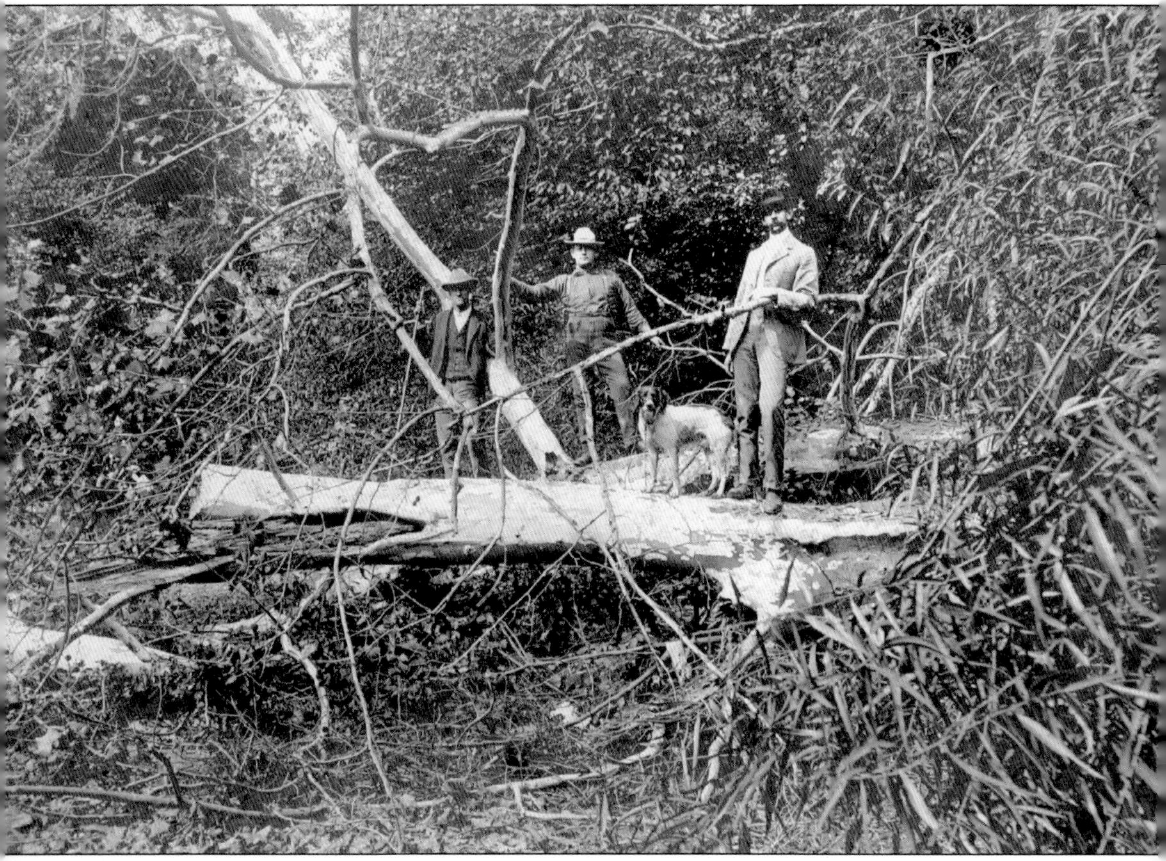

These fishermen with their dog seem to be exploring the driftwood deposited by a recent flood. The location may be Kinniconick Creek, but the date is unknown.

Shortly after the Civil War, William Birely came to Vanceburg, where he owned and operated the old mill most of his life. He loved hunting and fishing and claimed that was his reason for coming to Lewis County. He never married, and it is said that his betrothed died of typhoid fever and her dying wish was for him to always take care of her little brother, James Gardner. Indeed, Birely brought Jimmy Gardner to Vanceburg and raised him. Birely was perhaps the wealthiest man who ever lived in Lewis County. In his will, he left money to many institutions and to some of his relatives, the Delaplanes, in Baltimore. He died at the home of the Gardners on Second Street and is buried in Woodland Cemetery.

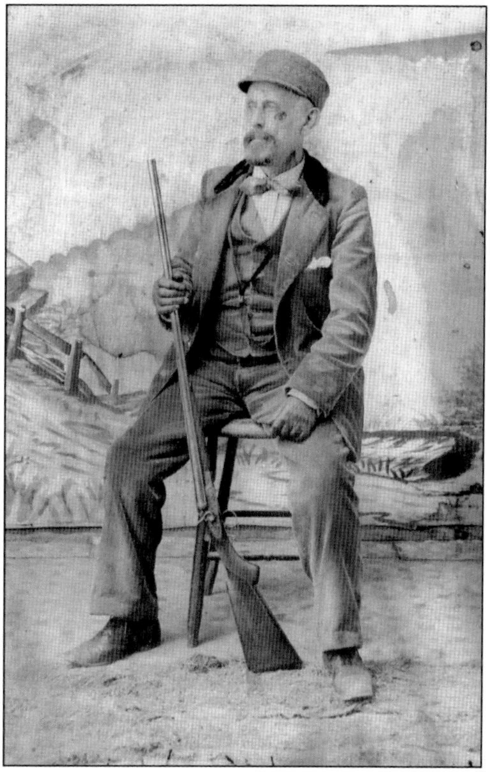

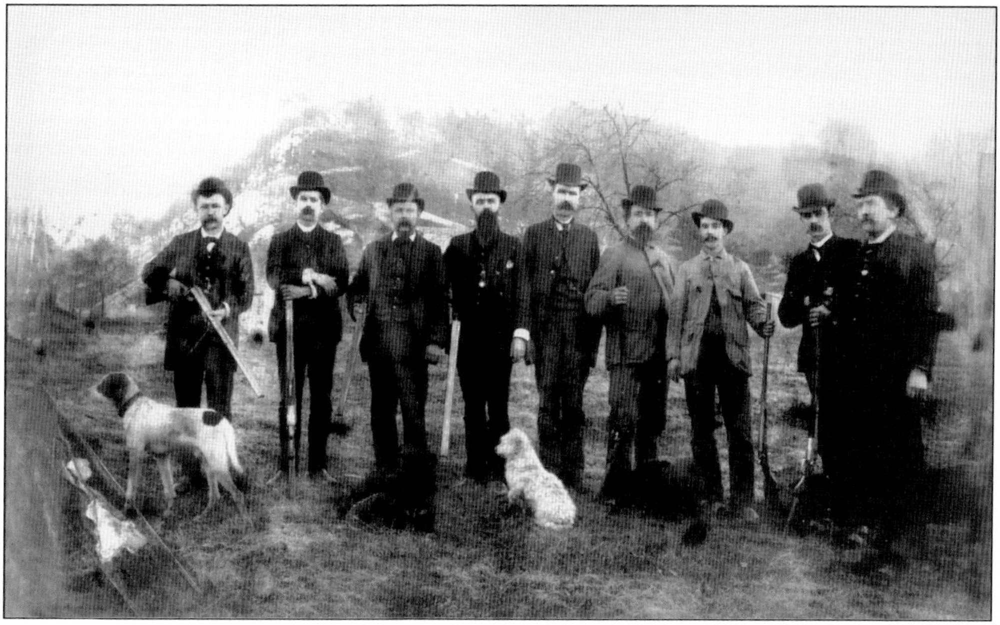

This undated picture of a hunters' club and their dogs was taken near the O.P. Pollitt home on Dry Run. Pictured from left to right are Frank Carter, Robert D. Wilson, Paschal Conner, Joseph A. Sparks, Abe McKay, Dr. William H. Campbell, Ed Sample, T.M. Eames, and Thomas B. Bullock. This was the original site of William Beverly "Red Buck" Parker's hunting lodge in the early days of Vanceburg.

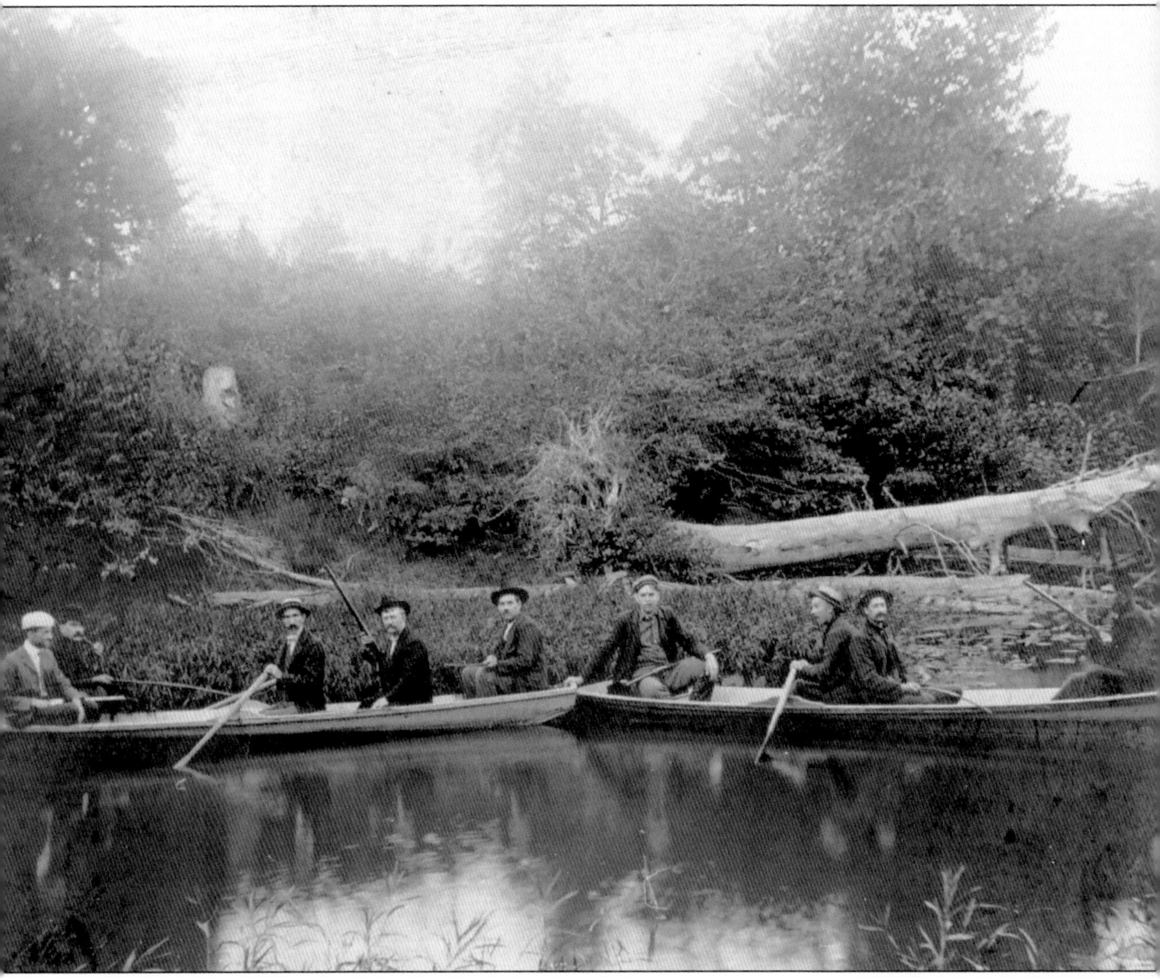

These unidentified men are leisurely rowing their boats on a calm stream, most likely Kinniconick, in the early 1900s.

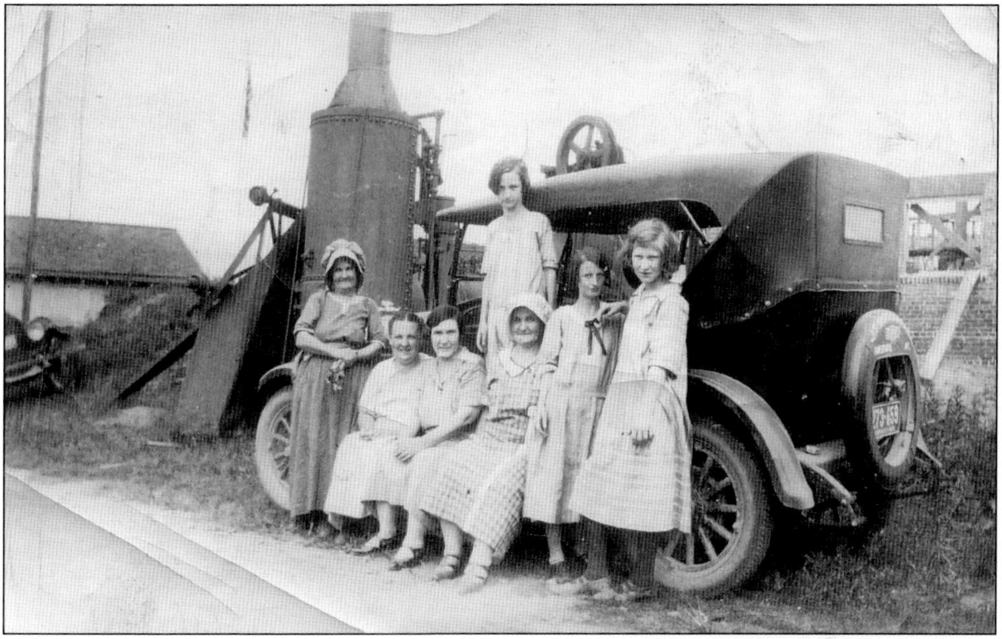

A group of various ages is standing by an early car sometime in the 1920s. They may have been part of the group that picked strawberries near Neal's Cafe. Pictured from left to right are Flora Liles (with bonnet), Blanch Boyd, Jessie Stevenson, Annie Falkner, Hazel Falkner (standing on car), Dollie Falkner, and Bernice Liles (Conley). In the background are the partially built walls of a new building, perhaps the L.V. Marks Shoe Company.

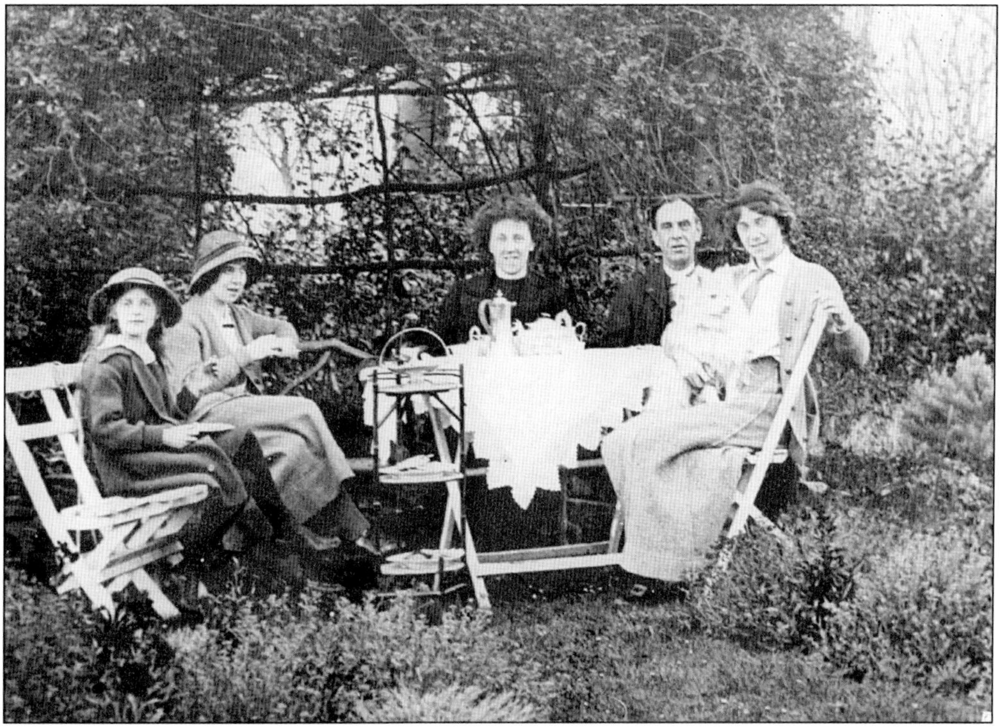

This alfresco tea party is typical of Victorian-age young ladies in Lewis County.

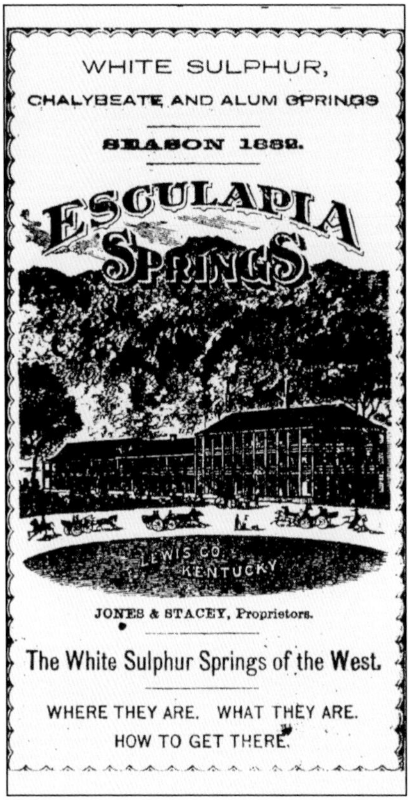

In Greek mythology, Esculapius (Aesculapius), the god of medicine, was often associated with mineral springs, which were believed to bring good health to those who drank from them. As with the Greeks, many people of the 18th and 19th centuries attributed various healing and restorative qualities to the waters of mineral springs, such as at Esculapia Springs and at nearby Glen Springs.

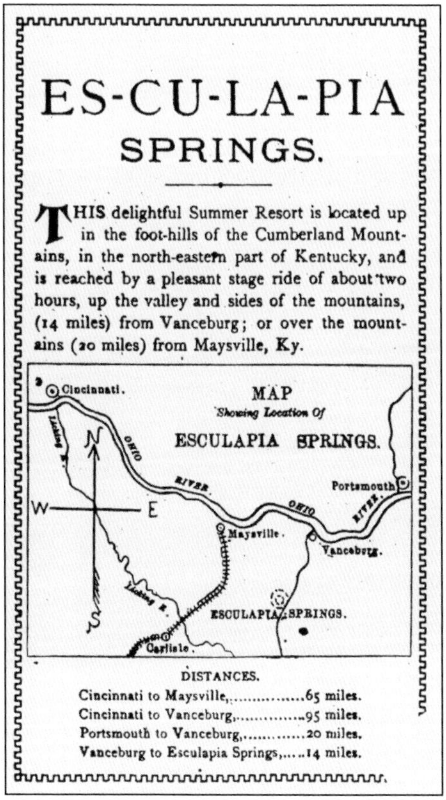

Esculapia Springs, located near the foot of Esculapia Mountain at the head of Big Salt Lick Creek in central Lewis County, was known and visited by hundreds of people from distant cities throughout the summer months. The first resort was built here in 1846.

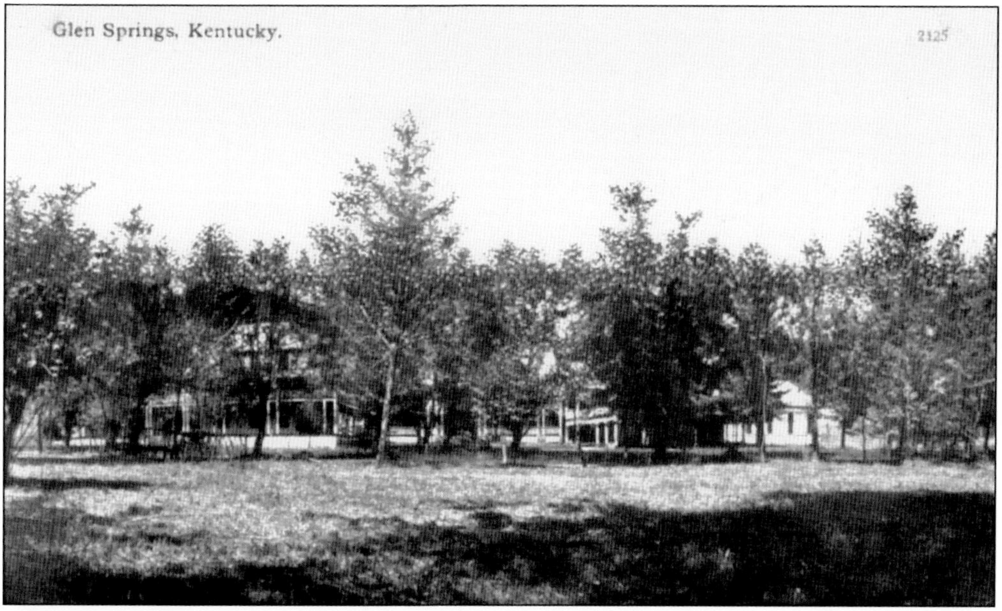

Glen Springs Resort is seen here as it appeared in 1908. Several health resorts and spas were located near the Charters area, which had many sulfur springs that were touted for healthy properties.

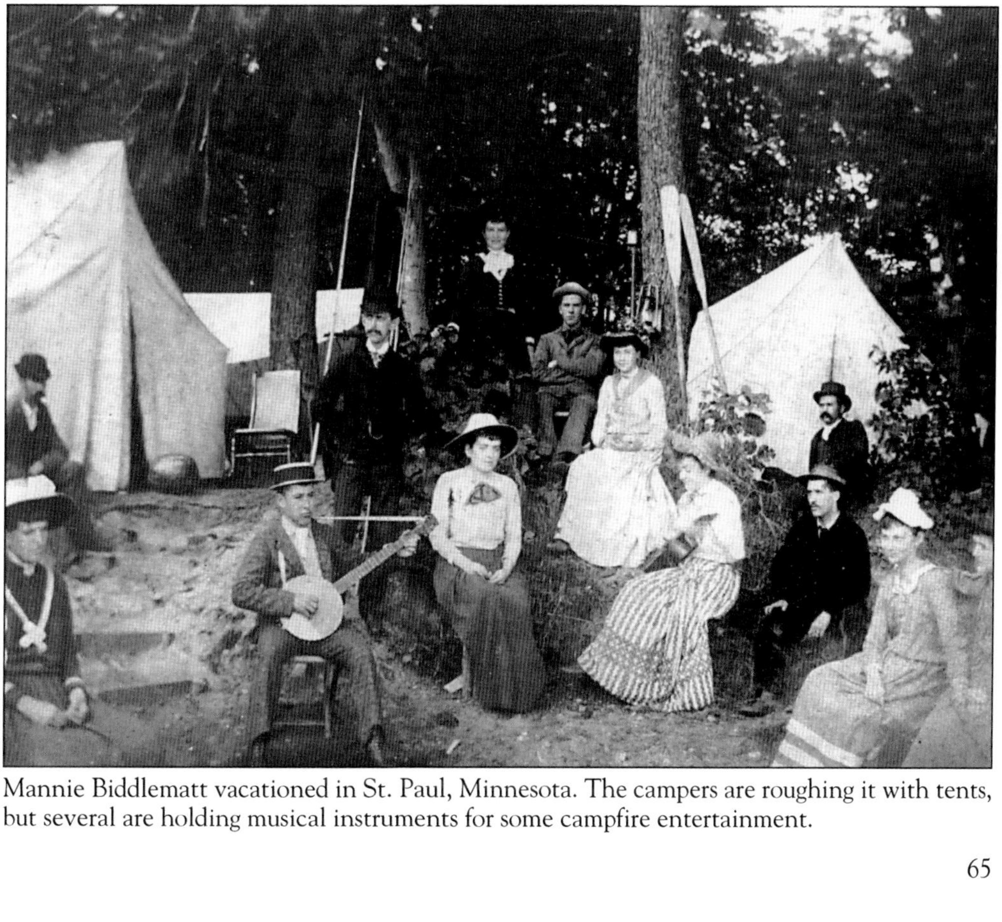

Mannie Biddlematt vacationed in St. Paul, Minnesota. The campers are roughing it with tents, but several are holding musical instruments for some campfire entertainment.

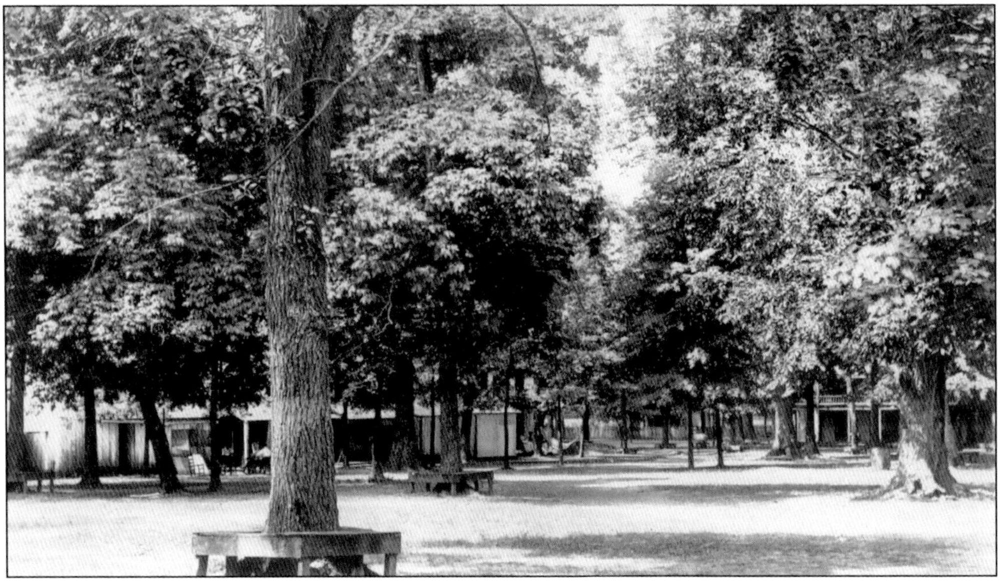

This shows Ruggles Camp Ground as it appeared in 1911. It was and is used by the Methodist Church for summer "camp meetings."

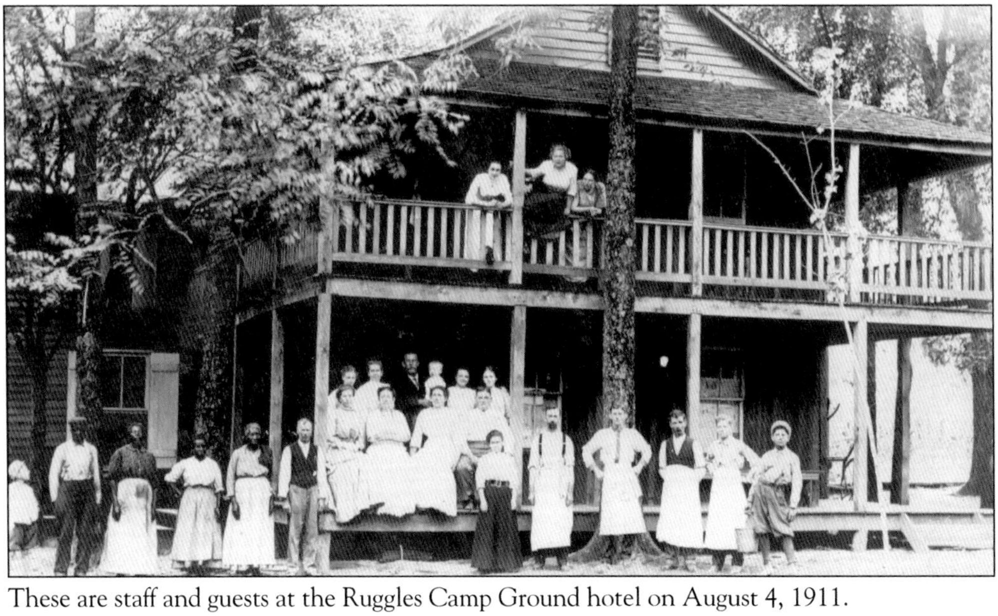

These are staff and guests at the Ruggles Camp Ground hotel on August 4, 1911.

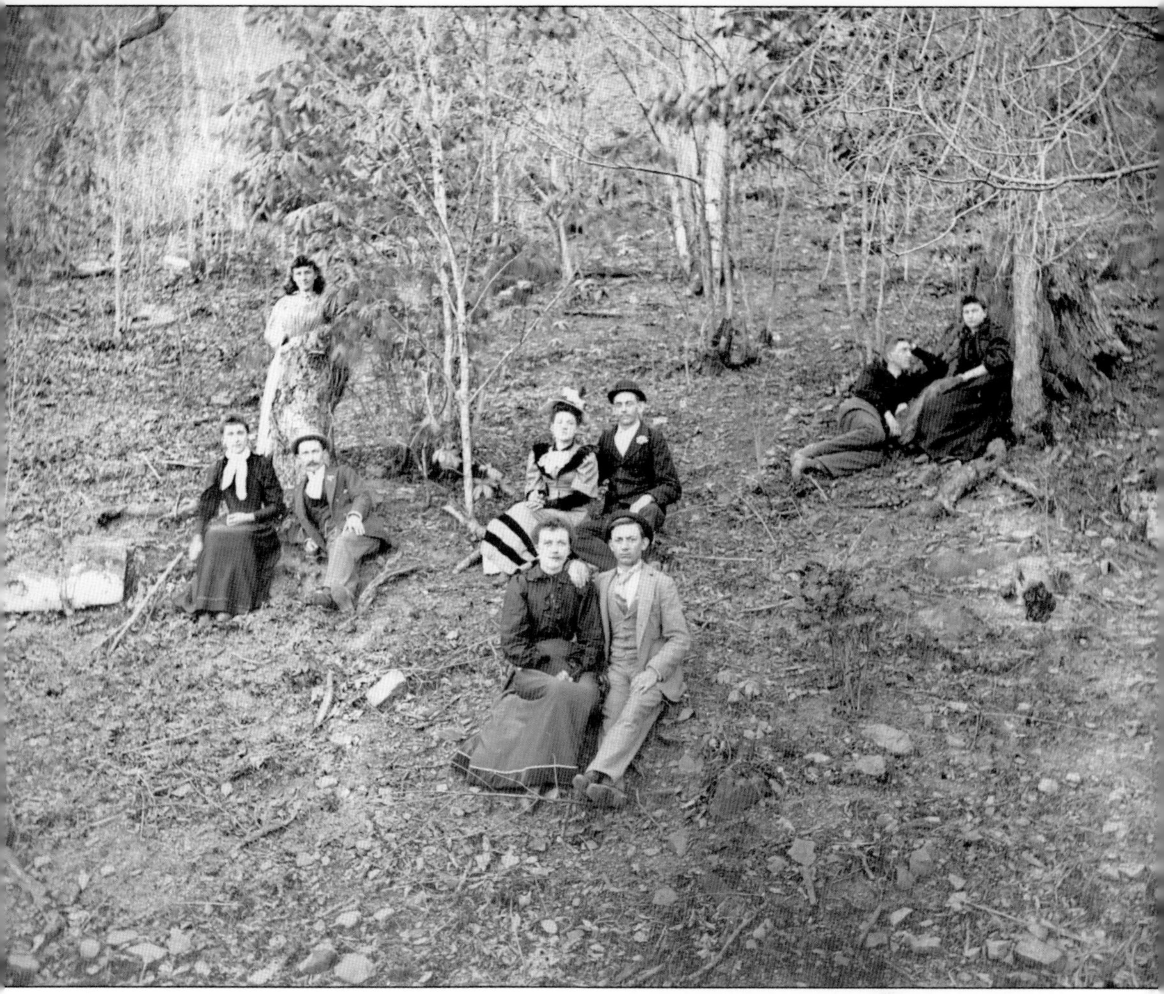

This group of young people seems to be out on a Sunday afternoon stroll in 1895. The location is the beech woods on the Clark farm below Vanceburg. The people are, from left to right, Kate Holderness (standing); Nannie Pugh and Ben Davis below Kate; Blanche Cottingham and A.H. Holderness, in the front of the picture in the first row; Jessie Jeffers and Charles Hammond in the top row; and Charles Eames and Eva Trenary, the couple on the extreme right. Notice how well-dressed the young people are.

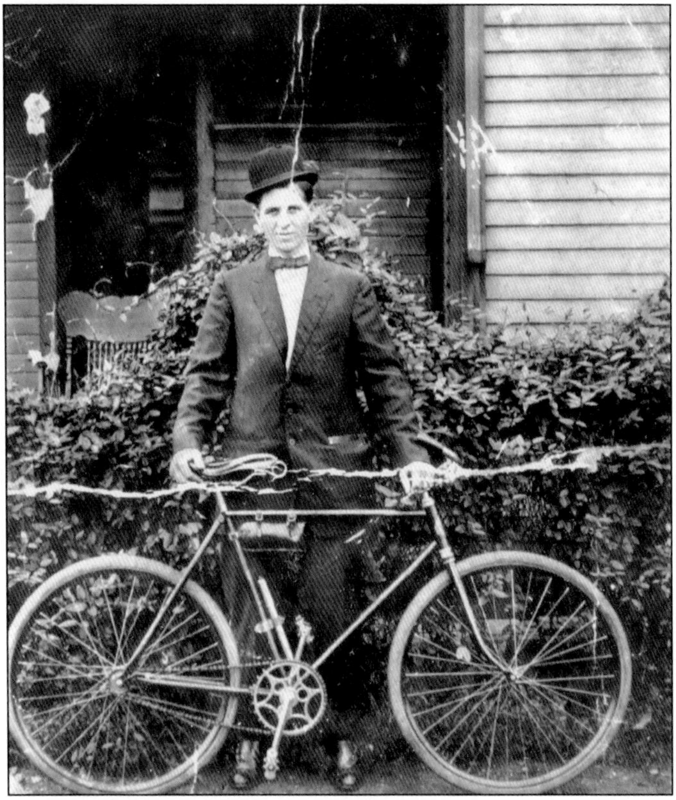

Edward Lewis, son of William and Nicie Bloomfield Lewis, poses here with his bicycle. The photograph was taken at Portsmouth, Ohio, where Ed lived after he married Nellie Bell. He later married Audrey Carver, daughter of Albert and Marybelle Carver.

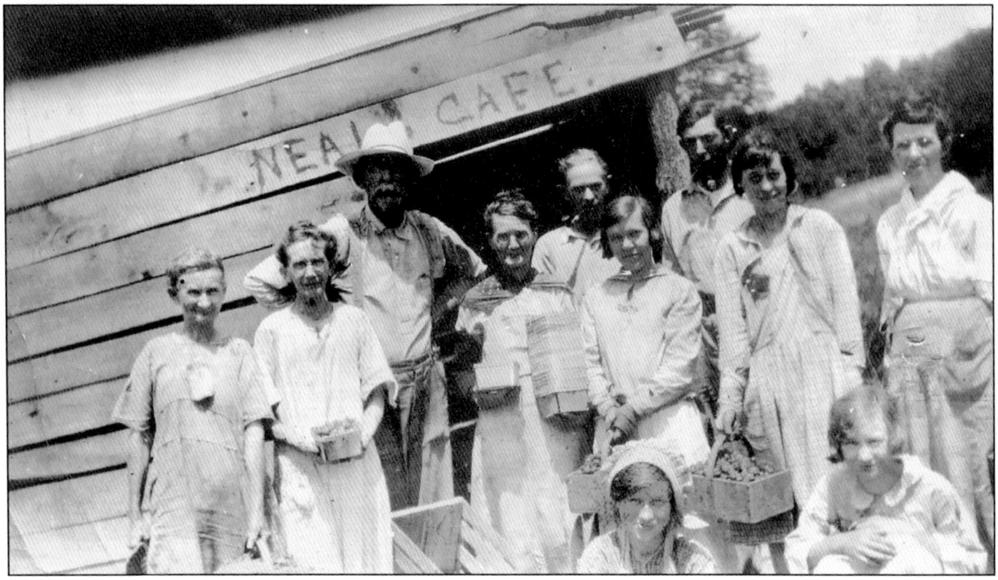

"Neal's Café" was a humorous title given to this shack that a group of strawberry pickers used for a lunchtime gathering. Included in the picture are Lizzie Jane Runyon, Mary Neal, Frank Neal, Berta Runyon, Bird Heath, Vivien Ruckle, Orville Ruckle, Delpha Conley, Molly Huff, Bernice Liles, and Opal Huff. This was taken near the Neal home on Route 3037 in the 1930s.

Five

Schools and Churches

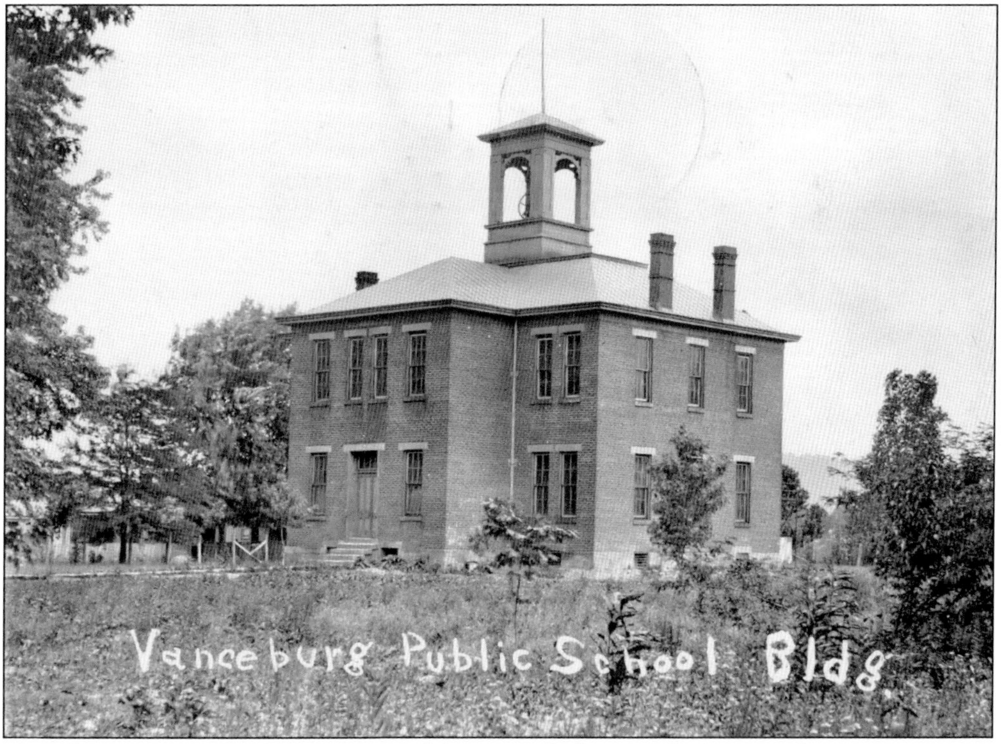

Vanceburg Lower School was on Second Street, with this view looking northwest.

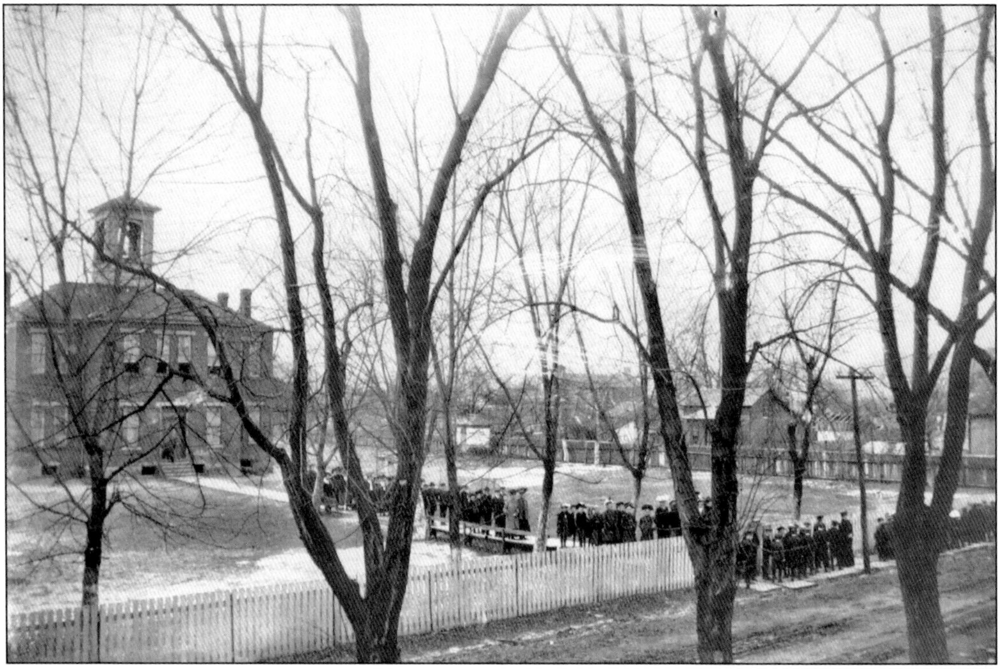

This is the front view of the Vanceburg Lower School about 1900. It appears that the students are lined up for a parade. The front of the line is at the corner of Harper Avenue and Second Street.

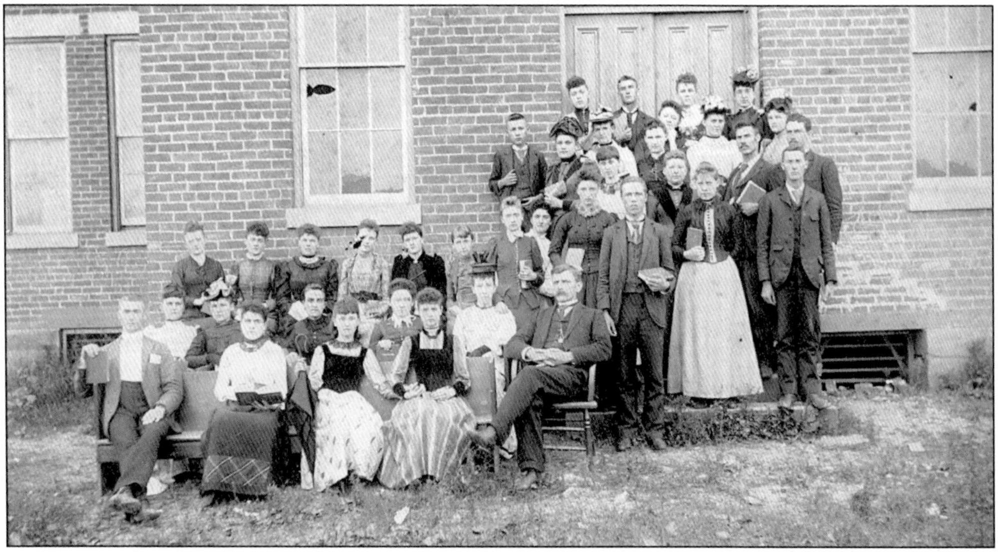

This group of "normal school students," taken sometime in the decade of 1880–1890, is standing behind the Vanceburg Lower School on West Second Street in Vanceburg, facing the river. Only some of the people in the photograph could be identified: those under the window with a broken pane are Emma Jones (Willim) and Grace Fisher (McDaniel). In the center of the picture, seated in a chair, is professor T.M. Games. In the group on the steps (in no order) are Cora Lykins (Bowman); Sudie Clark (McDaniel); Mary Waring (Grimm) in a white skirt; and U.C. "Crave" Thoroughman, holding a book. W.C. Dugan said of them, "After 40 years, one of the group could not recall the names of the others, though she remembered their faces."

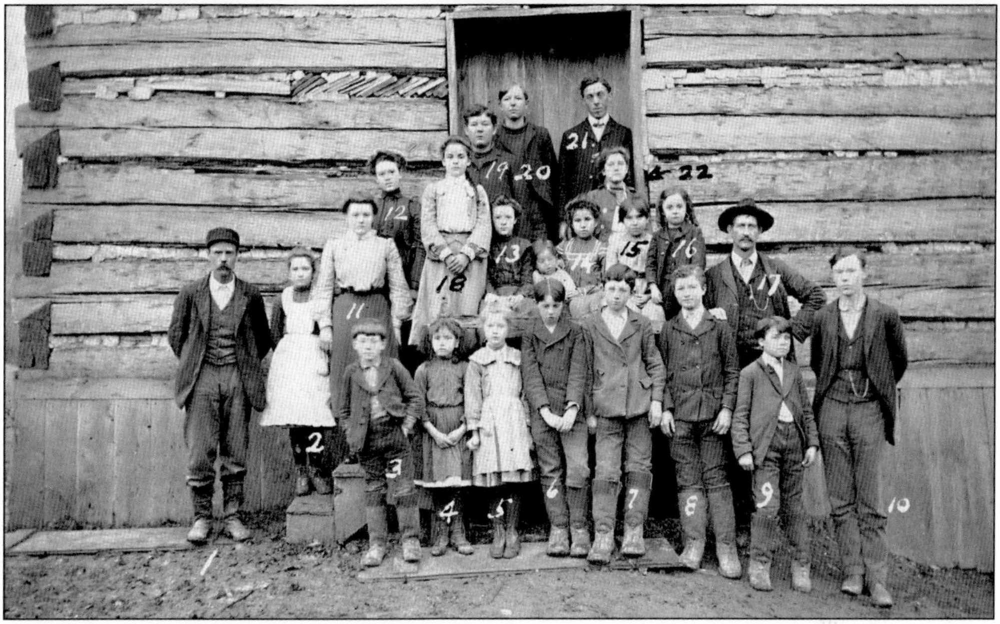

This view of a one-room log school at Martin (sometimes known as Queens) was taken about 1890. At one time, W.C. Dugan and Gus Doyle identified the names of students with numbers, but their notes have been lost. This, probably the first school at Martin, preceded two wooden frame schools, one of them known as Kissick's School.

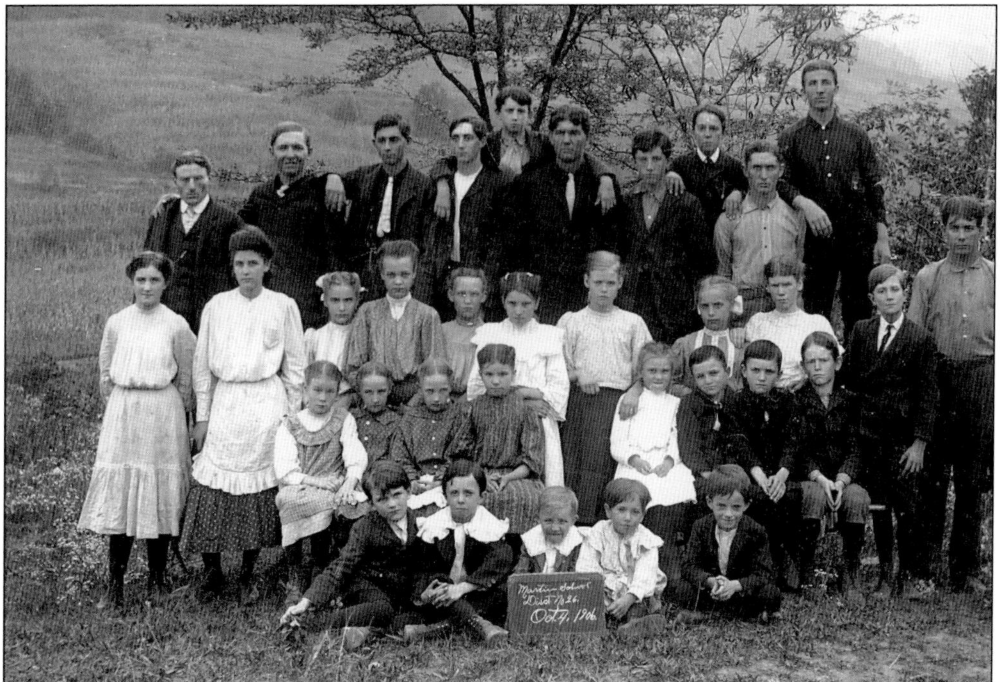

This picture of the student body of Martin School, District No. 26, was taken October 4, 1896. These children seem to be especially well-dressed for a country schoolhouse. We do not know their identities.

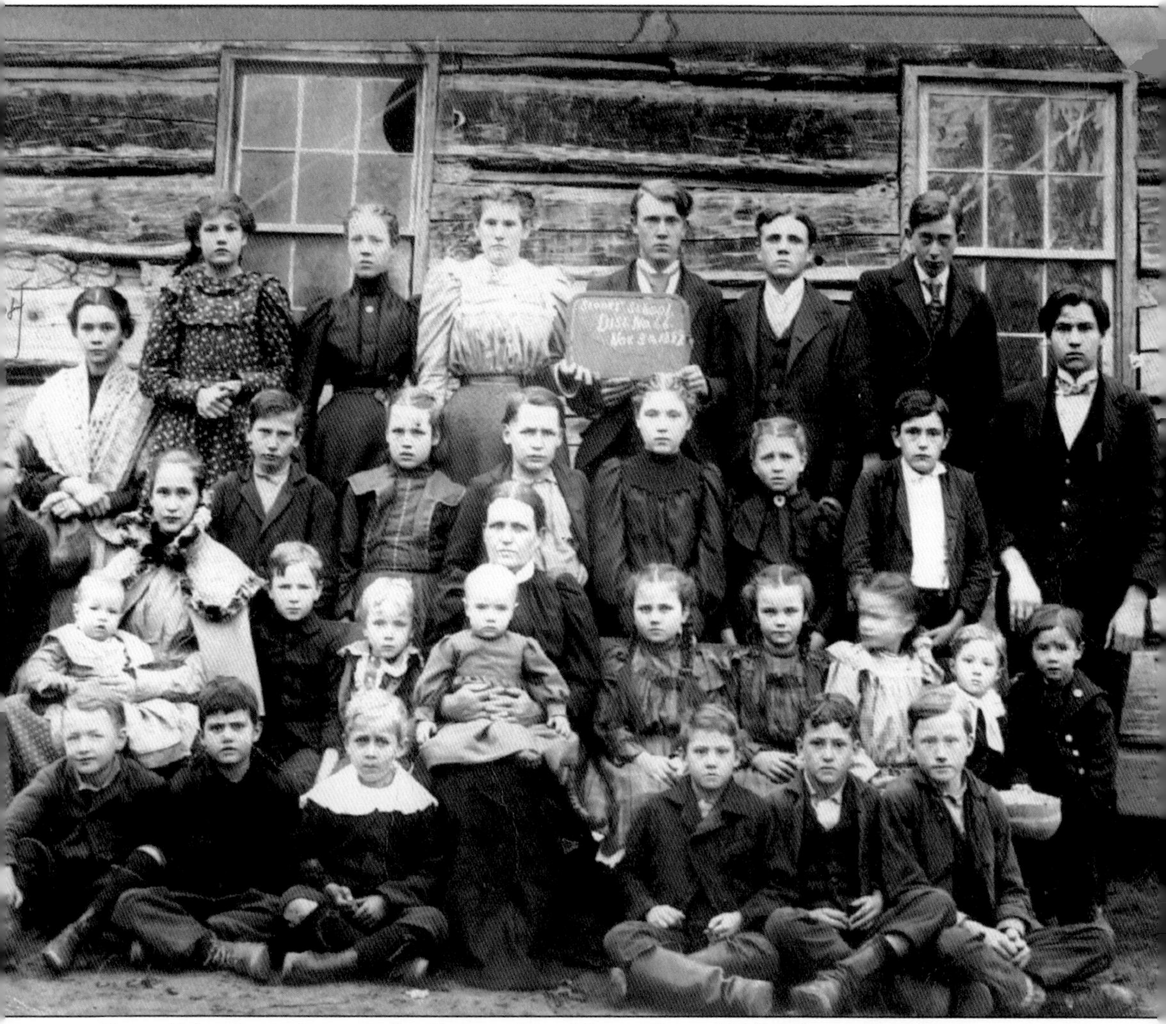

Stone School was designated as District No. 66 as early as 1879 and was later known as Scott's Branch. The picture was taken November 3, 1898. Shown from left to right are (first row) John A. Bloomfield, "Cornett" Stone, James R. Lewis, Ezekial Stone, James E. Stone, and Willie Stone; (second row) Clarinda Liles Kilgallin, with Frank Kilgallin on her lap, John Harlan Roe, Charles H. Roe, Calista Roe with Oma Roe (Cooper) on her lap, Cynthia Stone (Stafford), Rebecca R. Stone (Bates), Grace Mathewson (Cooper), John Kilgallin, and Olney Cooper; (third row) William Ray Roe, Alexander Bloomfield, Sophie J. Bloomfield (Fannin), James Ralph Bloomfield, Cynthia J. Roe (Horsley), Etta J. Lewis (Rayburn), Lewis O. Hinton, and Willie Pitts (teacher); (fourth row) Abigail Cooper Liles, Eva Stone (Bates), Minnie Roe, Eda Laura Stone (Edington), James I. Roe, Charles A. Roe, and Sylvester W. Lewis.

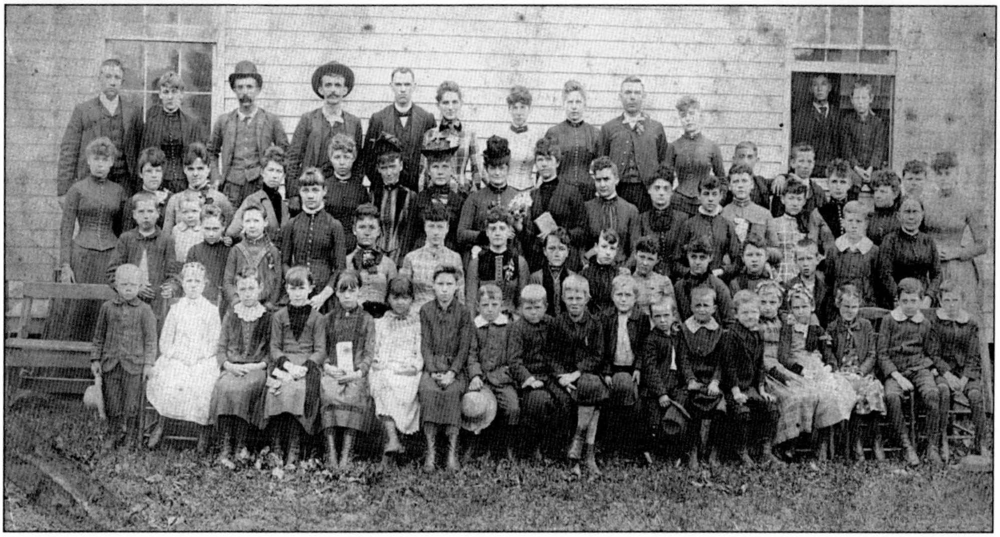

Prof. Lawrence Rolf came to Vanceburg to operate the Riverside Seminary in the fall of 1890. This picture is believed to have been taken the previous year, when the seminary was operated by Lee and Shockley, who had acquired it from the Strother family. Included in the picture are Bruce Plummer, Nellie Fisher, Ella Sparks, Nellie Pugh, Beulah Pugh, Mary Donehoo, Soc Plummer, Alma Agnew, Carrie Burriss, Ella Fryer, Bessie Pugh, Sallie McClellan, Sallie Green, Mary Bruce, Mrs. Anna Wells (wife of Dr. J.M. Wells), Kate Willis, Mintie Plummer, and Lillie K. Fountain—the central woman of the three in the middle of the fourth row. Take note of the two boys in the window.

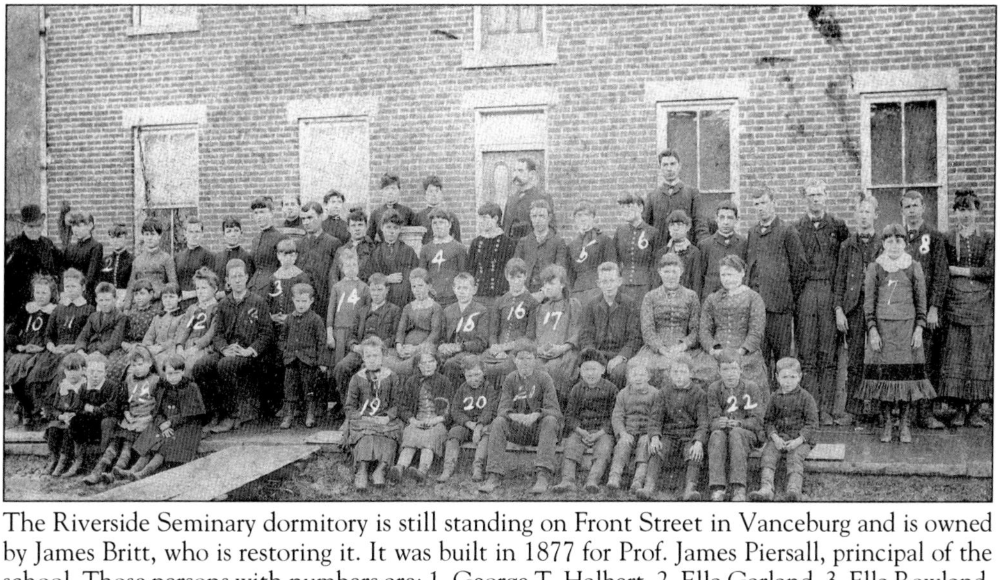

The Riverside Seminary dormitory is still standing on Front Street in Vanceburg and is owned by James Britt, who is restoring it. It was built in 1877 for Prof. James Piersall, principal of the school. Those persons with numbers are: 1. George T. Halbert, 2. Ella Garland, 3. Ella Rowland, 4. Rebecca Stamper Roe, 5. Emma Paula Arganbright, 6. Jenny Wood Gill, 7. Cinda Stamper Dunbar, 8. Ernest Bruce, 9. Mary Donehoo, 10. Nellie Pugh Hanford, 11. Sallie McClellan Plummer, 12. Grace Fisher McDaniel, 13. Will Stricklett, 14. Adelia McClellan Holderness, 15. Charley Hammond, 16. Jessie Stricklett Hammond, 17. Minta Plummer, 18. Nell Donehoo Ruark, 19. Maggie Sparks Cox, 20. Claud Staggs, 21. Harry Donehoo, and 22.Will Donehoo.

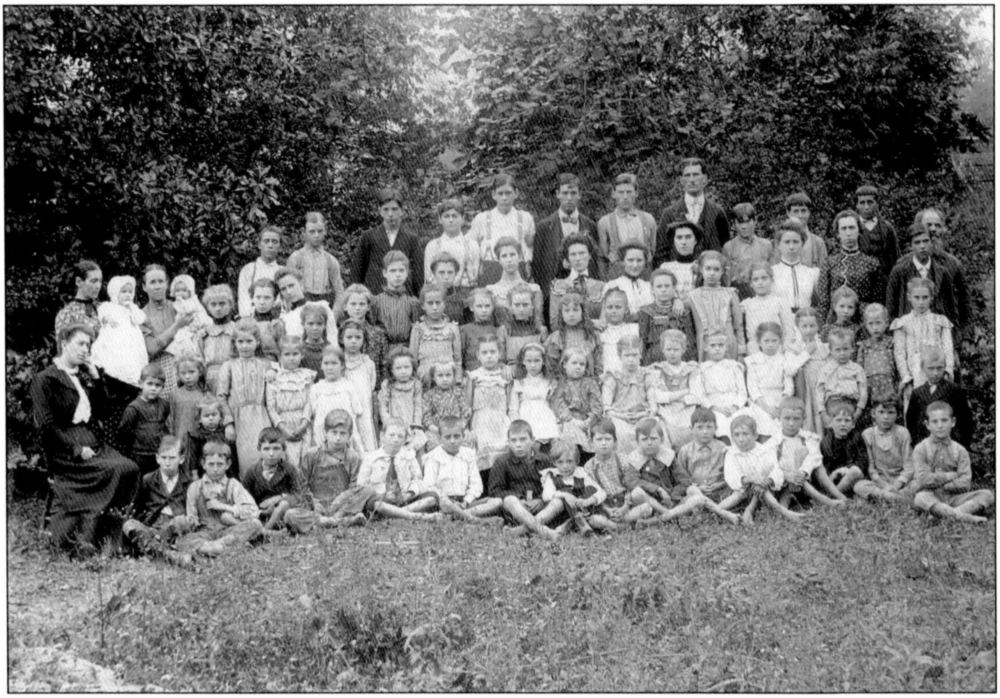

This picture of an unidentified group of students, almost all of them barefooted, was taken at a school on Quicks Run Road in the late 1890s or early 1900s.

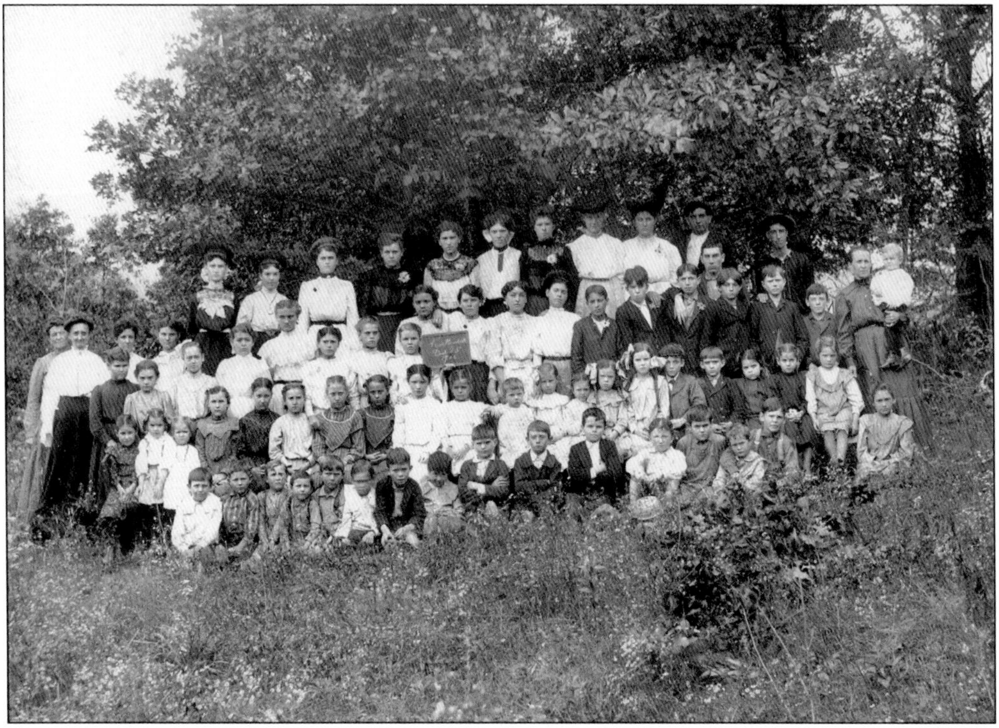

This is a 1906 class photo of the students of Kirkendall School, which sat on the northwest side of Quicks Run Road, a short distance from Muses Chapel.

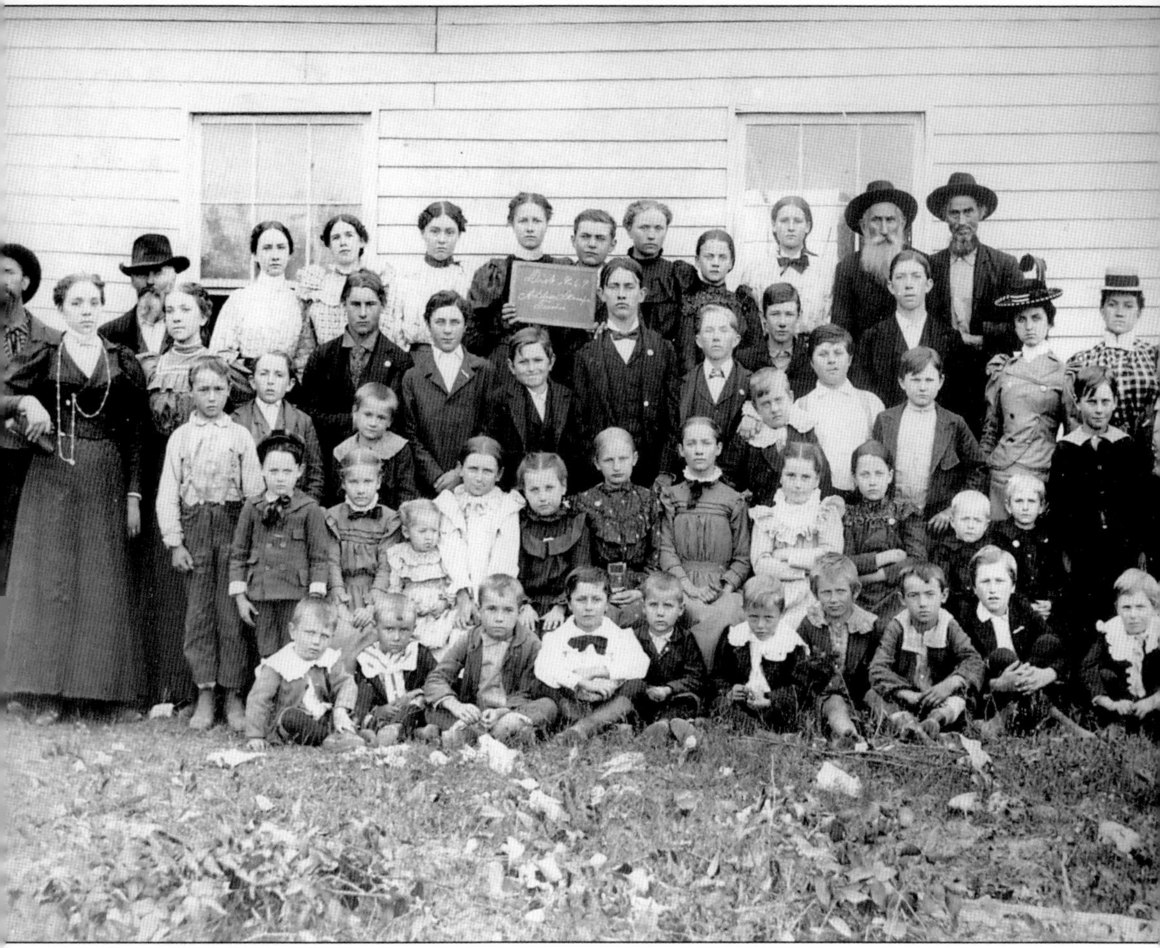

Orange Valley School, known as District No. 69, was located on what is now the Kenneth and Donna Carver farm near Petersville.

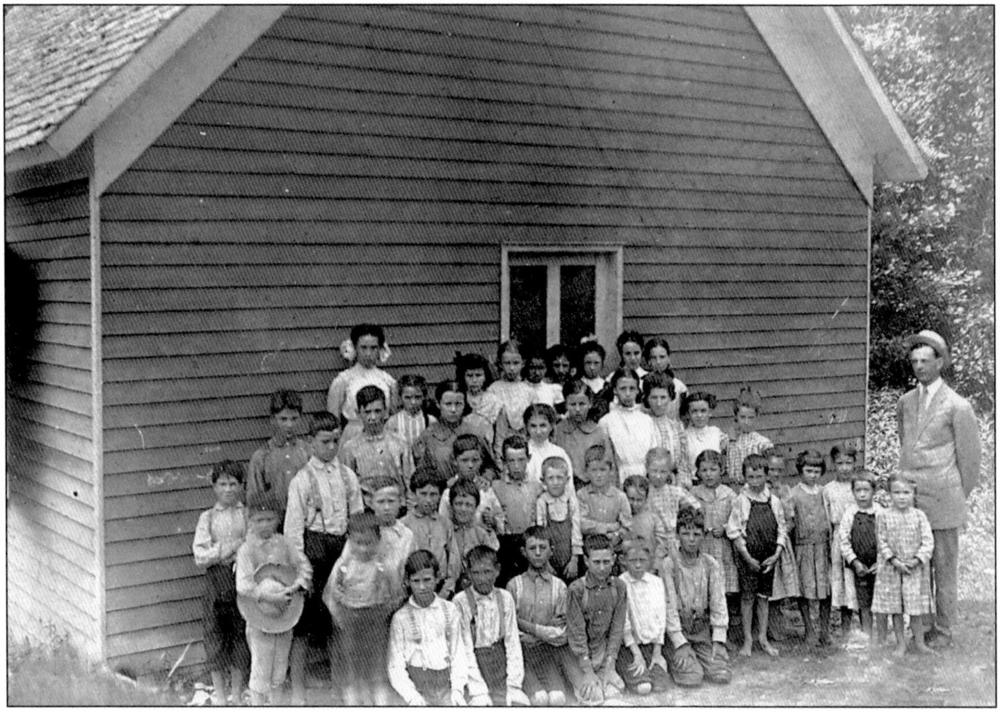

This unidentified school picture, taken around 1911, shows Bruce Thomas Lykins (1891–1935) and his pupils.

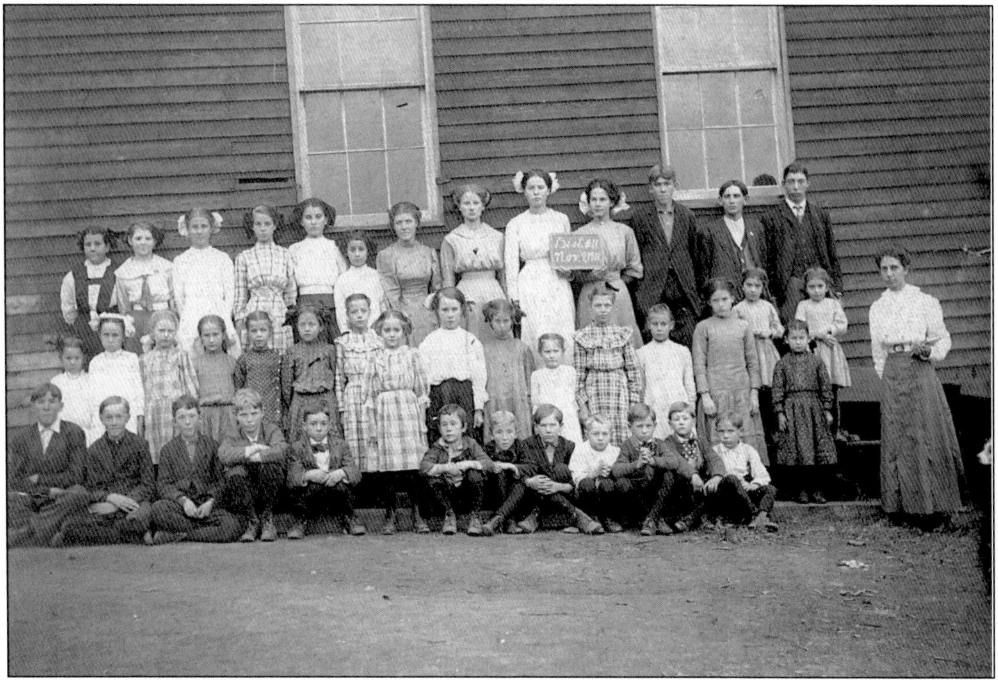

This is the student body of District No. 11, Aills School, on Quicks Run Road, taken November 9, 1911. Notice the dog peeking into the picture on the far right. The school has been painted, perhaps red. The shutters have been removed, leaving only the hinges.

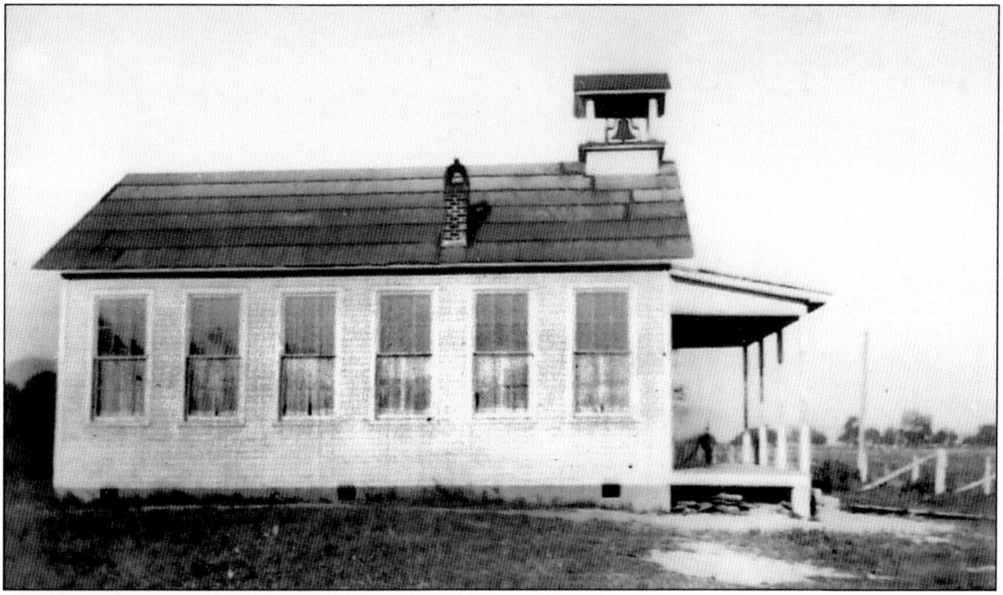

This was one of a series of Carrs schools. The building shown here is complete with bell and belfry in 1923. It is thought this building stood facing Route 8 near the Carrs-Fairmount Road.

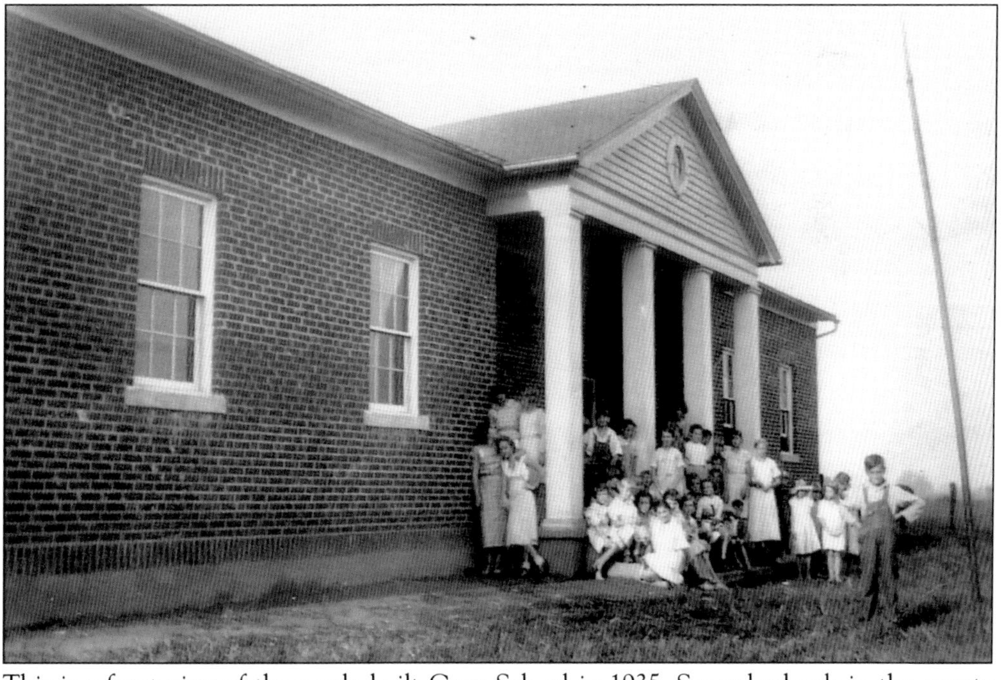

This is a front view of the newly built Carrs School in 1935. Several schools in the county were built in the same style in the 1930s, but most of them, including Carrs, have been destroyed (Valley School by storm, Glen Springs School from neglect; Kinniconick School is used for storage).

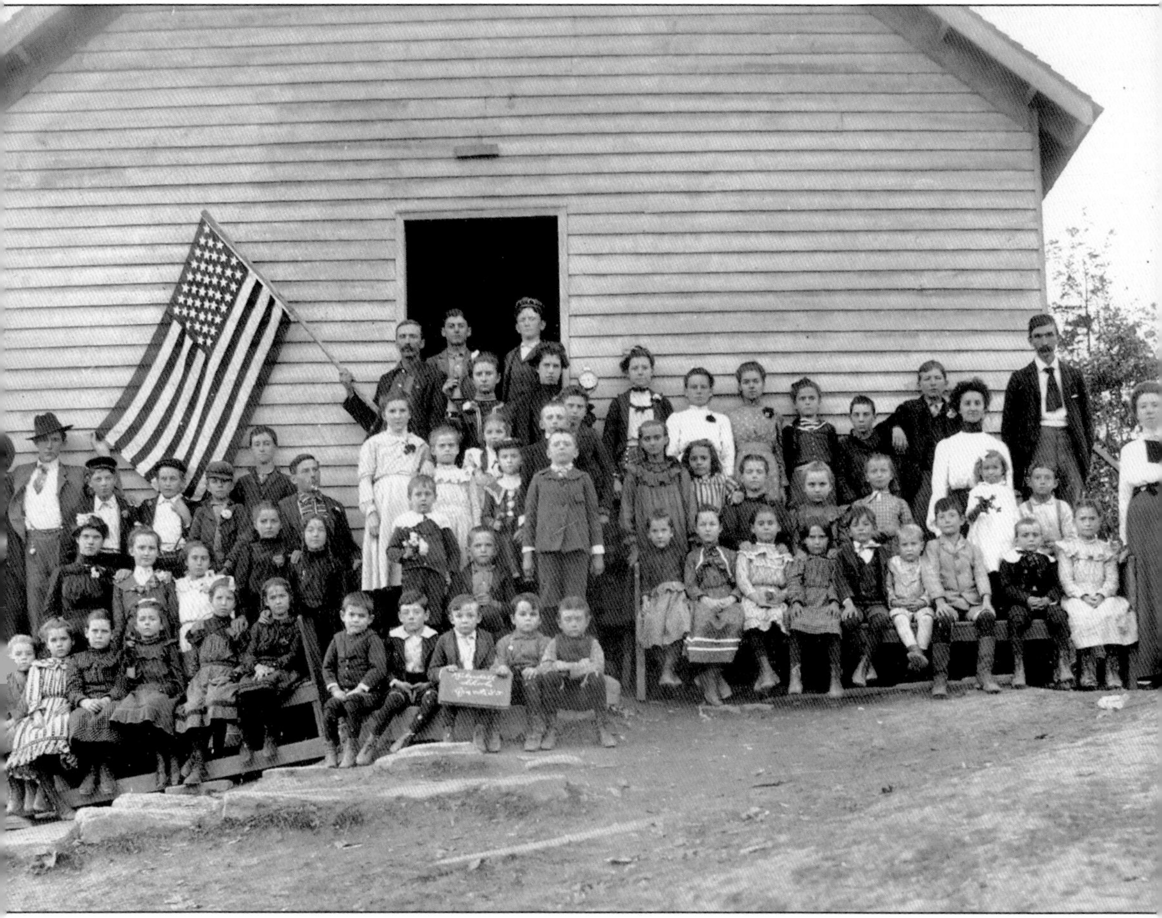

This Kirkendall School class photo is undated, but it appears to be in the early 1900s. One young lady in the doorway has an alarm clock and a small bouquet in her hands. The stars in the flag give a clue to its approximate date.

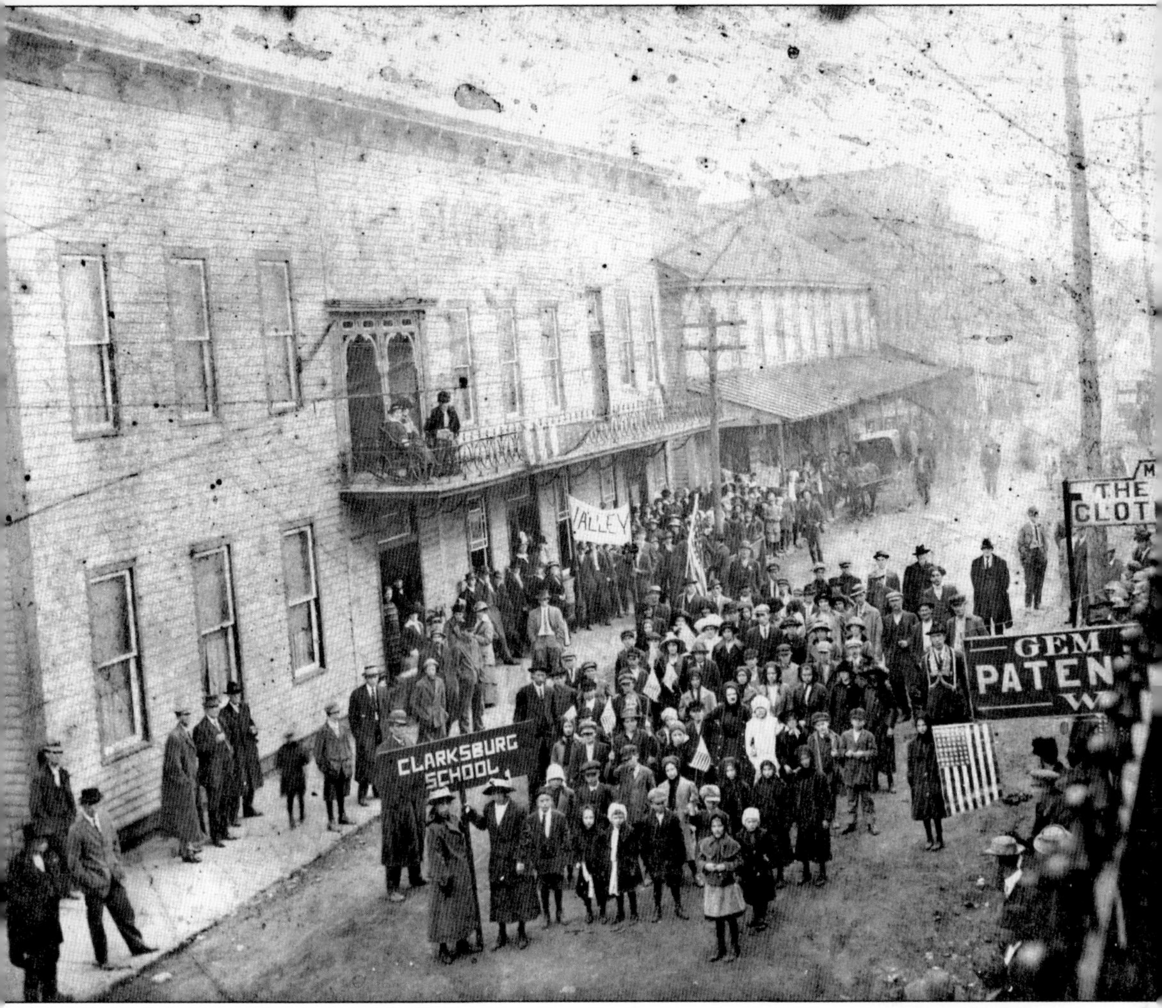

This is Vanceburg and Lewis County's first school fair parade. The fair was organized in 1903 as the "Lewis County Fair," and in 1913, the name was changed to "The Lewis County School and Agricultural Fair," during the administration of superintendent John Q. Adams. Close scrutiny of the picture reveals interesting people and objects. The picture was taken from the windows above the hair salon on the corner of Main and Second Streets. The building on the left is the St. Charles Hotel, which burned in March 1926, and the former gallery around the Citizens-Deposit Bank is visible in the right corner. Each school has its own banner. The parade was usually held in September, but everybody seems to be dressed for cold weather.

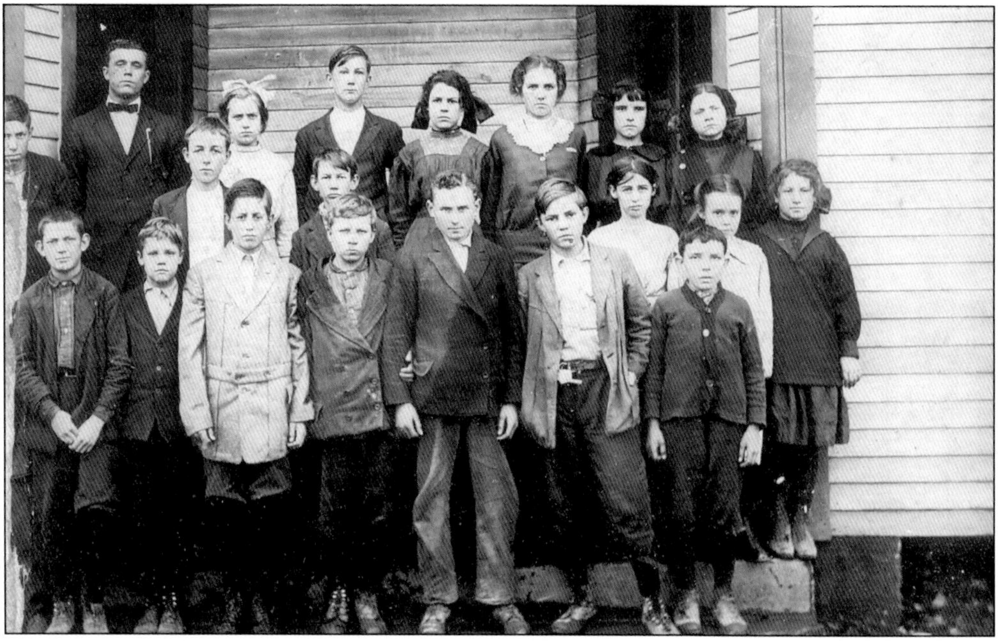

This Garrison School building preceded the brick building, which was dismantled several years ago. Robert "Bob" Brewer, who loaned this picture, says he does not know the names of the students, but his uncle, John Brady Lewis, was the teacher (with bow tie). Lewis taught there from 1909 to 1913, when he went to work for the railroad (1914–1955). Two students on the extreme left have been torn off.

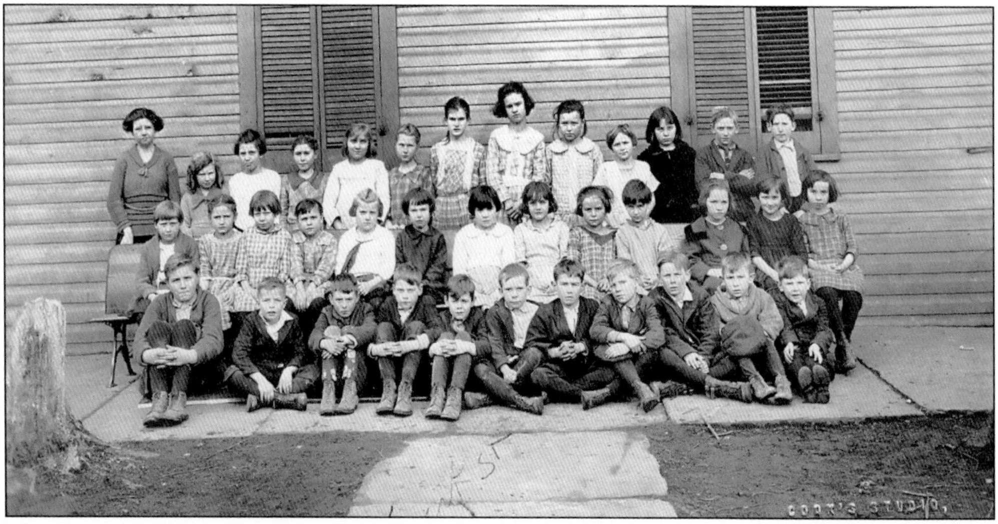

The Riverside Seminary School on Front Street in Vanceburg was established in the 1870s. This picture shows Sarah Keyser's third-grade class, taken about 1919–1920. From left to right are (front row) Orville Webster, Eugene Browning, Maurice Carroll, Roy Chamblin, Charles Hammond, George Irwin, unidentified, Roland Johnson, two unidentified, and Maurice Hamm; (middle row) Dolly Faulkner, Fannie Johnson, Viola Gilbert, Felicitas Keyser, Emma McKee, and eight unidentified students; (back row) Sarah Keyser (teacher), Ruth Plummer, Helen Plummer, Opal Lewis, Edna Webster, Bernice Liles, Dell Mofford, Nanny Stapleton, Beulah Boyd, Virginia Cobb, Dolly Bowlin, Donald Murphy, and Earl Lewis.

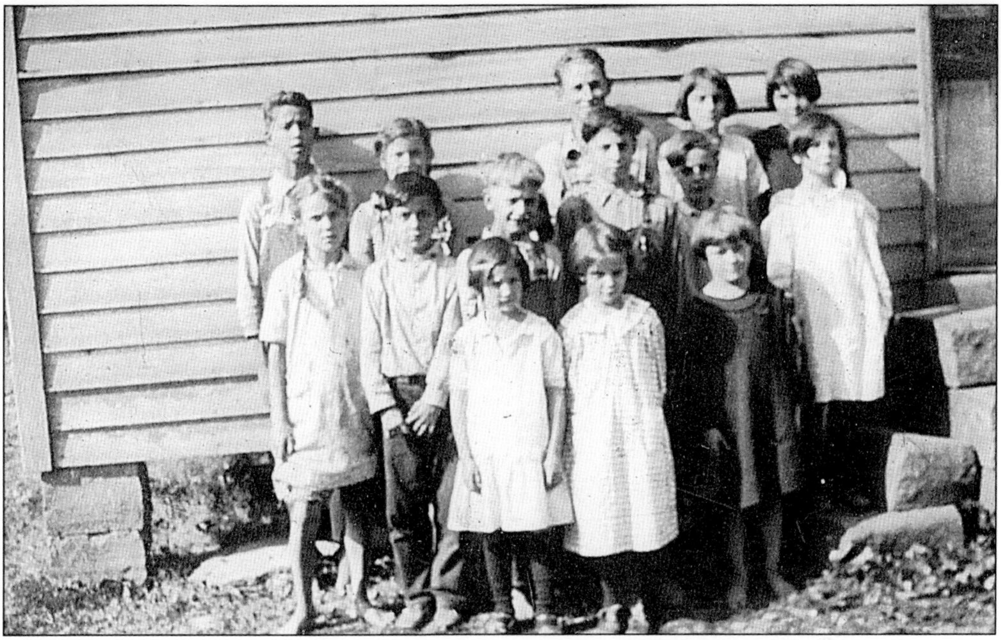

Taken about 1929, Scott's Branch School students are, from left to right, (front row) two McFarland girls and Naomi Stone; (middle row) Grace Roe Carver, ? McFarland, Earl Lewis, Ernest Smith, Nic McFarland, and Hilda Dummit; (back row) Vess Lewis, Minnie Roe (Stafford), Ward Lewis, Gladys Cooper, and Lucy Stone.

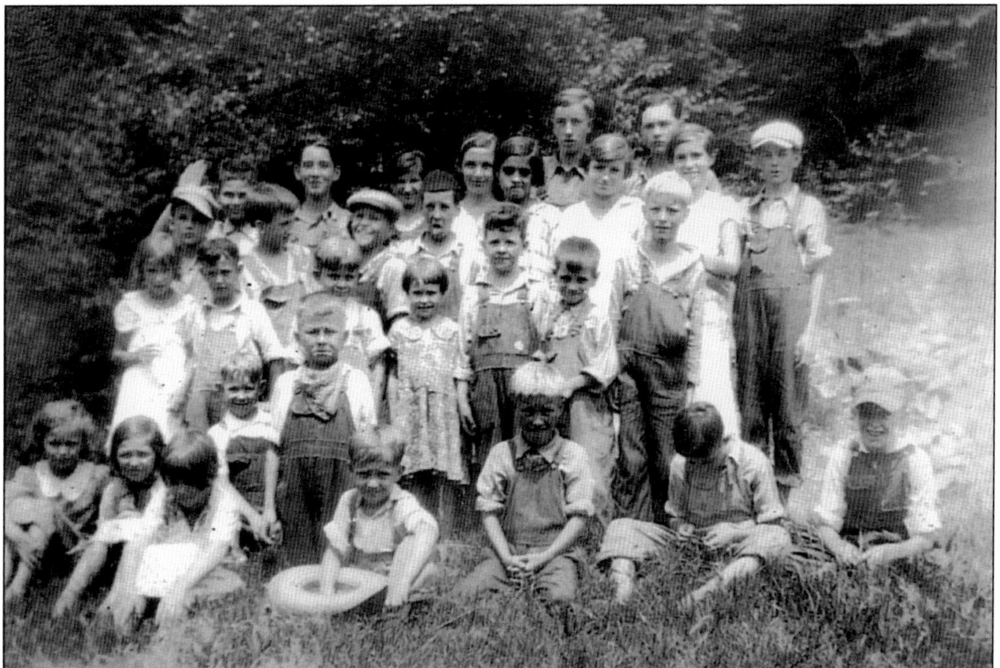

Family names of students in this Tannery School group in 1934 are Blevins, Lewis, Howard, Armstrong, McCleese, Osborne, Glover, Liles, and Riffe.

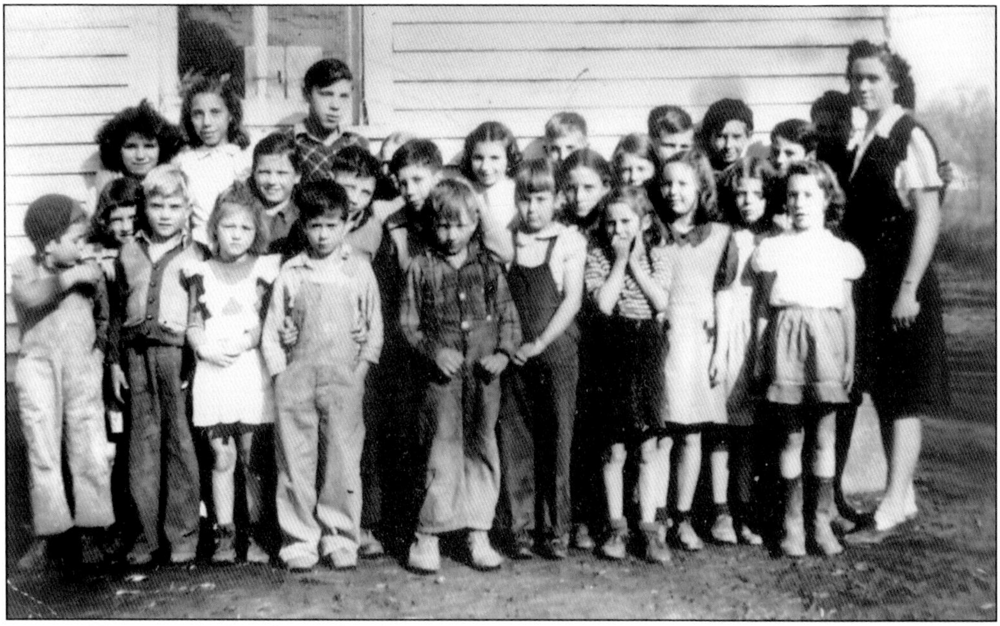

Pictured here is Blankenship School, set in the bottom lands near the foot of Stone Hill. The building in this 1945 picture was removed many decades ago. The inscription on the back of the picture said that Allen Walters, John Henry Blankenship, Karen Sue Stone, and Alton Walters were in the front row, and the only two identified in the middle row are Irene Carver and Betty Carver (the exact placement of students is not stated). The teacher, Elaine Stone, stands at the right.

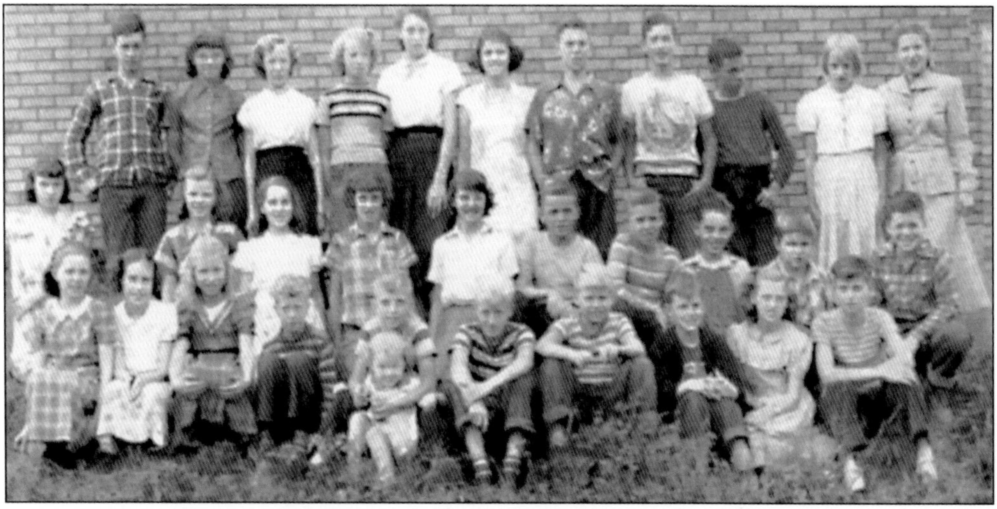

These are members of the fifth, sixth, seventh, and eighth grades at St. Paul School in 1951. From left to right are as follows: (front row) Patty Ratliff, Carol Walters, Francis Wells, Carl Morton Bradley, Tommy Hannah, Ernestine Hannah, Noah Sammons, Ralph Sammons, Gary S. Blaine, Carolyn Riffe, and Bobby Boggs; (middle row) Louise Pack, Edna Carol Bivens, Hildreth Blaine, Betty Walters, Dale Greene, James Robert Lute, Ronald Greene, Donald Walters, Elijah Greene, and Ronald Veach; (back row) Elmo Veach, Janie Smith, Carrie Bradley, Emma Wilburn, Frieda Ruth Greene, Sammy Joe Bennett, Paul Walters, Lloyd Pack, Phyllis Aldridge, unidentified, and Virginia Hannah (teacher).

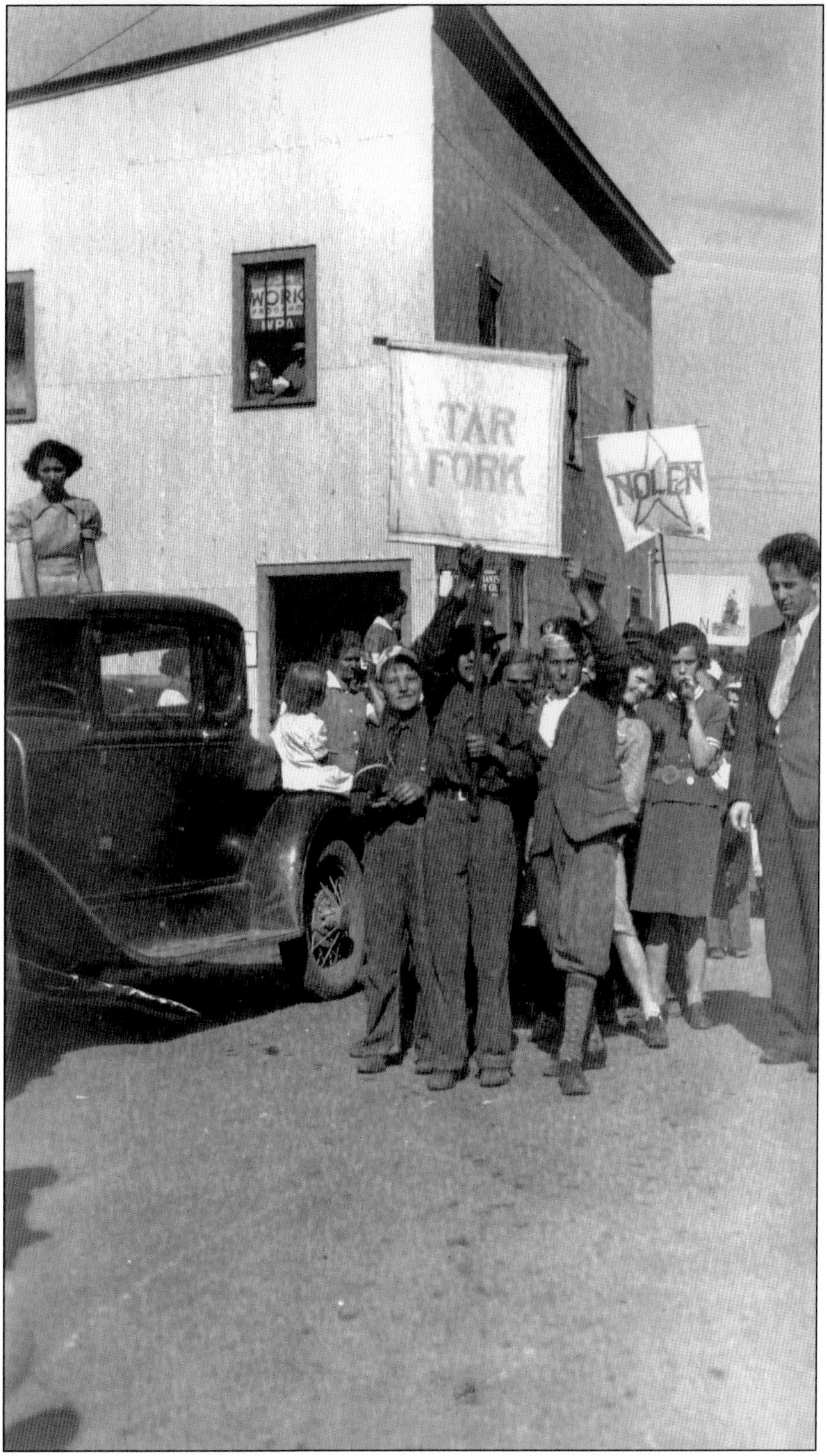

A 1930s view shows the annual School Fair parade assembling on lower Main Street in Vanceburg. Two of the schools—Tar Fork and Nolen—are shown with their signs. The old mill is in the background with a WPA sign in the window.

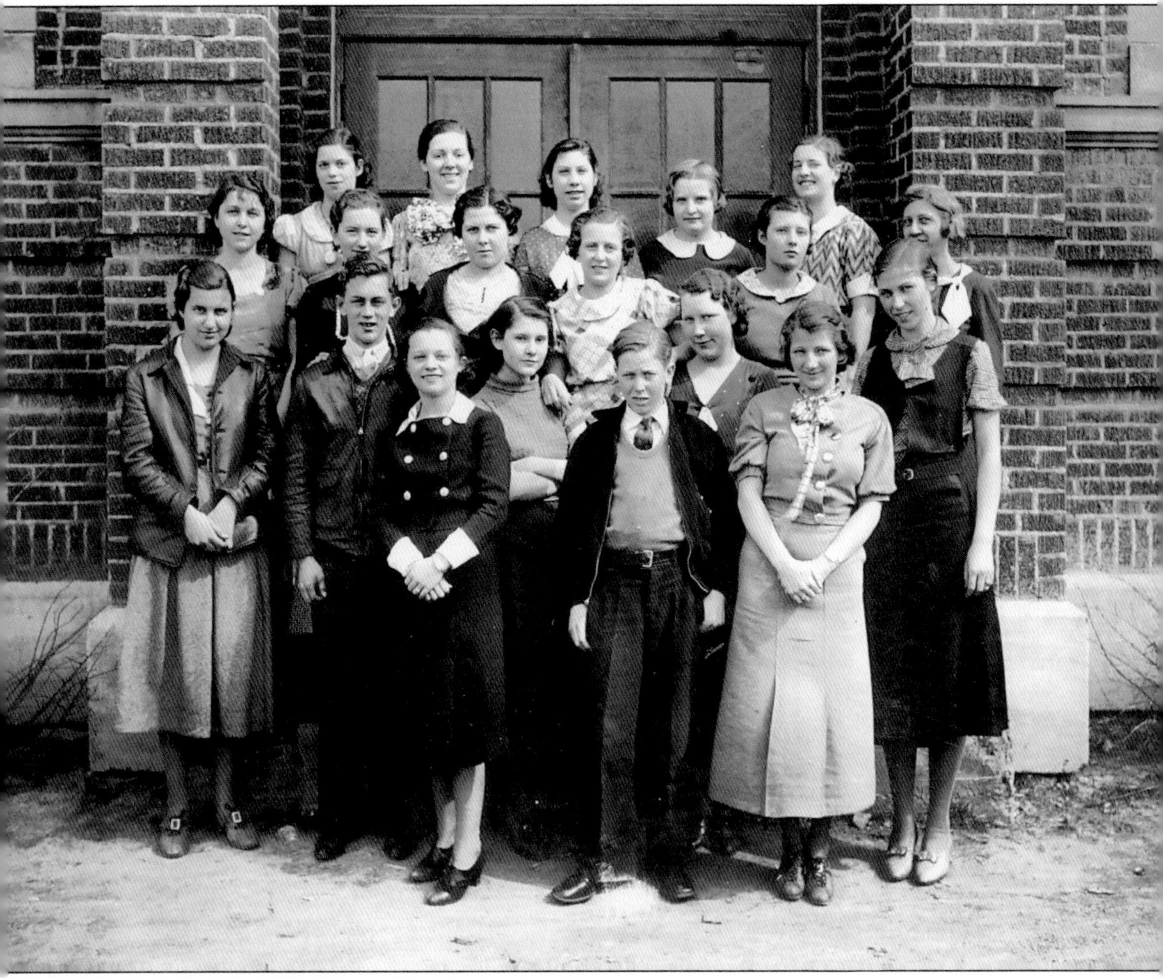

This picture, taken in the early 1900s, shows Carrie Goldenburg's Latin class.

This old report card shows the marks made by Clifford Liles when he was a young student in Carrie Goldenburg's class. Liles lost his life in a boat accident on the Ohio River at Vanceburg about 1960.

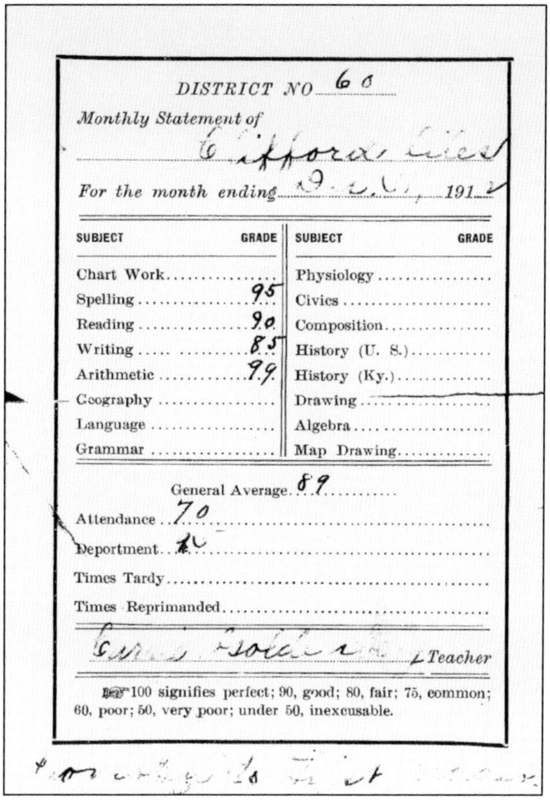

DISTRICT NO 60

Monthly Statement of

Clifford Liles

For the month ending ......, 191..

SUBJECT	GRADE	SUBJECT	GRADE
Chart Work		Physiology	
Spelling	95	Civics	
Reading	90	Composition	
Writing	85	History (U. S.)	
Arithmetic	99	History (Ky.)	
Geography		Drawing	
Language		Algebra	
Grammar		Map Drawing	

General Average 89

Attendance 70

Deportment

Times Tardy

Times Reprimanded

Teacher

100 signifies perfect; 90, good; 80, fair; 75, common; 60, poor; 50, very poor; under 50, inexcusable.

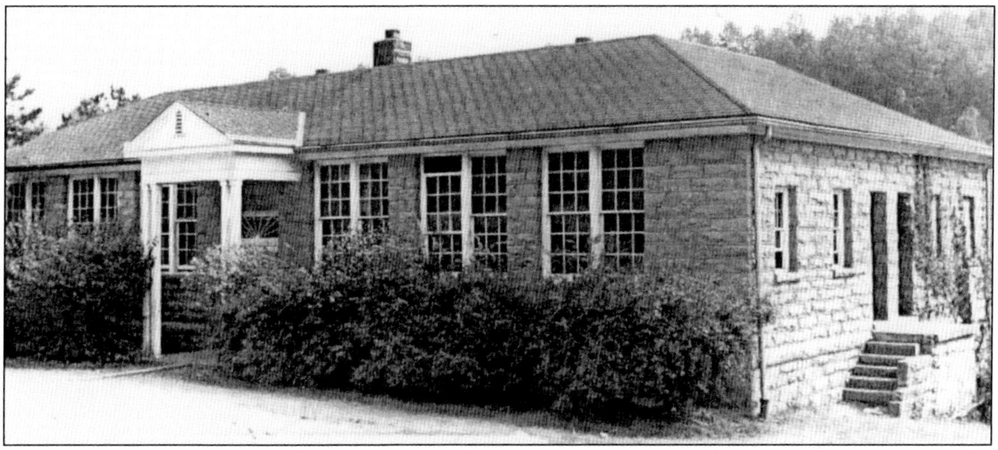

Laurel High School served the southern part of Lewis County until the late 1950s. It burned, and the students were then transported to Vanceburg. The 1930s-style building is quite similar to a school in Carter City, Kentucky.

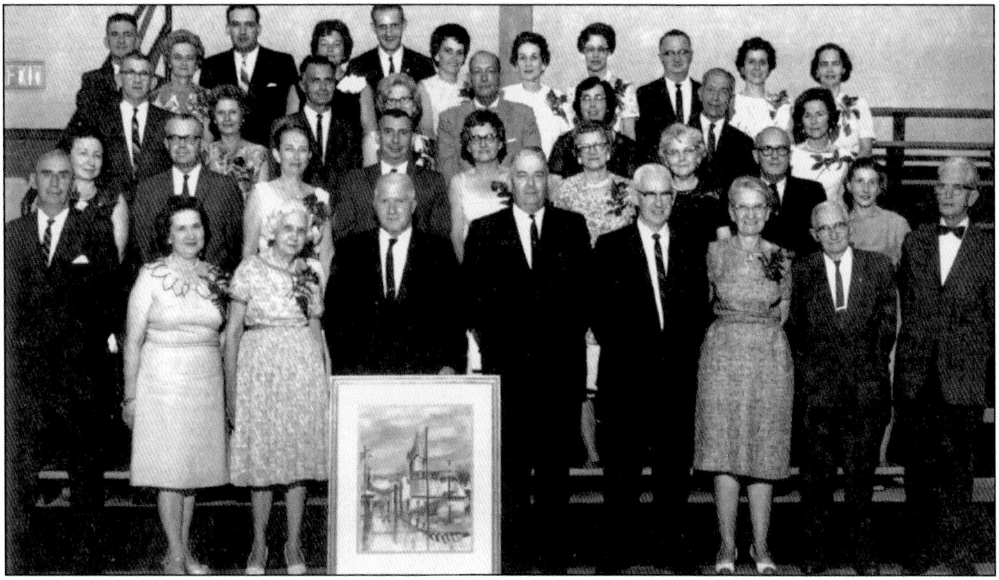

The Lewis County High School Class of 1933 had a reunion in 1965; former students and their guests included Robert Fabe and Miriam Timmer Fabe, of Cincinnati; Carrie Goldenburg, teacher; Charles Staggs; Lena Wells Voiers; Leroy Dorsey, teacher; Thomas Rowland, superintendent of schools; Anna Plummer Davis; Stella Webster Carver; Joe Carver; Winnie Staggs; Ned LeMaster; Hazel Lowder LeMaster; Ralph Davis; Harlan "Rub" Voiers; and Ann Staggs. The painting of Market Street in downtown Vanceburg shown in front was done by Robert Fabe, a well-known Cincinnati artist, and was presented by him as a gift to the school board.

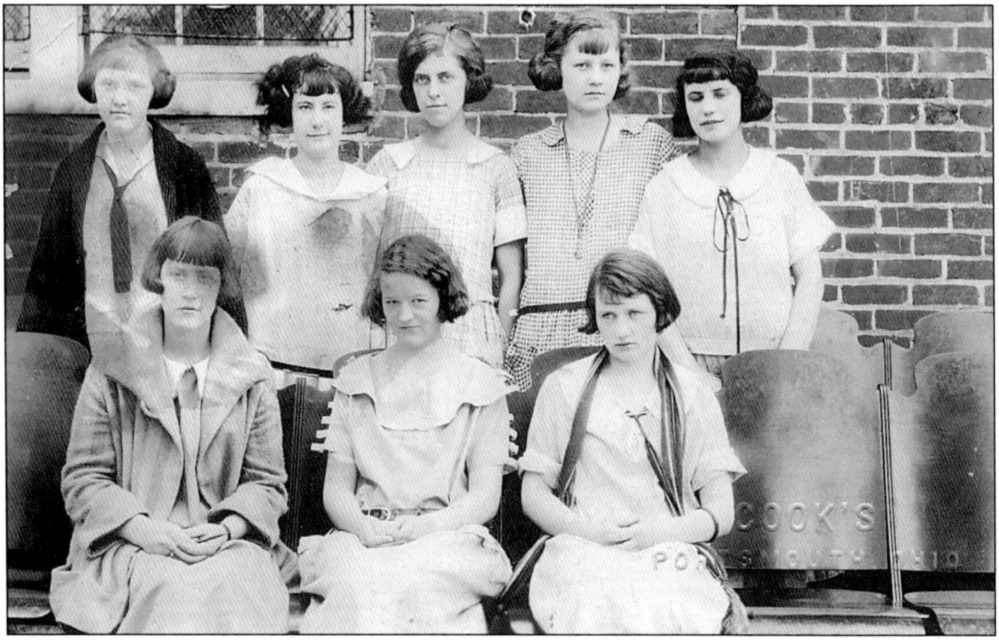

The students in this 1924 Lewis County High School picture are (front row) Evelyn Hays, Edith (Lykins) Hamm, and Margaret (Willim) Lykins; (back row) Bess Forman, Helen (Huffman) Rayburn, Velma Keyser, Audra Abbott, and an unidentified student.

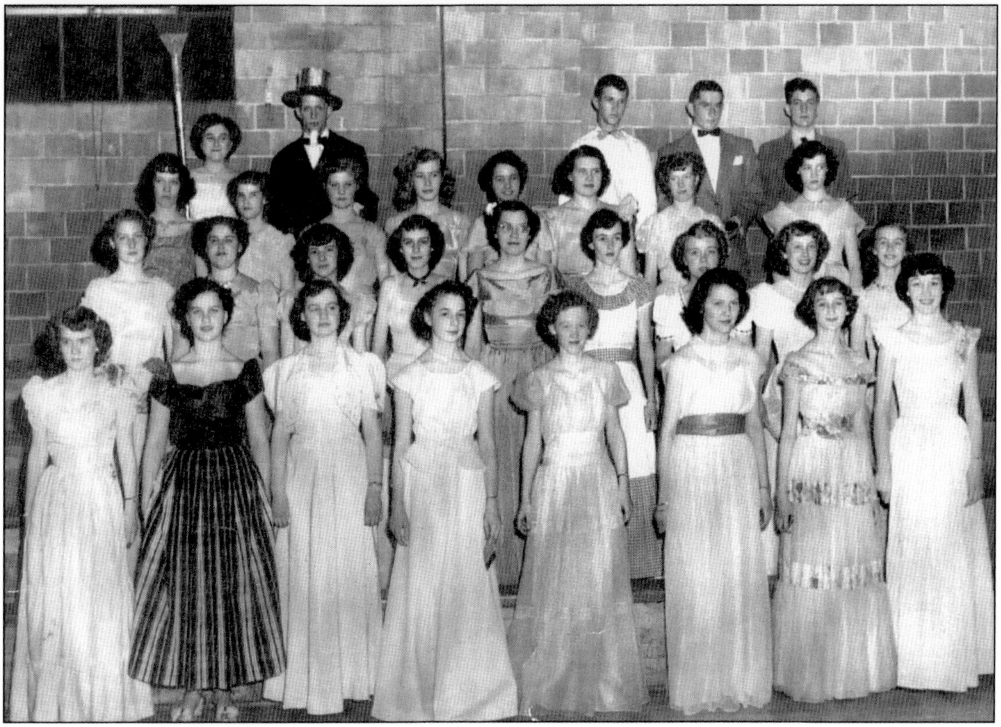

This singing group is the 1954 Glee Club of Lewis County High School.

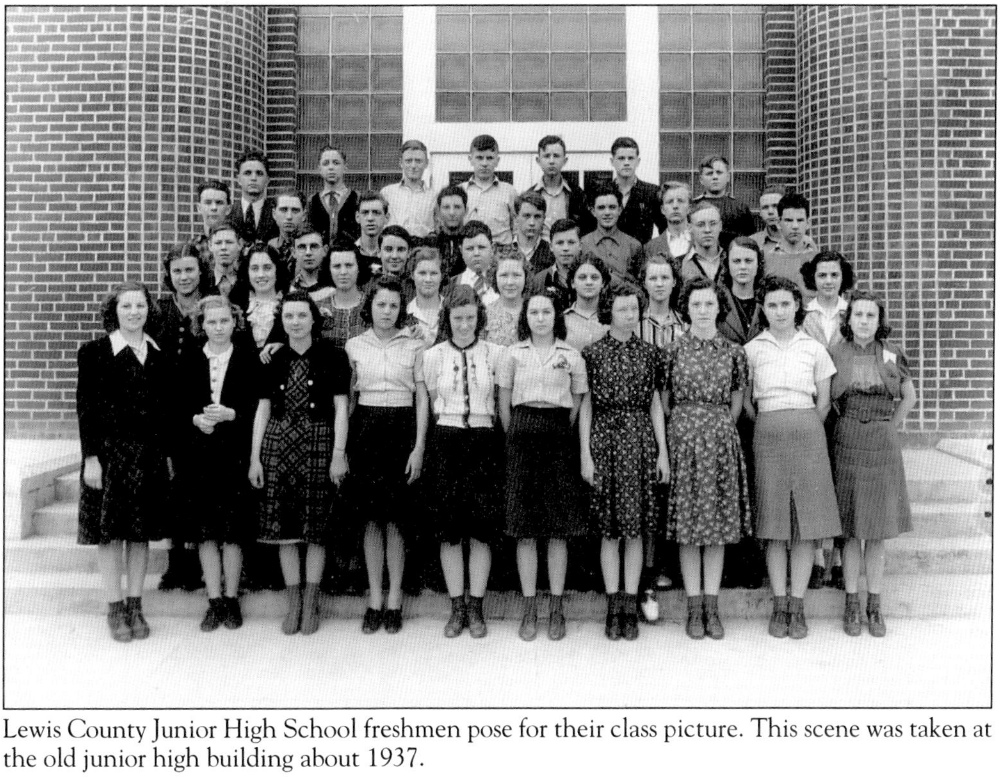

Lewis County Junior High School freshmen pose for their class picture. This scene was taken at the old junior high building about 1937.

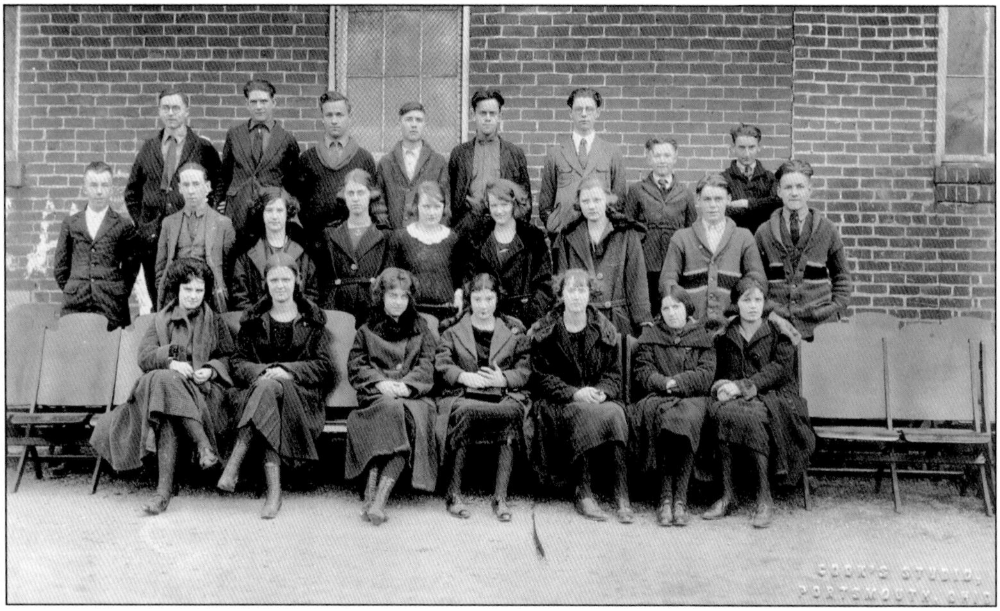

These are sophomores at Lewis County High School in 1923.

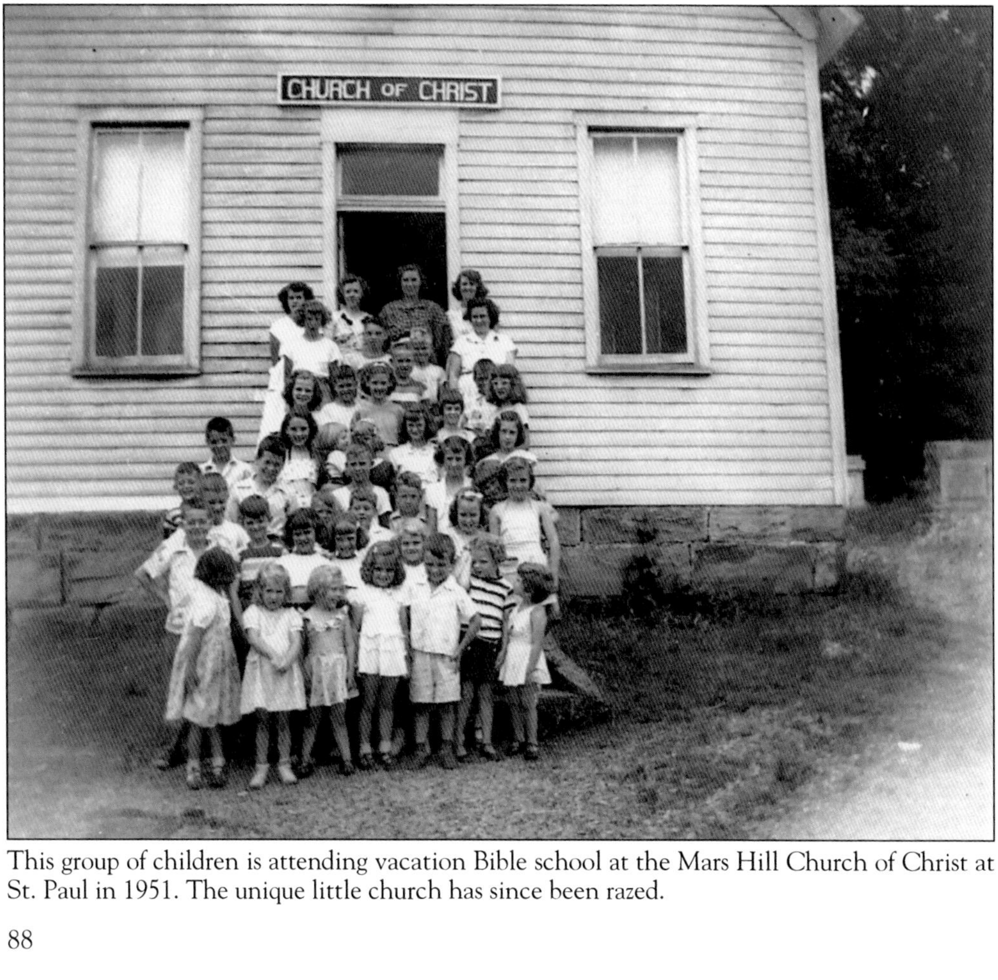

This group of children is attending vacation Bible school at the Mars Hill Church of Christ at St. Paul in 1951. The unique little church has since been razed.

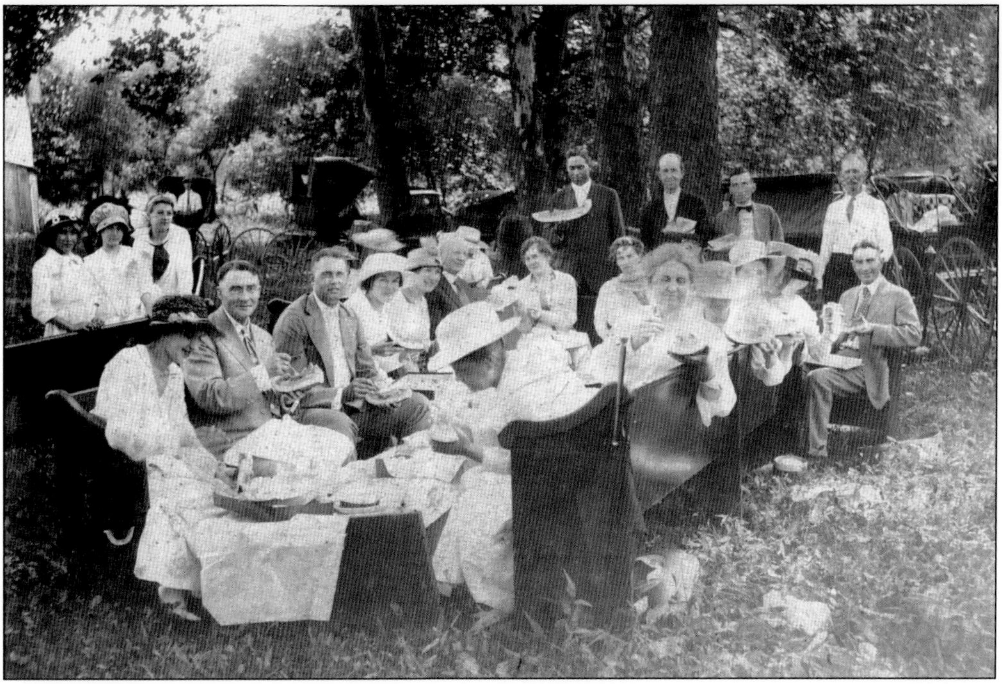

These people are eating watermelon on some church benches placed outside under the trees. There are at least four buggies shown in the picture. It is believed that Leland Cook is seated on the middle bench, third from the left. The location and date are not known.

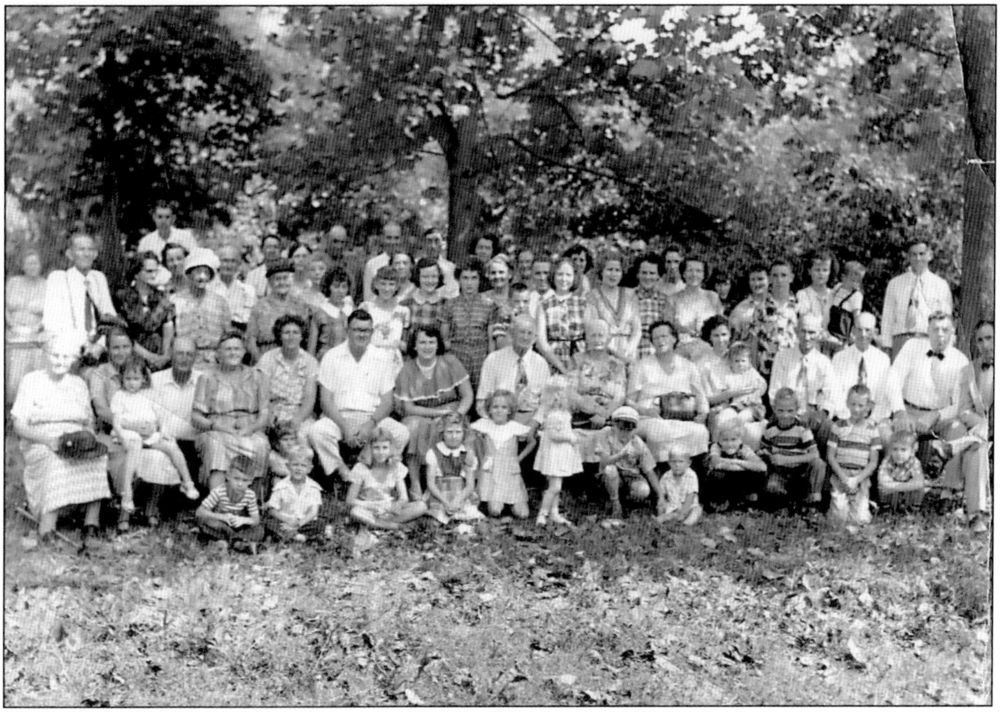

These were apparently members of the Quincy Christian Church at one of their special gatherings in the 1950s.

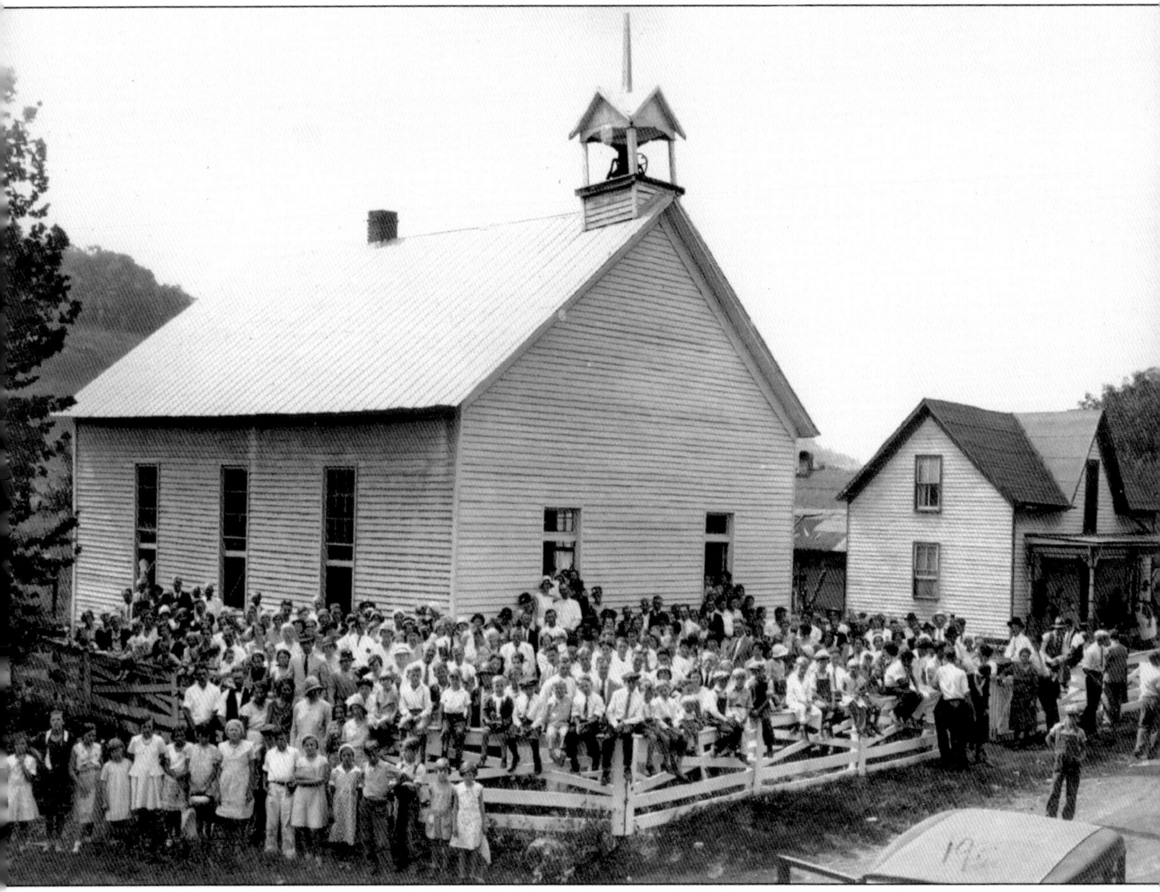

This Petersville Christian Church Homecoming in 1930 shows, at right, the Poynter house, which has been removed. The original church building has had two additions built onto it.

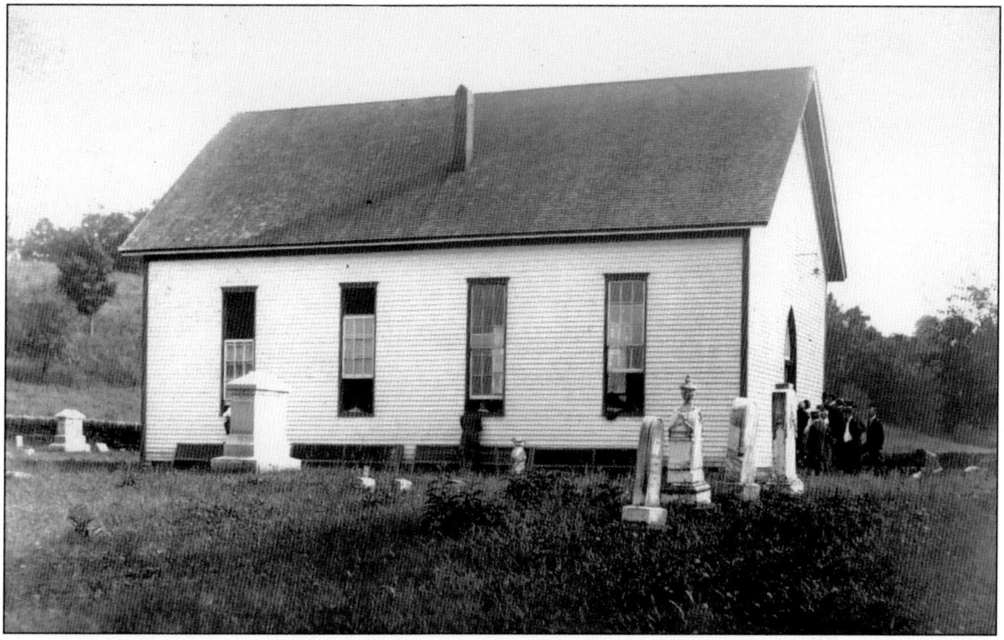

Ebenezer Presbyterian Church, located on Cabin Creek, was founded in 1798. This building (their third) was built in 1877. The picture was taken about 1910.

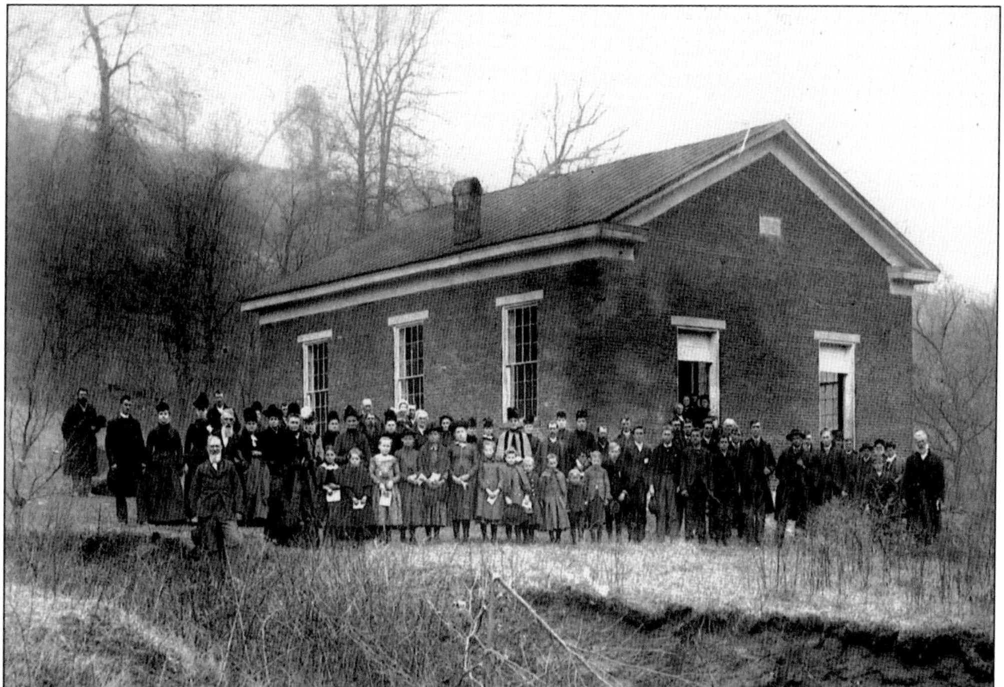

Sand Hill Christian Church was built in 1860 and is said to be a replica of Alexander Campbell's church in Bethany, West Virginia. This photograph was taken about 1890. The building is still standing and has regular services.

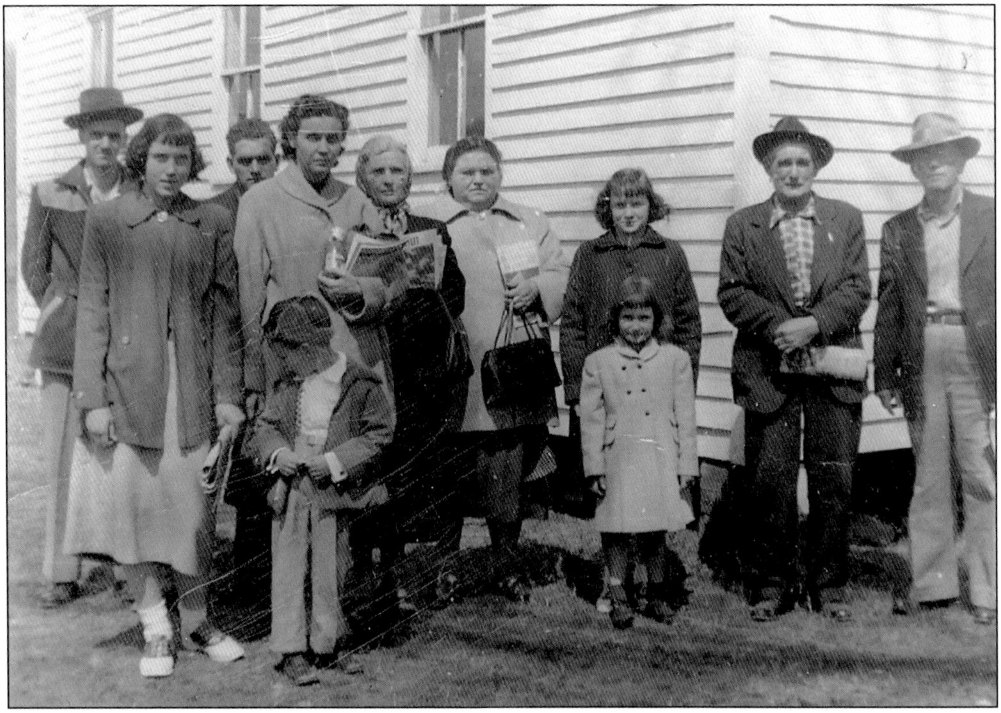

This picture, taken about 1955 at Scott's Branch Church of Christ, shows, from left to right, (front row) Edith Lewis, Ancil Lewis, Grace Roe Carver, and Gayle Carver; (back row) Benton Kilgallin, Ellis Carver, Anna Roe Kilgallin, Ida Carver Lewis, Shirley Lewis, Wyatt Fannin, and Herbert Roe.

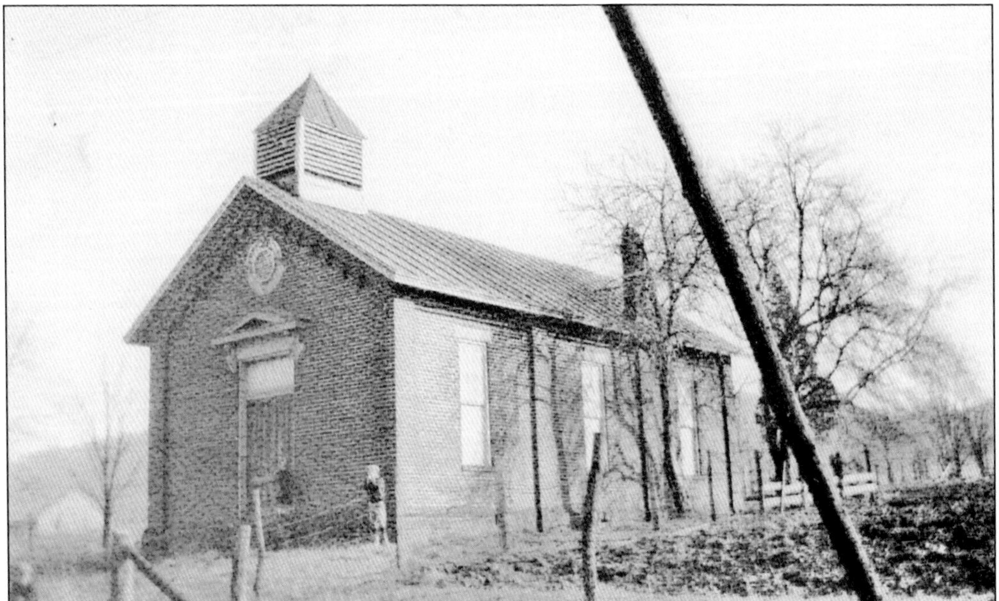

The Peter Taylor Methodist Chapel near Carrs had some unique architectural features. It was razed in the 1980s, and the graves in its cemetery were moved to Black Oak and Quincy cemeteries. The area was often referred to as Stout's.

Six

People

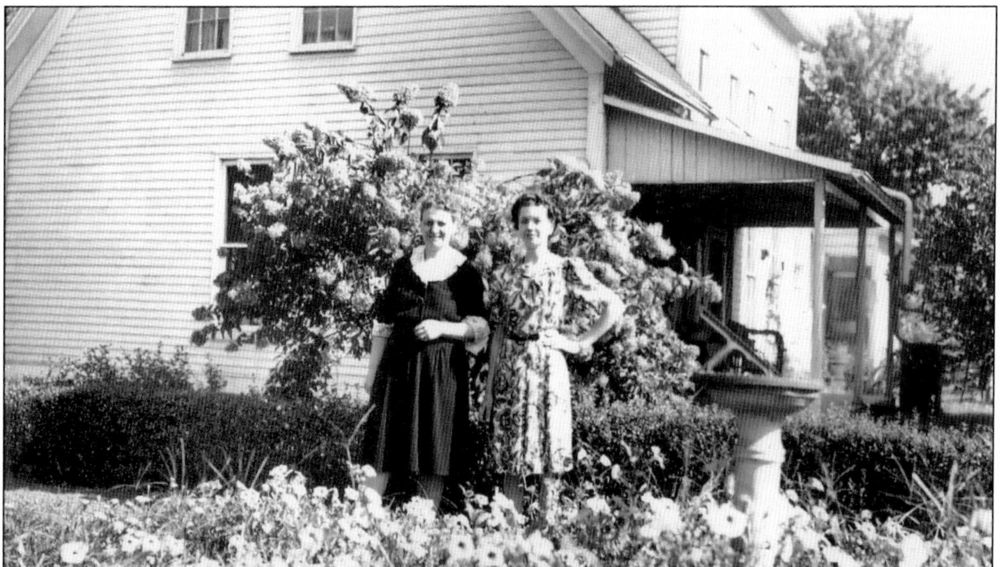

Lena Wells Voiers (left) and a friend are photographed at the Sam Pollitt home sometime in the 1940s. The house stood on the site of the Plummer Apartments, Front Street, Vanceburg.

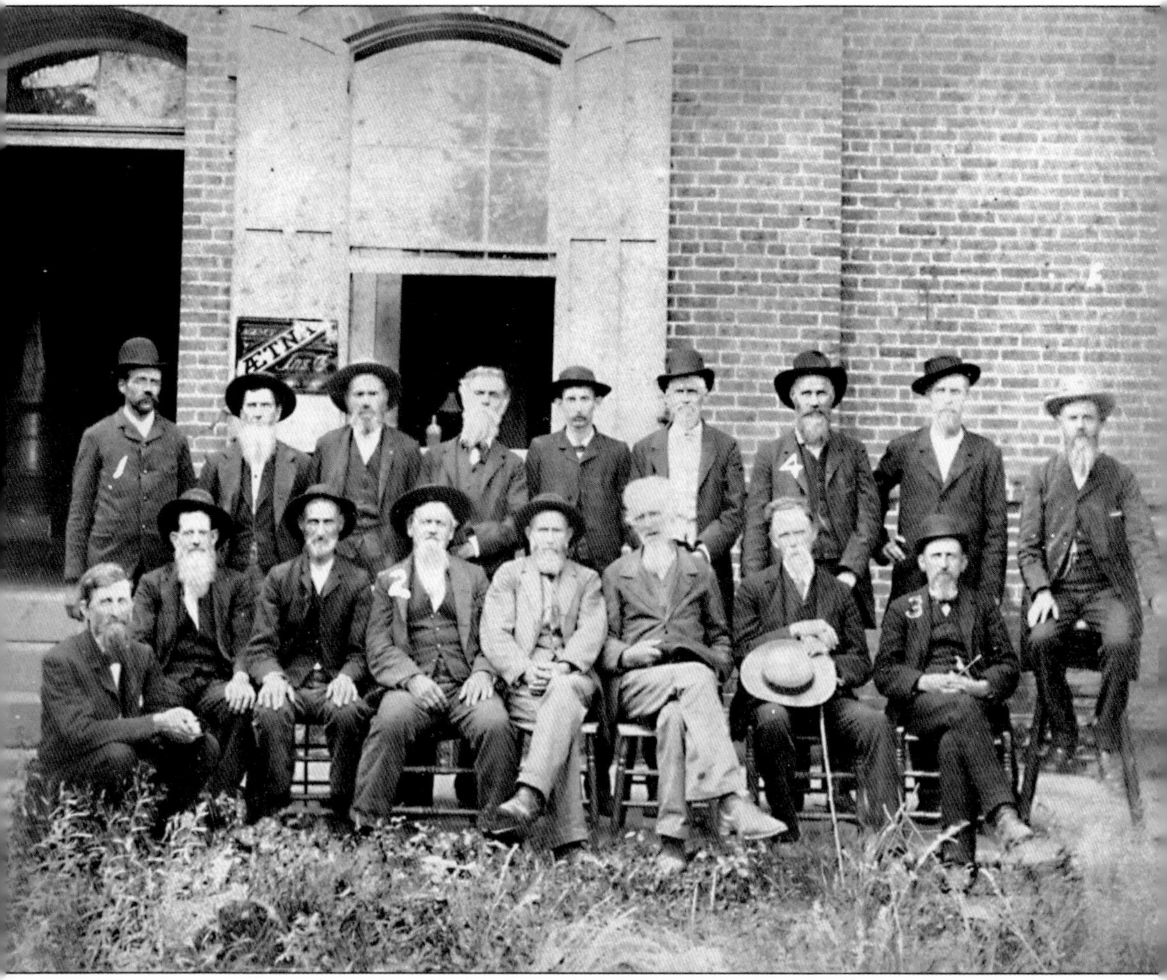

This picture of members of the Lewis County Fiscal Court was taken about 1902 or earlier in front of the old courthouse.

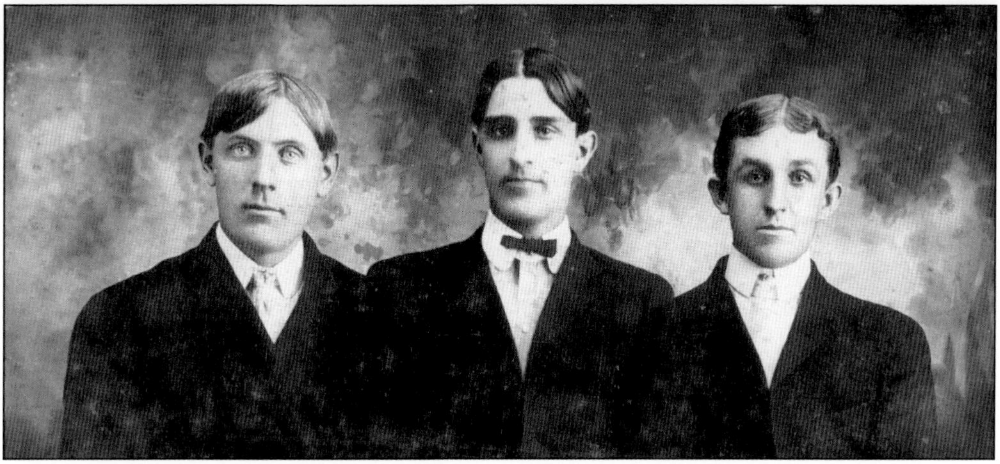

These well-dressed young men are, from left to right, Harry C. Plummer (1884–1916), ? Burriss, and Eugene Tannian.

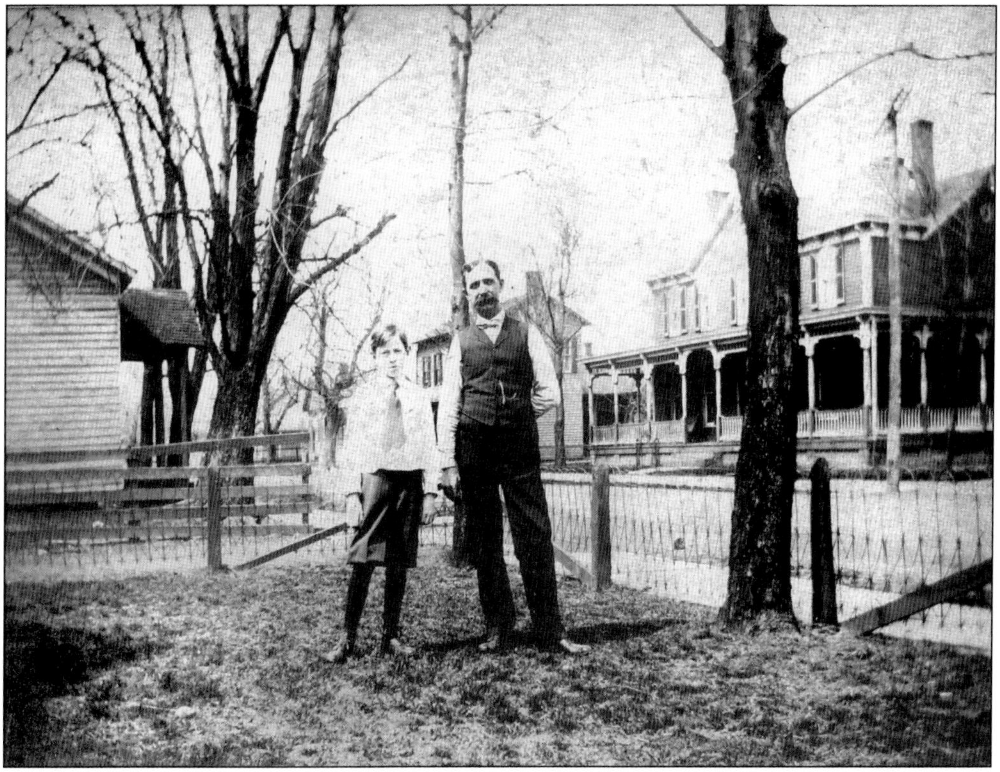

This picture of W.A. Voiers Sr. and his son, Gus, was taken about 1906–1907, across the street from the present-day Kenny's Restaurant on East Second Street in Vanceburg.

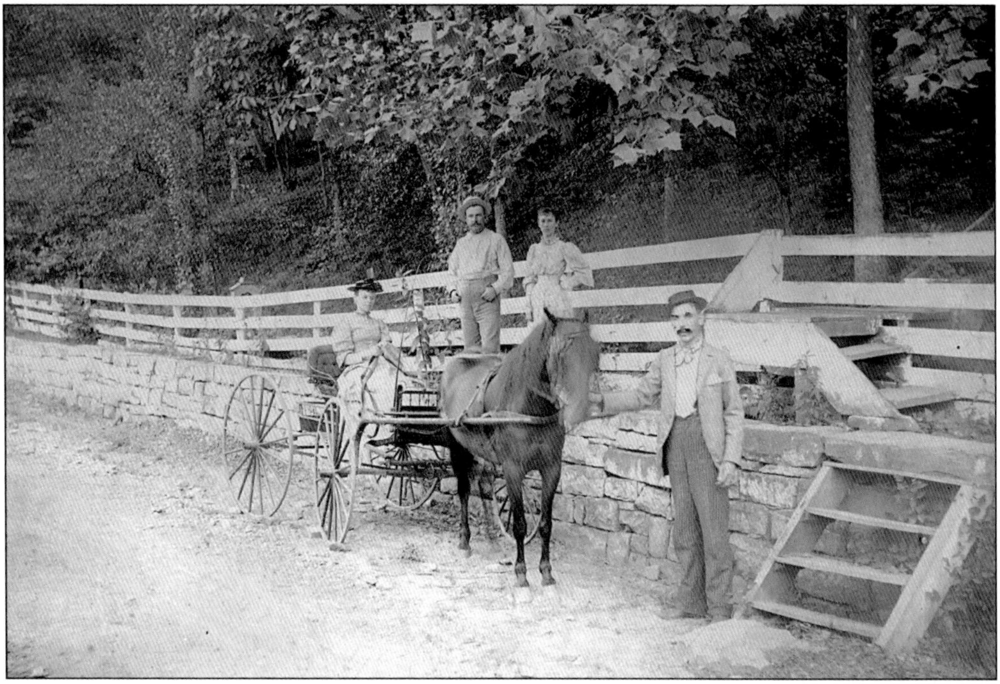

These two couples, one of whom is Mr. and Mrs. James Gardner, have been carriage riding on a summer day. It is believed that the Gardners are the woman in the carriage and the man leading the horse. The date and location are unknown.

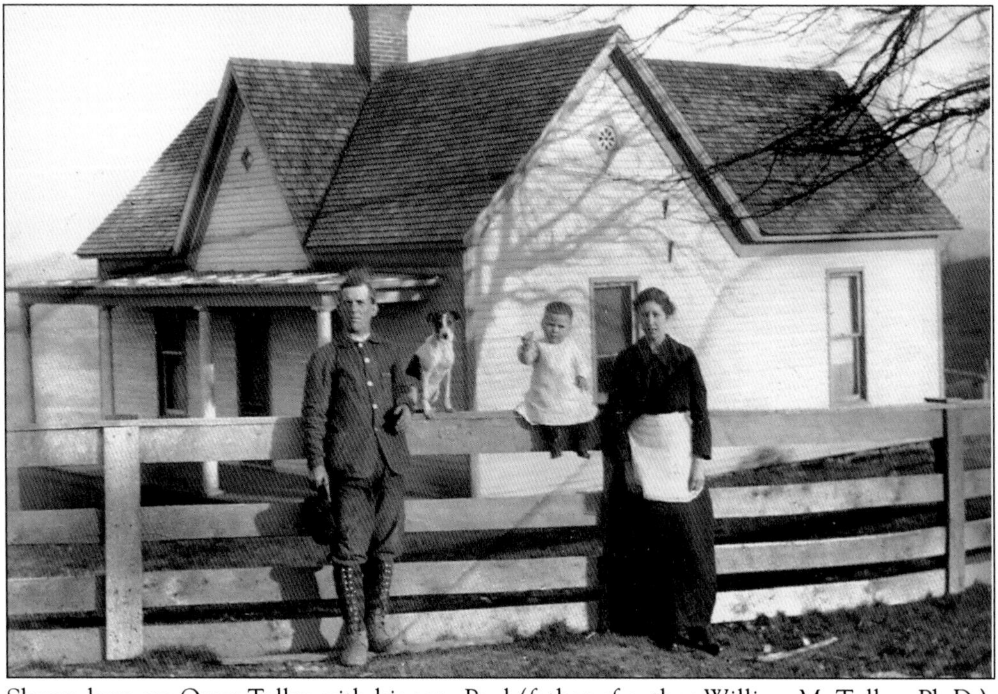

Shown here are Omar Talley with his son, Paul (father of author William M. Talley, Ph.D.), and his wife, Mary Elizabeth Crow Talley, near Sherburne. They are standing by the white-washed fence of their new home about 1914. It burned a few years afterwards.

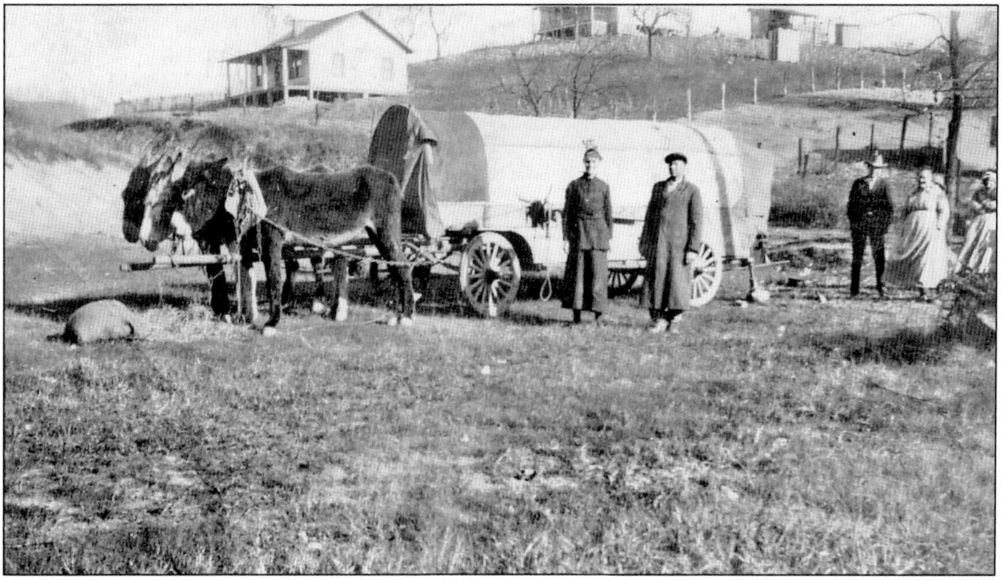

The Ratliff family was somewhere near the riverbank at Vanceburg with their covered wagon as they started their trip west in the early 1900s.

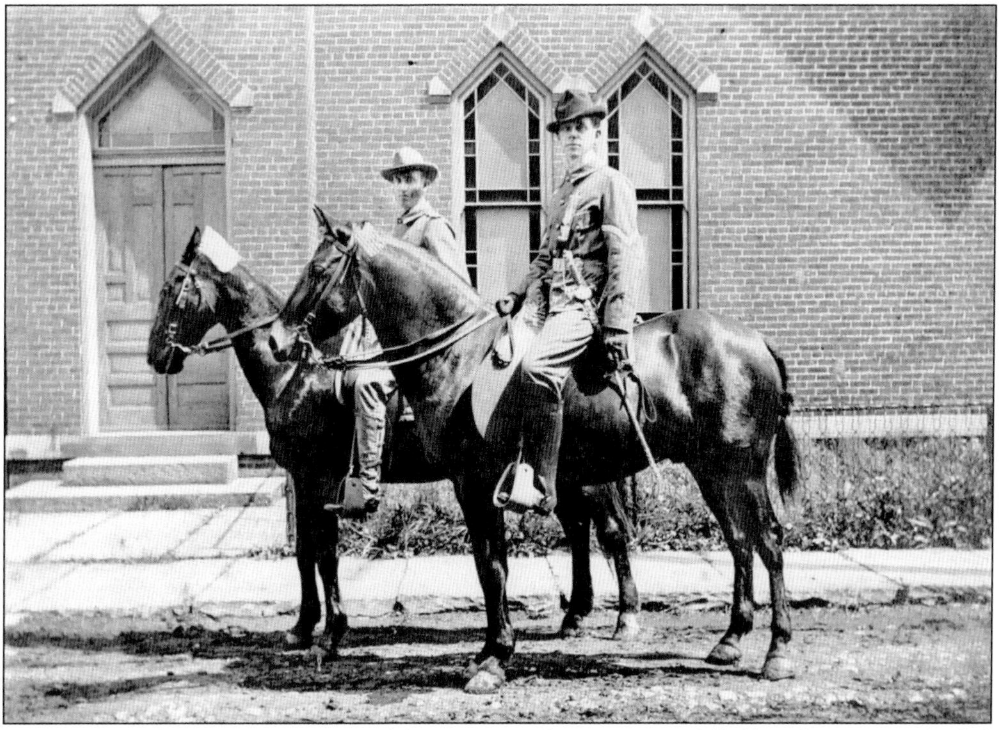

Getting ready for a Junior OUAM celebration, members Jim Carrol (left) and W.C. Cox (right) are shown on their horses in front of the Vanceburg Presbyterian Church (now Baptist) on Market Street in 1903.

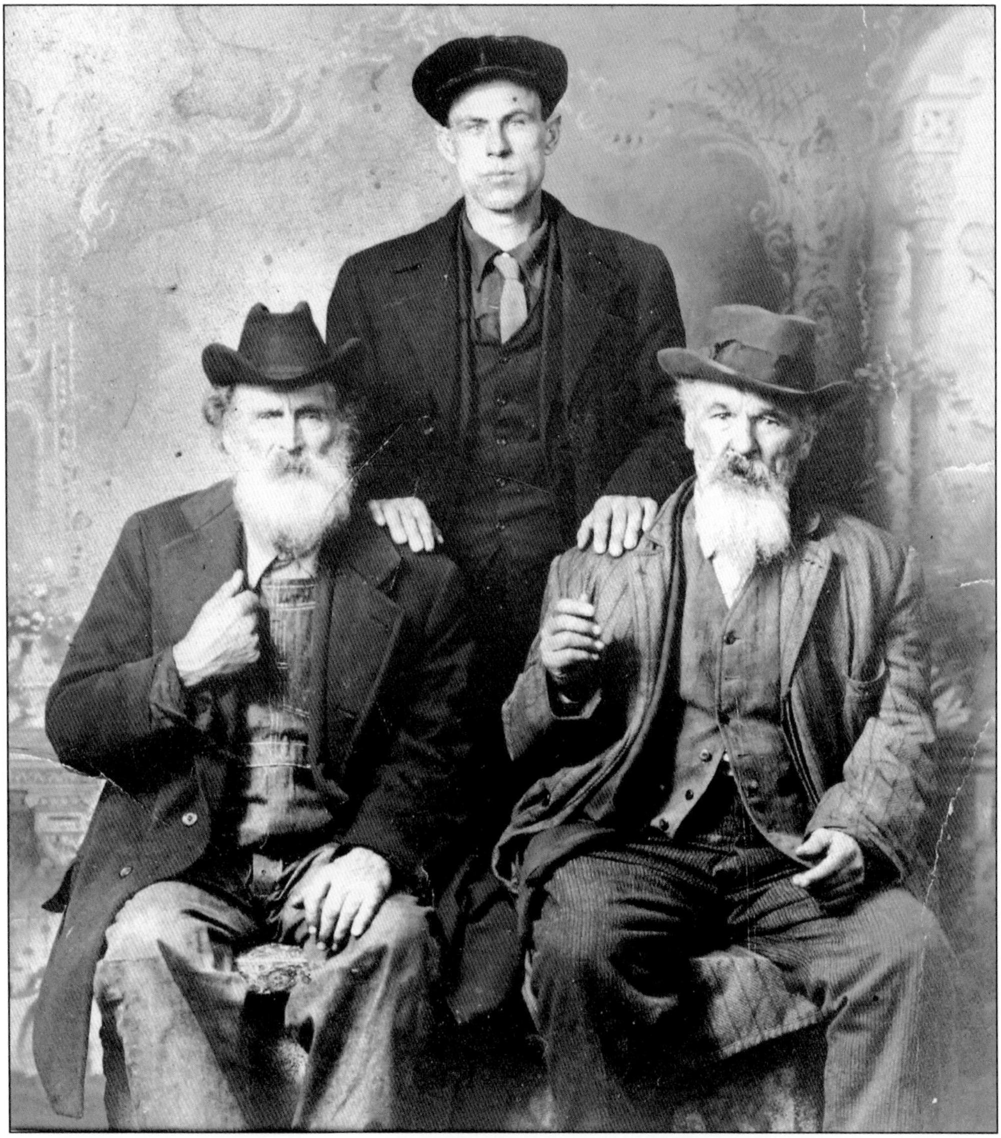

Seated here, from left to right, are Henry Bloomfield (1845–1928) of Trace Creek and Stephen Lewis (1842–1934) of Brushy Creek, Carter County; standing is Stephen A. Lewis (1878–1966) of Scott's Branch.

Lewis Plummer moved to Vanceburg from the Burtonville area at the end of the Civil War. He served as jailer at one time. His three sons—Angus "Cell" Plummer, William Allen Plummer, and Martin Luther Plummer—founded Vanceburg's first funeral home in 1870 or 1874.

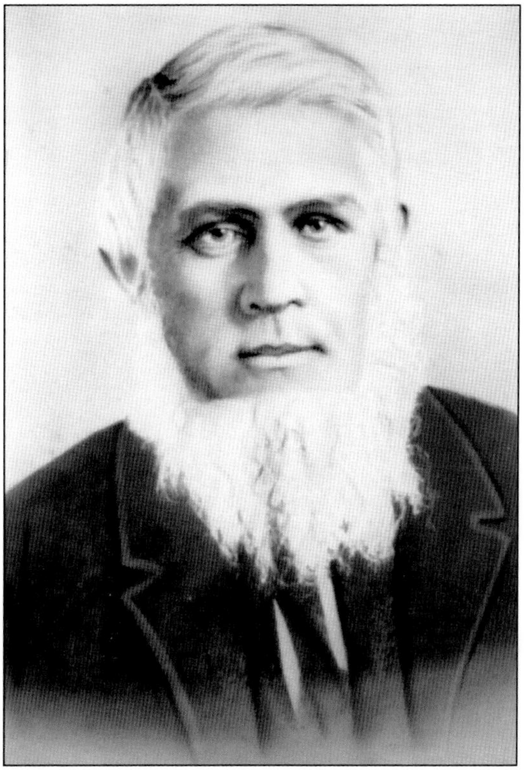

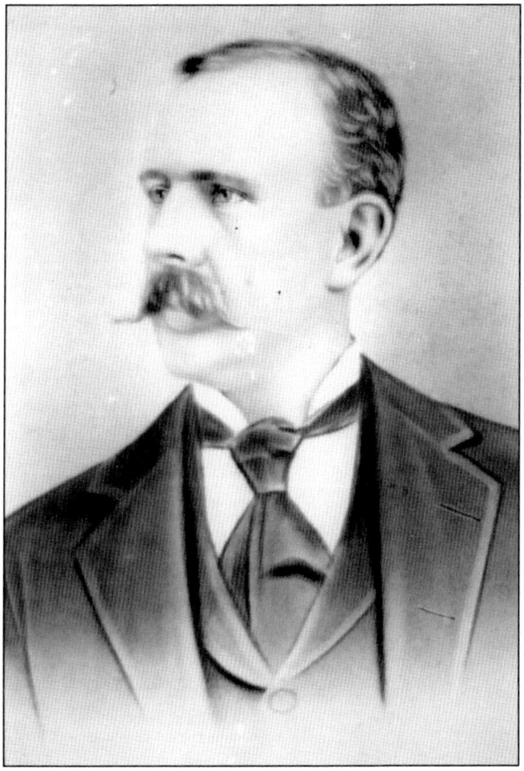

Angus Marcellus Plummer, also known also as A.M. or "Cell" Plummer, was a partner in the funeral home and monument business. His brick home on Front Street has been restored by Ed and Lois Taylor.

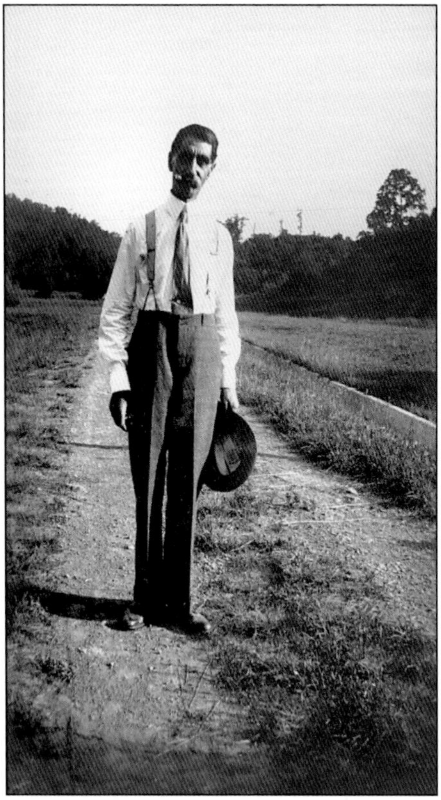

This is an undated picture of Max Block (1871–1941), who immigrated from Russia or Poland. His wife, Sarah, had first married a Mr. Timmer, by whom she had at least two children, David and Miriam. Mr. Block opened a department store here as early as 1913. In years previous, he traveled around the county as a peddler. His first store was in what is now Hickle's Pool Room on Second Street in Vanceburg; in 1920 he moved his store to the building on the northwest corner of Main and Second Streets.

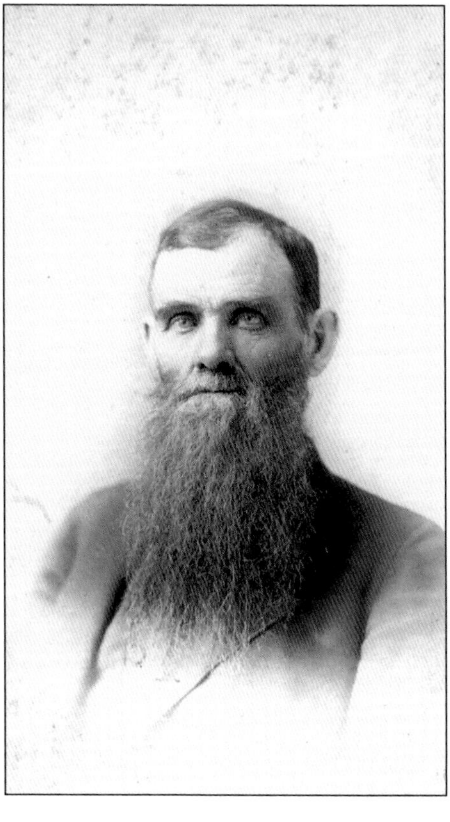

Judge George Morgan Thomas (1828–1914) married Catherine Willim. He served in several political offices, including solicitor of internal revenue under President McKinley, and at one time he served in the U.S. Congress. He built his home (later Commercial Hotel) in 1883.

This photo of Peter D. Lykins and his wife, Eveline Stacy, was taken from a tintype made in 1884. The family came from Morgan County to Lewis County to settle around the time of the Civil War. Petersville was named for Peter D. Lykins.

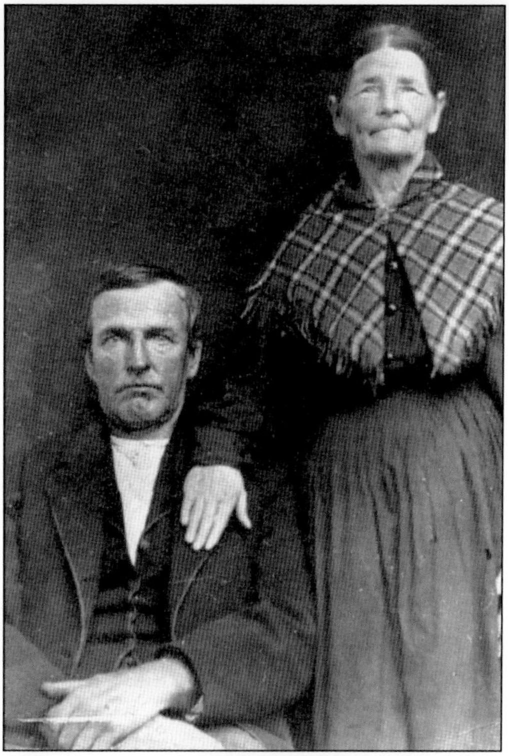

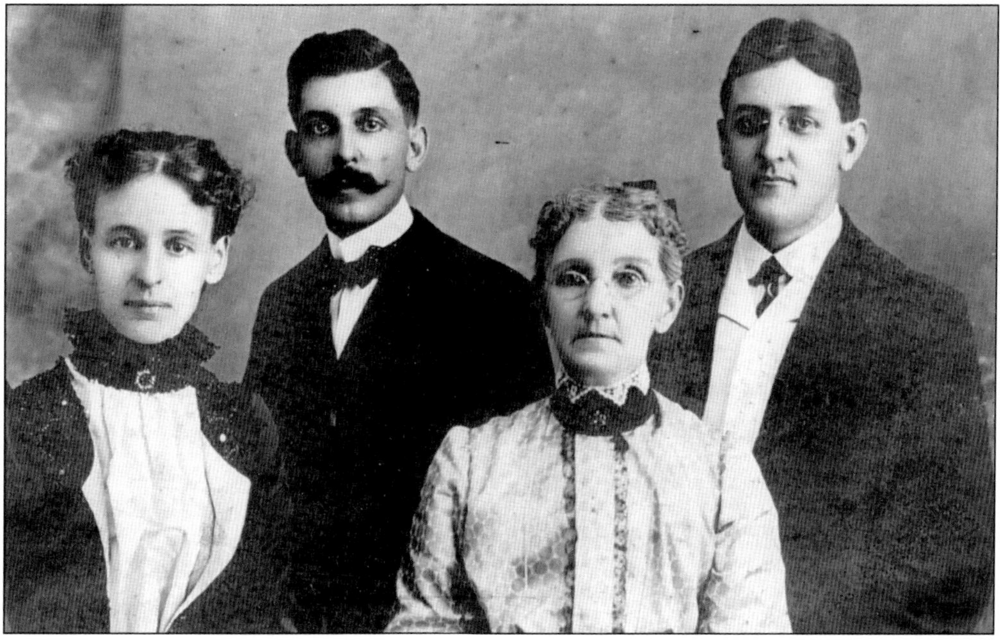

George Morgan Stricklett (1840–1920), at far right, was an accomplished musician who lived most of his professional life in New York City; he came back to Vanceburg in his later years, where he died. He is buried in Woodland Cemetery. Pictured with him around 1897, from left to right, are Maggie Fryer Stricklett; L.M. Stricklett; and his mother, Georgia A. Stricklett, widow of Pleasant M. Stricklett.

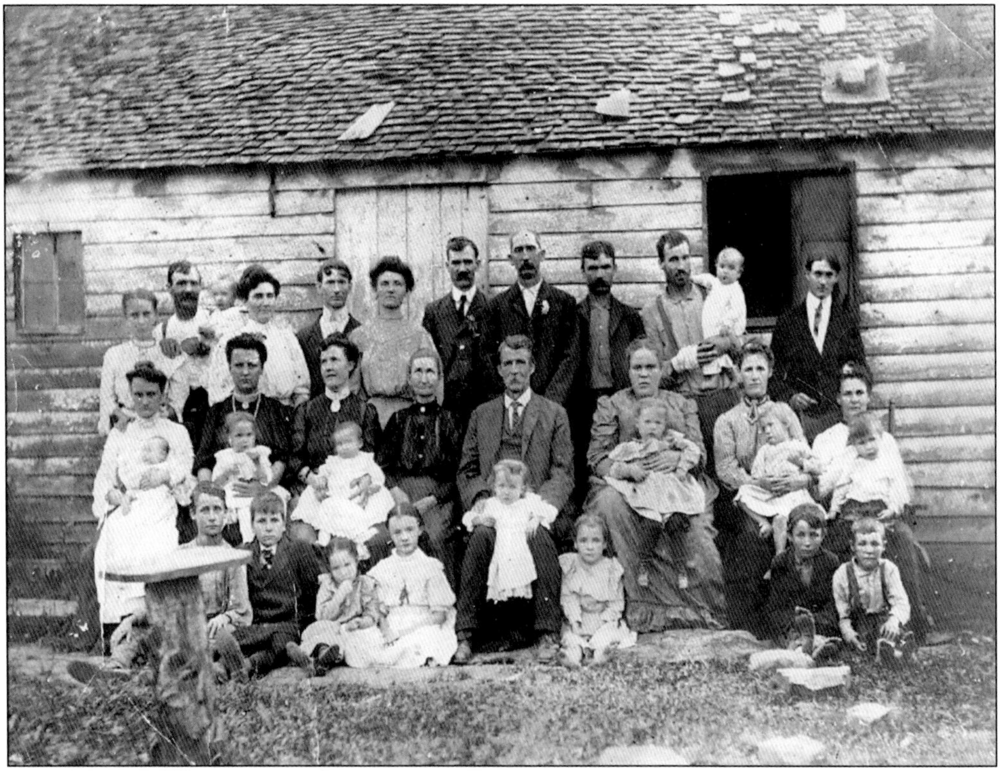

The Falkner family is gathered beside their home near Clarksburg. In this group are Civil War and Spanish-American War veterans. Many members of the family are buried in the Clarksburg Cemetery. Note how small shingles to stop leaks are held in place by large stones.

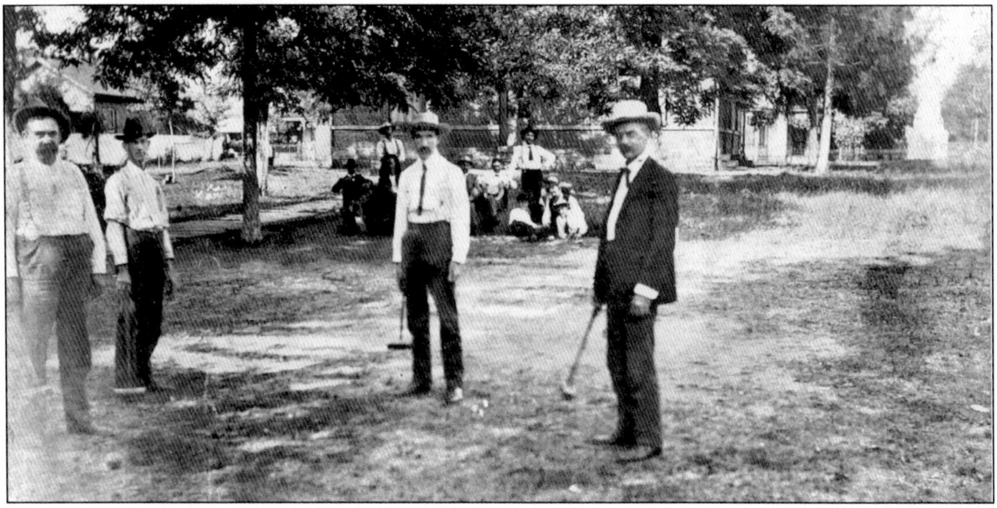

These men are playing croquet on the lawn of the old courthouse, facing the railroad. They are, from left to right, Col. C.L. Tannian (jailer); an unidentified man; Judge J.M. Lee in the center; W. Roch Henderson, standing with the men in the background; and Prof. T.M. Games, superintendent of the old Vanceburg Lower School from 1881 to 1904. W.C. Dugan fixed the date of this picture about 1903, as the first named officers were the incumbents from 1901 to 1905, and Professor Games left Vanceburg in the summer of 1904.

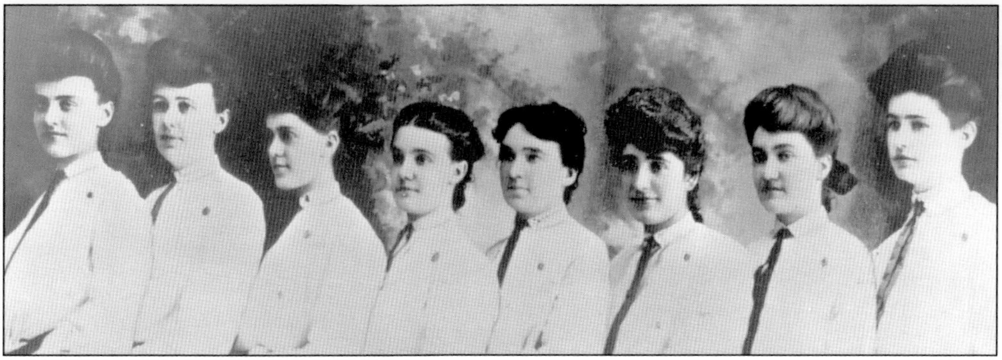

The Allegresse Club, pictured before 1905, consisted of a group of young women socialites. "Allegresse" is the French word for joyful. These young ladies, from left to right, are Nina Mathewson, Maude Bate, Cora Stamper, Nellie Clark, Ollie Politt, Priscilla Parker, Lena Parker, and Julia Stamper. Other members not shown are Louise Cottingham, Nellie Cooper, Blanche Cottingham, Mildred L. Pugh, Myra Rolfe, and Flora McEldowney.

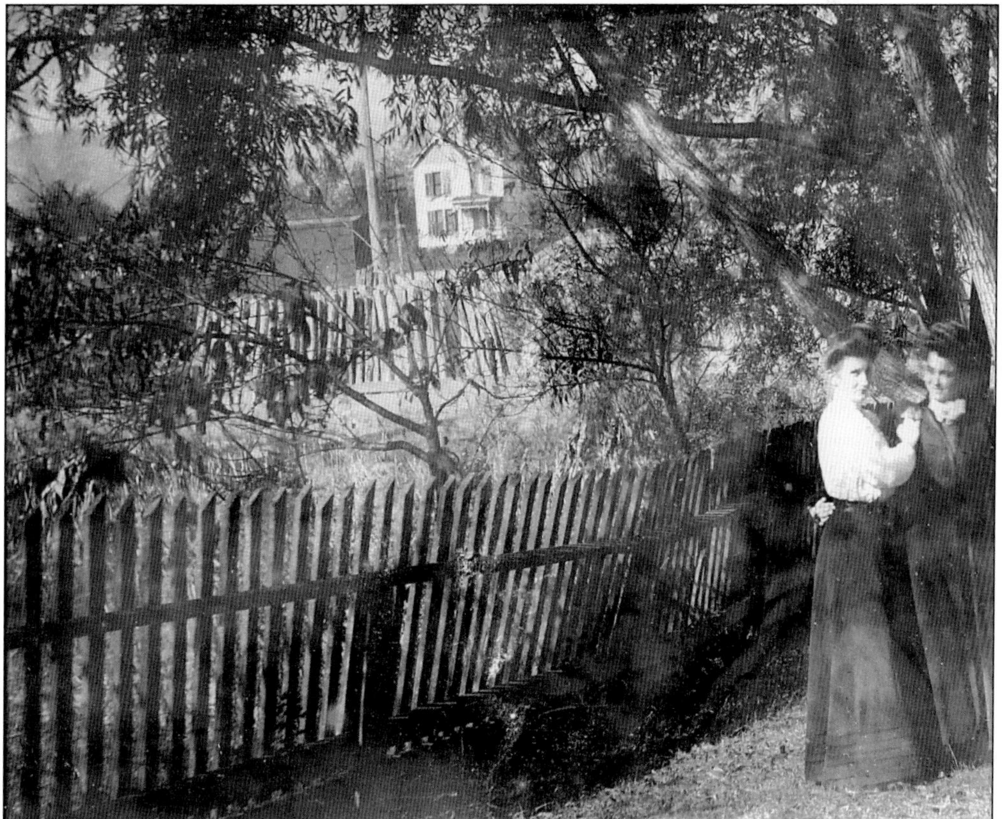

A 1908 view shows two young women in an enclosed garden. In the background can be seen more picket fences and a large house. The pose seems to indicate the young ladies were reluctant to be photographed.

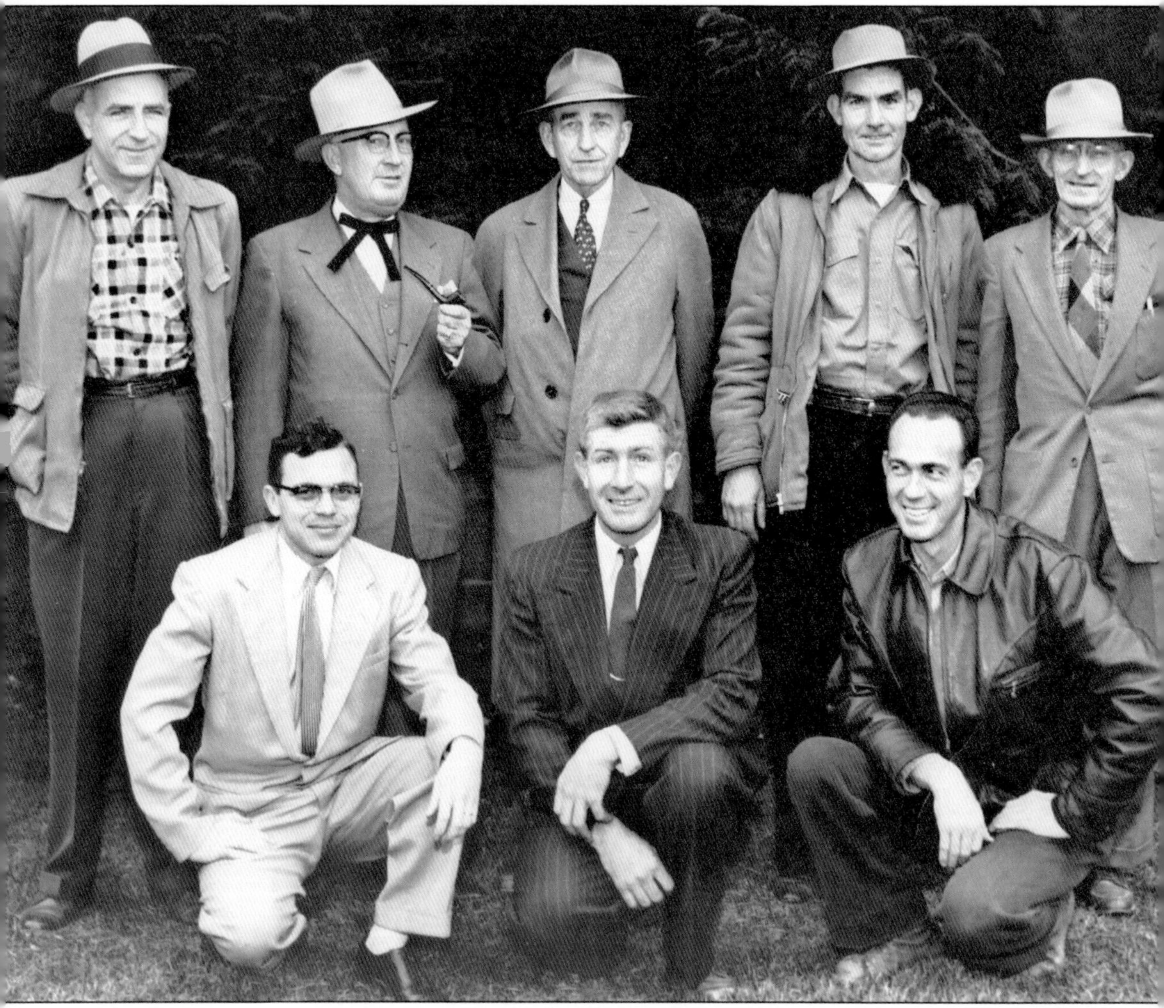

These men made up the Agricultural Board of Lewis County. The date may be in the 1950s. The men are, from left to right, (front row) Mike Duff, county agent; Julian Gillespie, county member of Agricultral Stabilization and Conservation (ASC); and Ted Allen, soil conservation supervisor; (back row) Mr. Haines, Farmers Home Administration (FHA) supervisor; Newell E. Rudder, Tollesboro farmer; O.P. "Pat" Tannian, land owner and banker; James Theodore Gardner, county infirmary; and T.M. Ruggles, Tollesboro farmer.

Tom and Isabel Burns of Concord grew up as slaves in Fleming and Mason Counties. In their later years, they settled in Lewis County, where they reared their children. They are buried in the Mt. Tabor Methodist Church Cemetery, but no stones mark their graves.

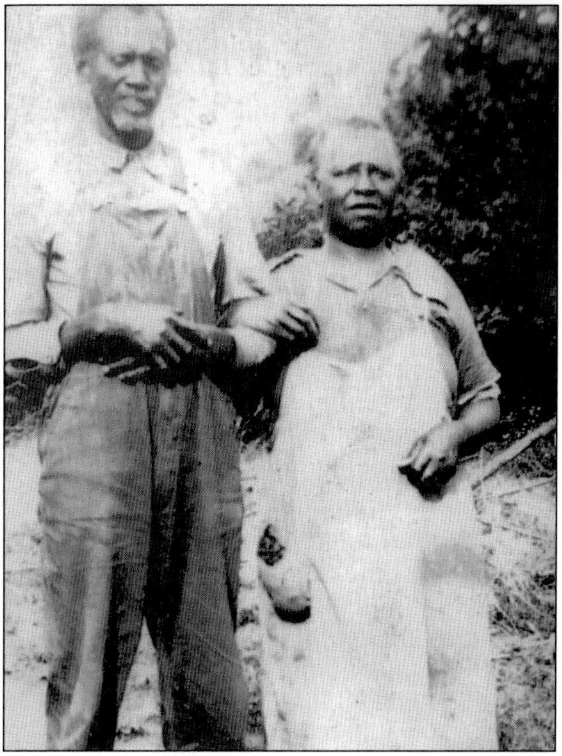

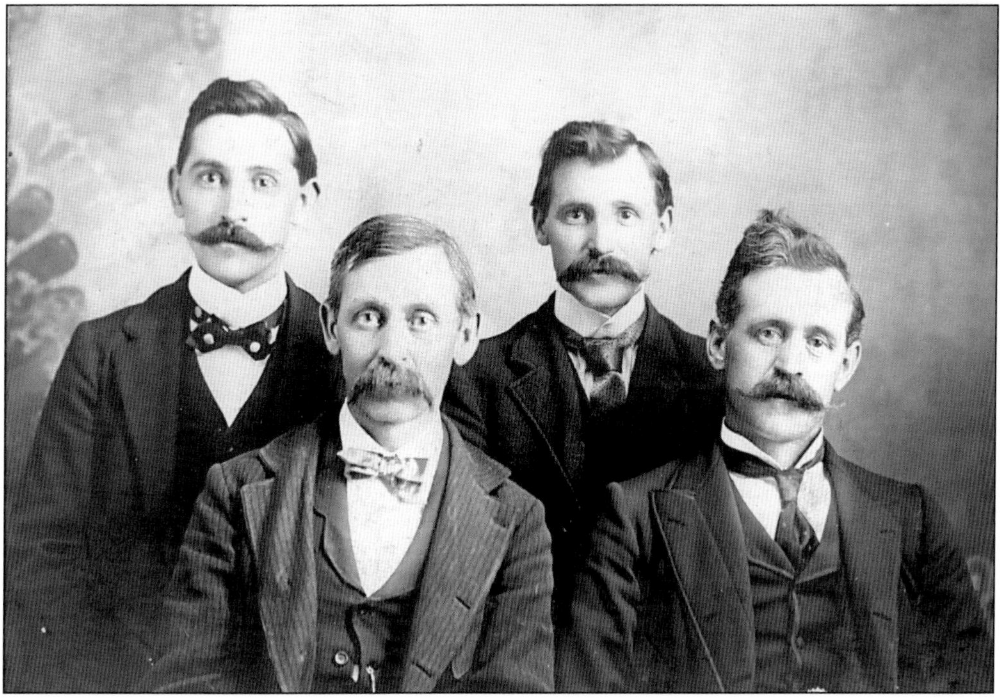

These Grandison brothers, the sons of John and Isabelle Bertram Grandison, are shown on May 25, 1901. From left to right are (front row) Jack Grandison and Henry Grandison; (back row) James Grandison and Pete Grandison.

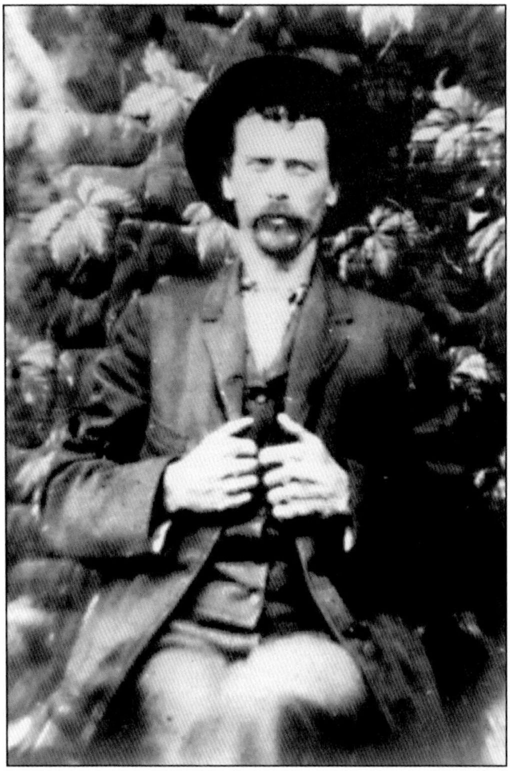

Jacob Richmond, a young man from the Laurel area, strikes a jaunty woodsman's pose surrounded by bushes and vines.

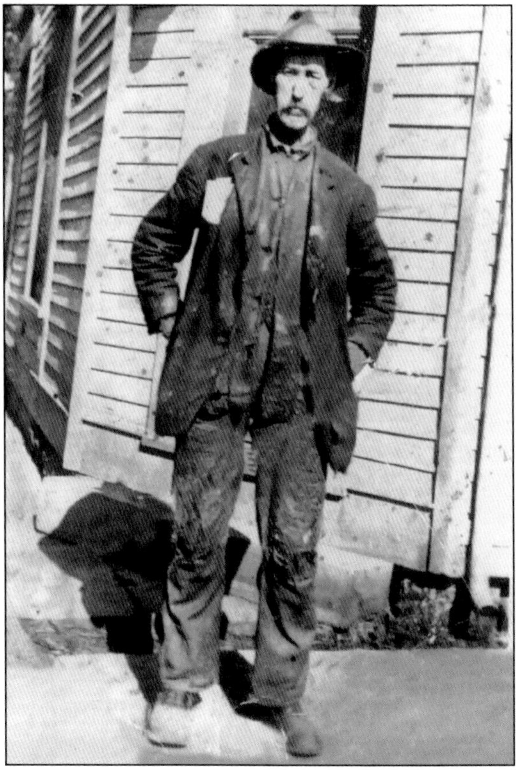

James Qualls, popularly known as "Jim Crow," was born in 1861 and died in 1933. Qualls was a "town character," a harmless and wise man who lived with his mother in a little house on East Second Street. He was immortalized in the writings of Capt. William C. Dugan, previous editor of the *Lewis County Herald*. He and his mother, "Mammy," are buried in Slate Point Graveyard.

Karl Beckwith Chapman and Nettie Howland were married about 1902 and lived all their lives in Quincy.

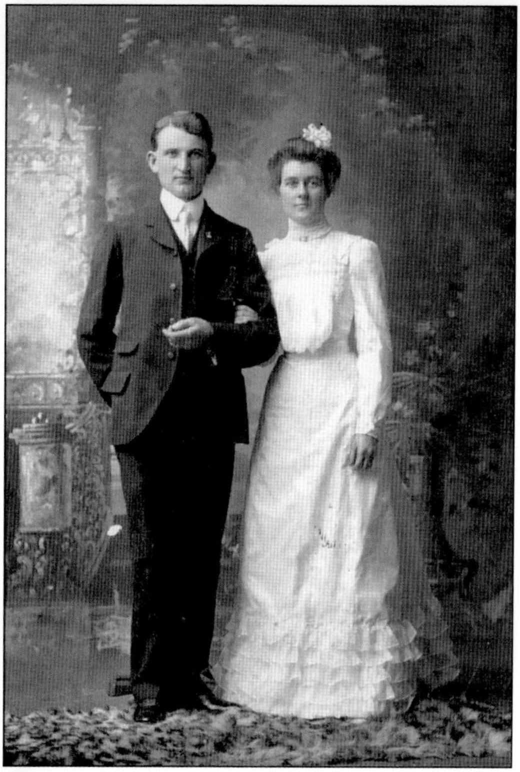

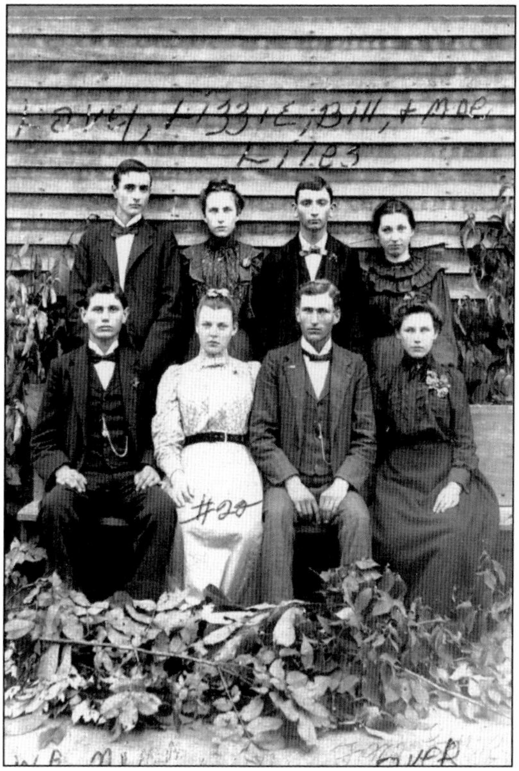

This photo, taken in 1900 behind the old Tannery School, includes, from left to right, (front row) Lovell Liles, Lizzy Liles (who married Lawrence Osborne), Bill Liles, and May Liles (who married Jess Lewis); (back row) Will Arthur Lewis, Mimia Lewis, Tom "Zig" Lewis, and Laura Horsley.

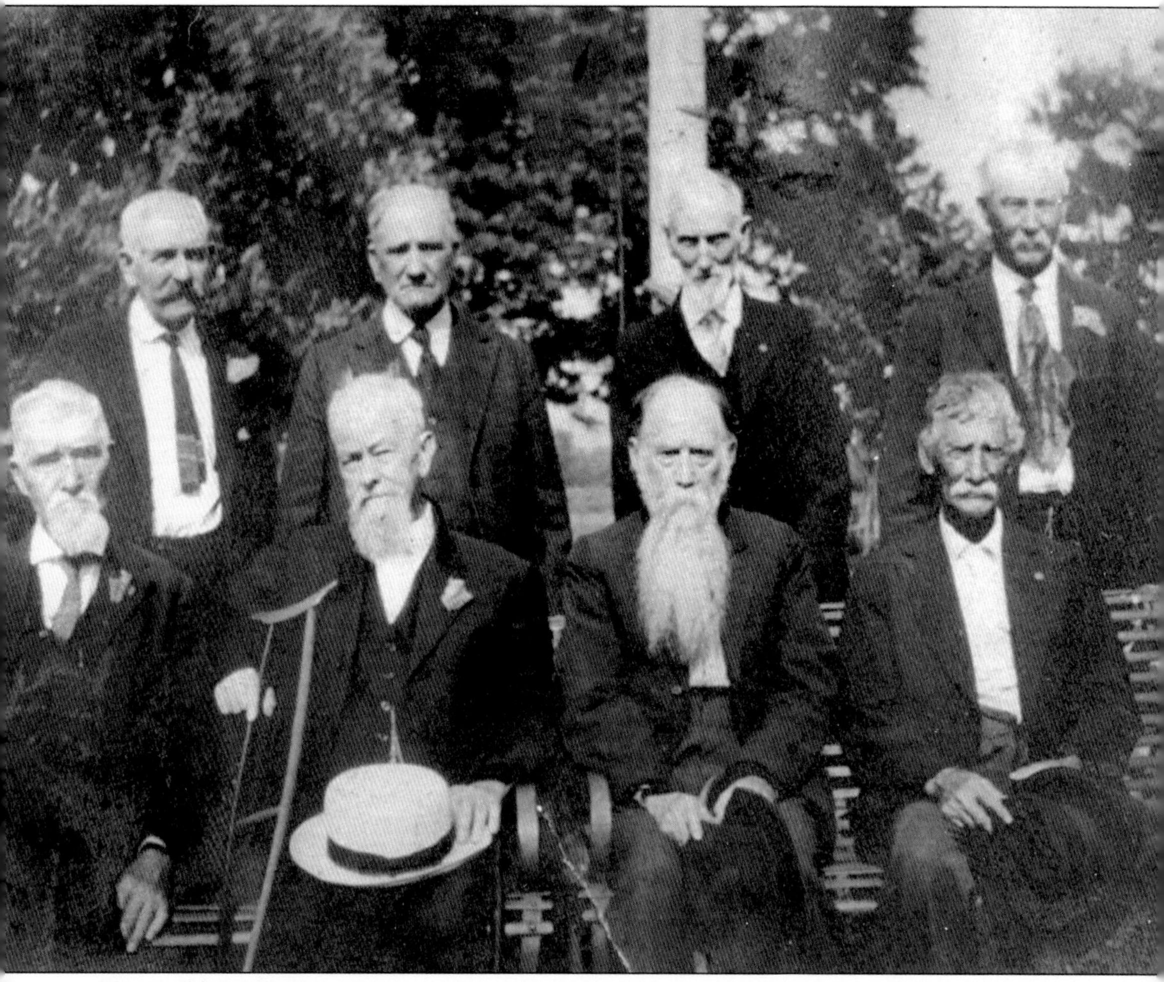

These old Civil War Union soldiers (here in about 1919) are, from left to right, (front row) Ephraim Moore, John Schofield, unidentified, and Wiley Arthurs; (back row) Thad Hendrickson, Rev. B.N. Anderson, John S. Mavity, and E.R. Lindsey.

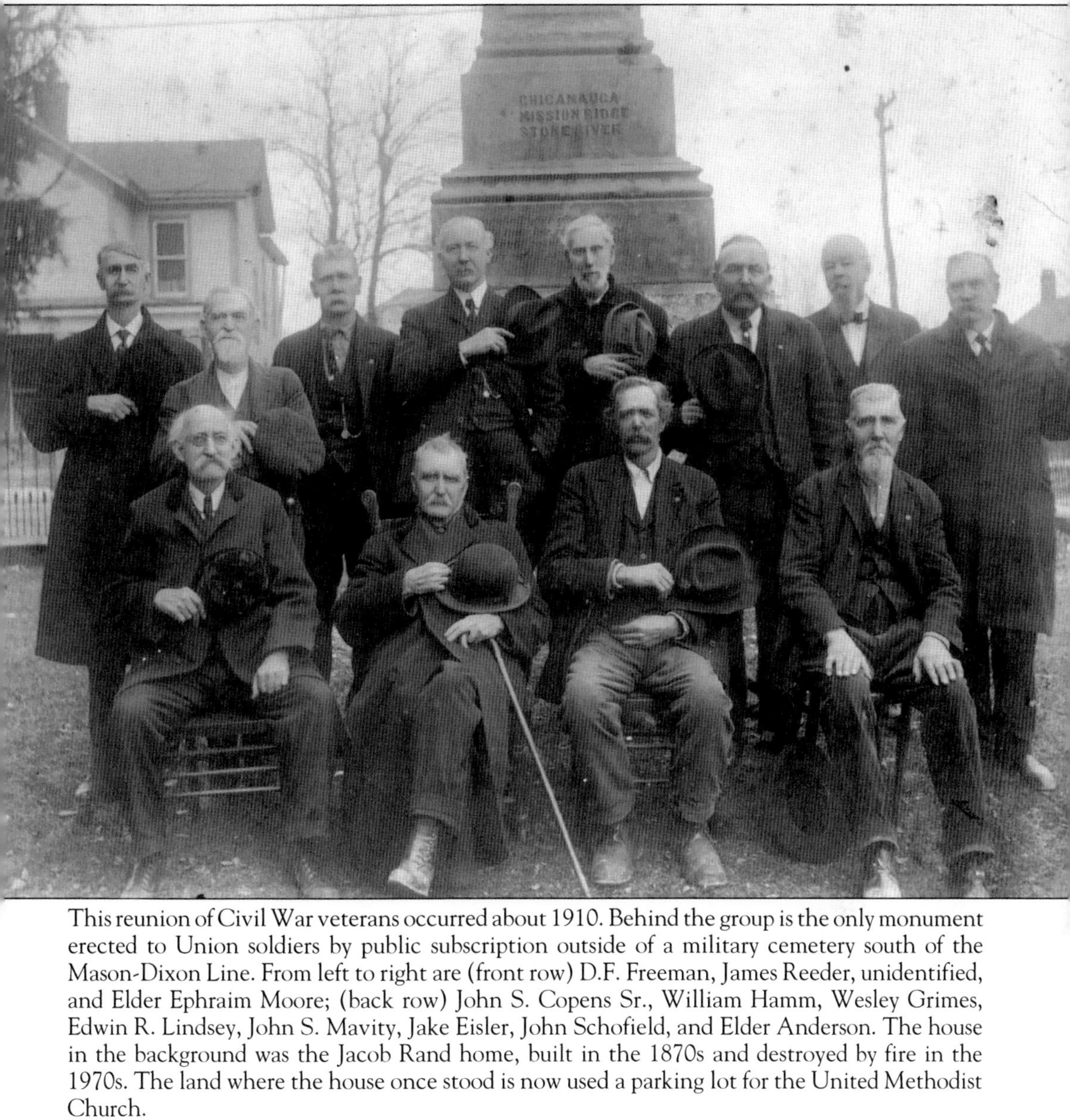

This reunion of Civil War veterans occurred about 1910. Behind the group is the only monument erected to Union soldiers by public subscription outside of a military cemetery south of the Mason-Dixon Line. From left to right are (front row) D.F. Freeman, James Reeder, unidentified, and Elder Ephraim Moore; (back row) John S. Copens Sr., William Hamm, Wesley Grimes, Edwin R. Lindsey, John S. Mavity, Jake Eisler, John Schofield, and Elder Anderson. The house in the background was the Jacob Rand home, built in the 1870s and destroyed by fire in the 1970s. The land where the house once stood is now used a parking lot for the United Methodist Church.

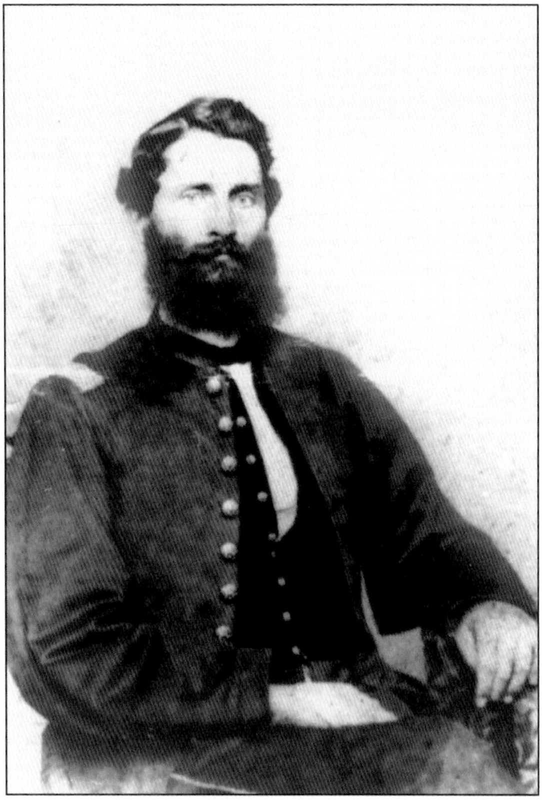

Cpl. Abraham Dillow (July 29, 1939–January 30, 1910) was a Civil War veteran, serving in the Union Army, Co. A, 5th Regiment, West Virginia Volunteer Infantry.

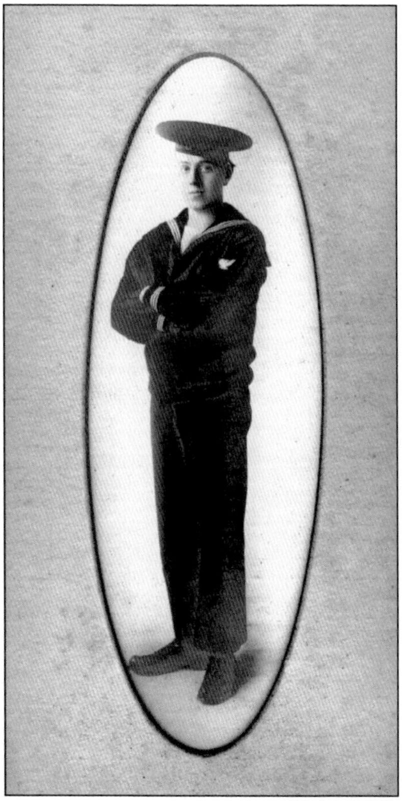

W.A. "Gus" Voiers Jr. is shown here in his World War I navy uniform. After his discharge, he came back to Vanceburg to operate the shoe store his father had opened.

Jacob Eulett (1895–1964), a young man from Laurel, is pictured in his World War I uniform. He is buried in Morgan Cemetery. He has many descendants in Lewis County.

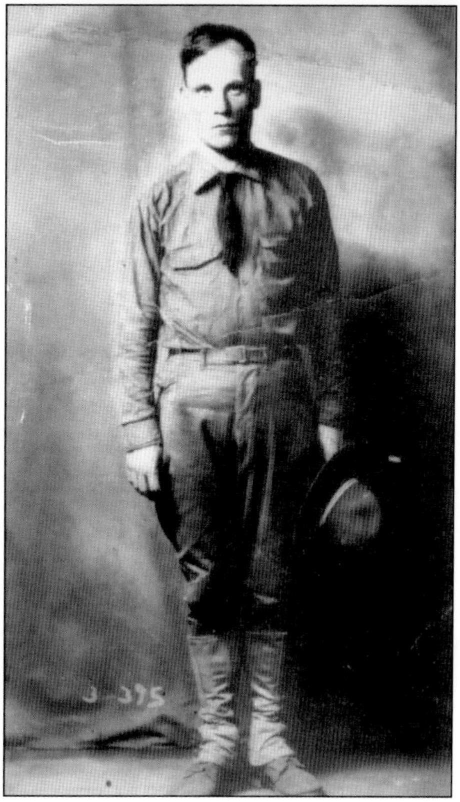

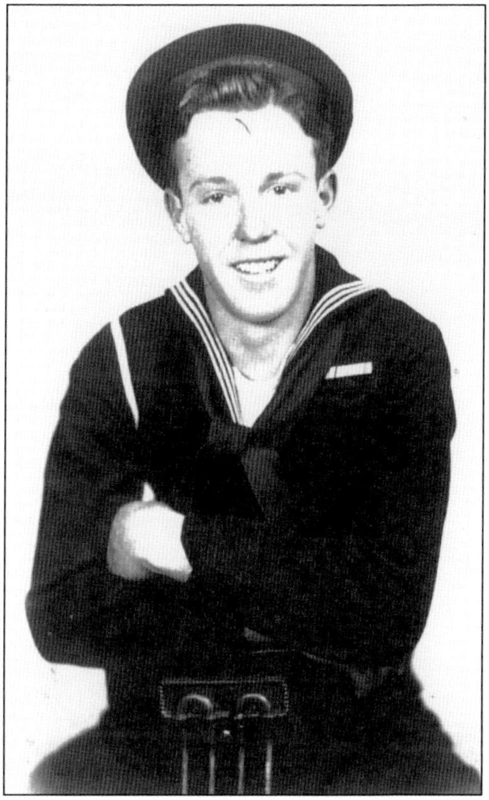

This is a smiling young Albert Cadwallader in his World War I navy uniform. He and his family lived on Quicks Run, where the family settled in the early 1800s.

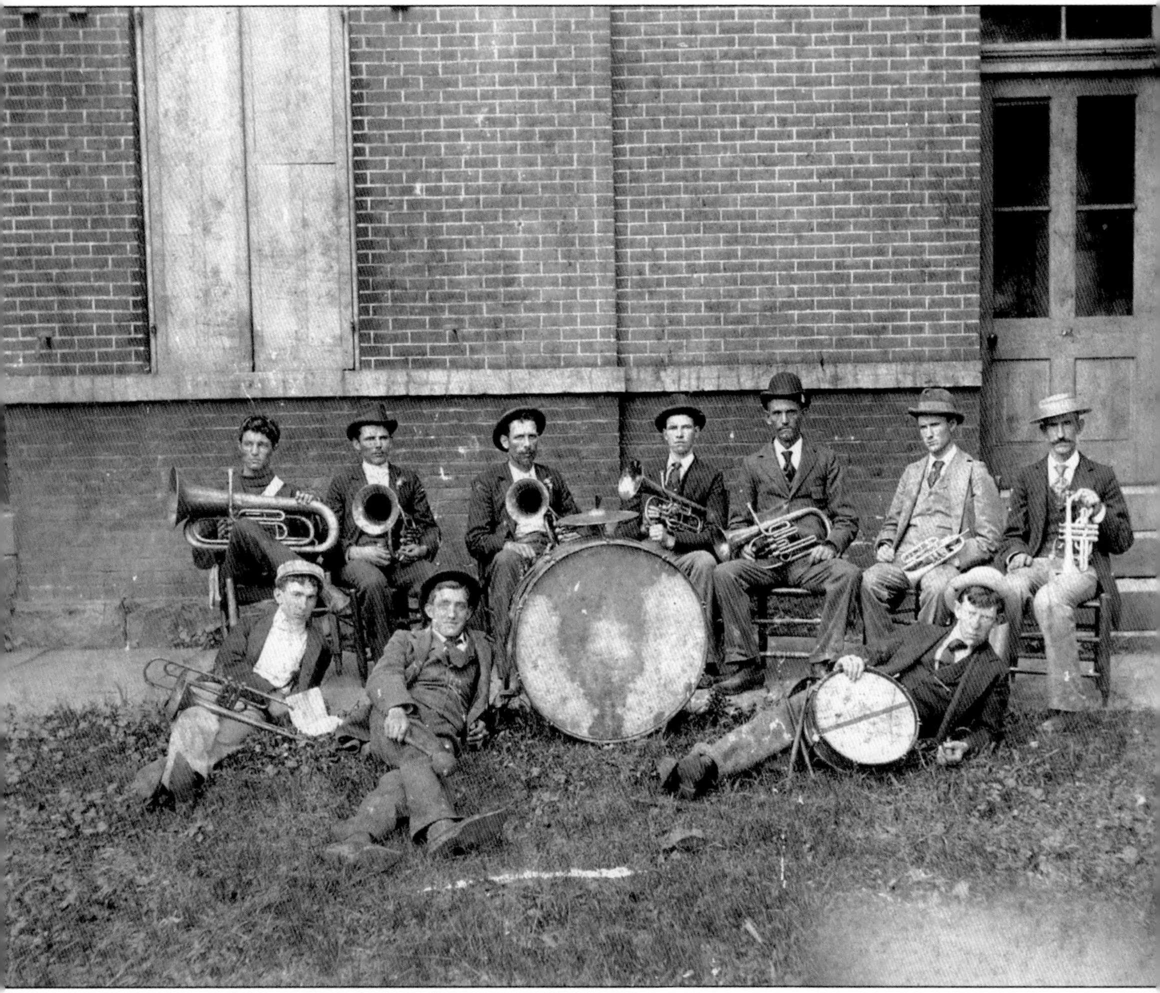

The First Vanceburg Band was photographed on the west side of the old courthouse about 1893. Shown here, from left to right, are (on the grass) Hugh Lawill, Vergne Ingrim, and W.A. "Billy" Plummer; (seated) Oscar Ruark, three unidentified men, Dude Manning, Will Donehoo, and an unidentified man. The shuttered window was the vault in the county clerk's office. The door on the extreme right was later bricked up.

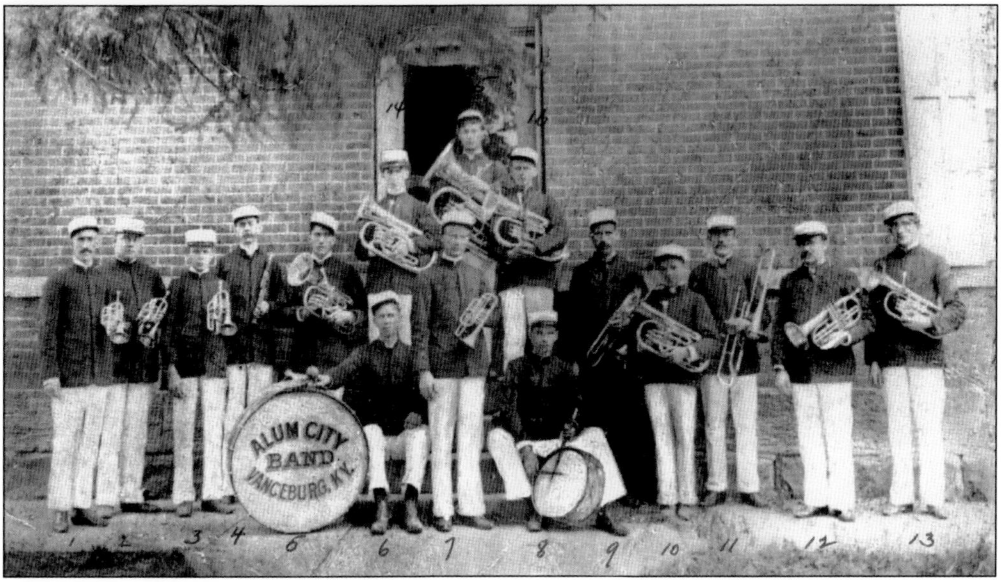

This picture of the Alum City Band of Vanceburg was taken about 1896 at the back of the old courthouse, facing the railroad. From left to right, the members are numbered (front row) 1. Charlie Greenhow, 2. Ernest Applegate, 3. Earl Fite, 4. Charlie Hammond, 5. Ted Adams, 6. Billy Plummer, 7. W.A. Frizzell, 8. Bill "Duke" Donehoo, 9. Harry Jeffers, 10. Kib Ruark, 11. John Greenhow, 12. George Paynter, and 13. Vergne Ingram; (back row) 14. Hugh Lawell, 15. Oscar Ruark, and 16. Mike Niscius. The numbers for the men on the steps—14, 15, and 16—are obscured by the tree limb.

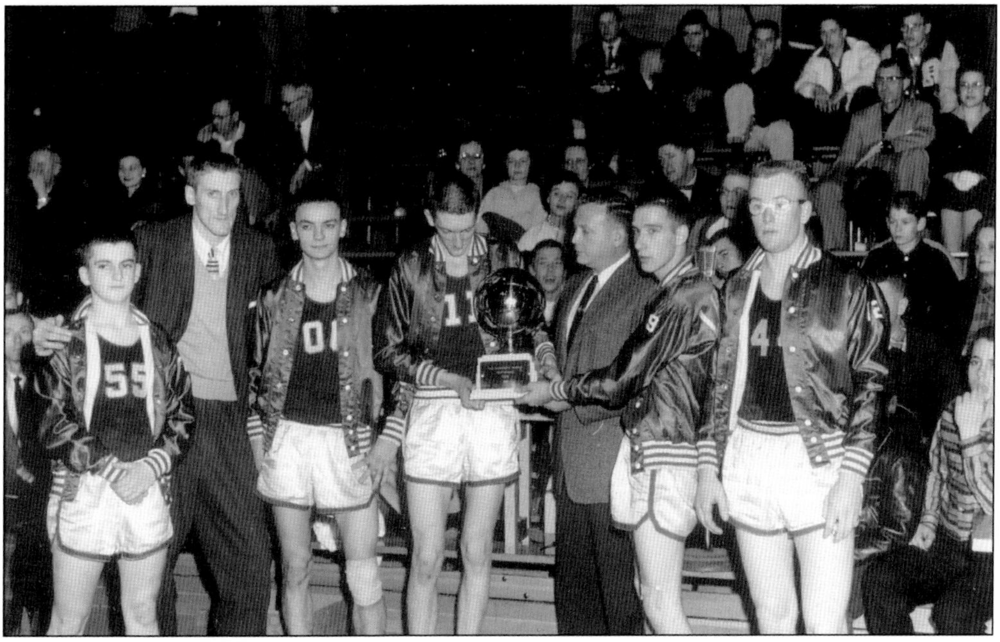

These 1956 Eastern Kentucky Conference basketball champions, from Lewis County, played in the armory field house at Ashland, Kentucky. They are, from left to right, Charles J. Riedinger, Coach Shelby Linville, Paul Jordan, Ralph Davis, unidentified official presenting trophy, Tom Kennard, and Lovell Pack.

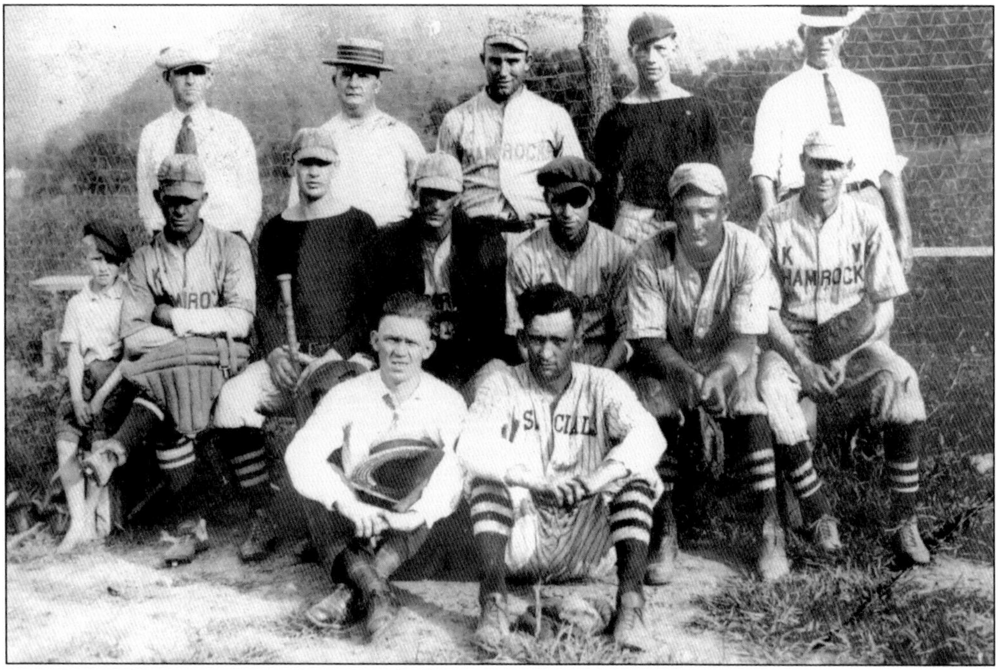

Members of a 1920s Vanceburg baseball team are, from left to right, (front row) Bill Brown and Hobe Cottingham; (middle row) "Tippie" Staggs (mascot), "Cook" Staggs, Denny Lykins, Leroy Lewis, "Whitie" Johnson, Raymond Ruark, and Lloyd Woods; (back row) Pat Tannian, "Tidy" Staggs, "Swatter" Heinisch, "Wid" McDaniel, and "Buddy" Staggs.

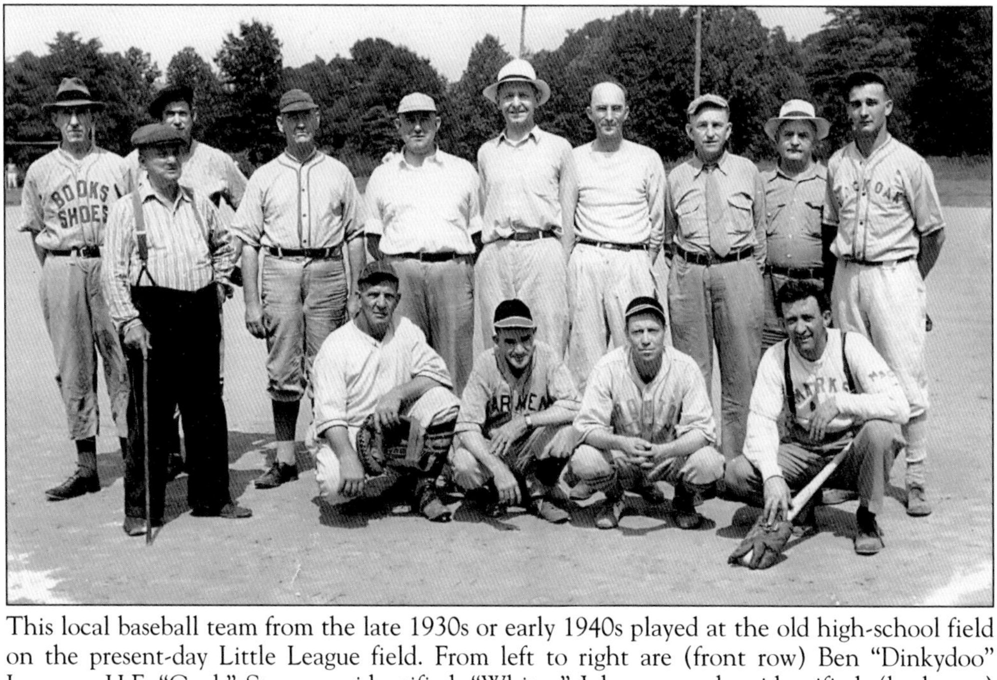

This local baseball team from the late 1930s or early 1940s played at the old high-school field on the present-day Little League field. From left to right are (front row) Ben "Dinkydoo" Layman, H.F. "Cook" Staggs, unidentified, "Whitey" Johnson, and unidentified; (back row) Jesse Henderson, unidentified, Ernest Truitt, Reinhold "Swatter" Heinisch, G.R. "Poke" Queen, Leroy Lewis, O.P. "Pat" Tannian, Ithiel W. "Tidy" Staggs, and unidentified.

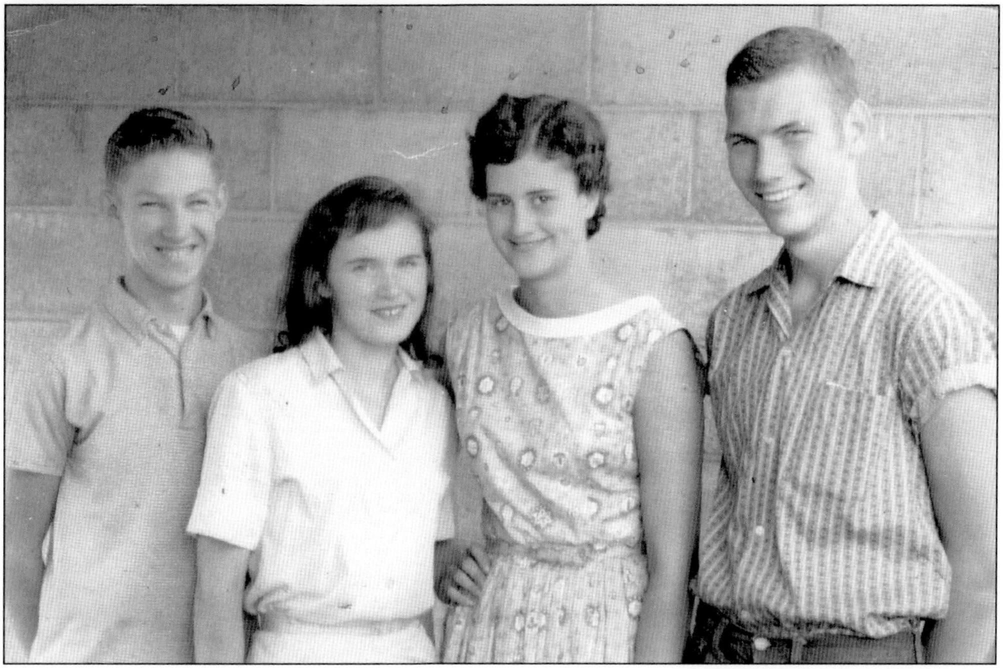

Lewis County's 4-H poultry judging team, under the supervision of County Agent Ed Strong, won second place in state competition in 1960. From left to right are Mitchell Truesdell, Shirley Lewis, Avanell Kidwell, and Bruce Roe.

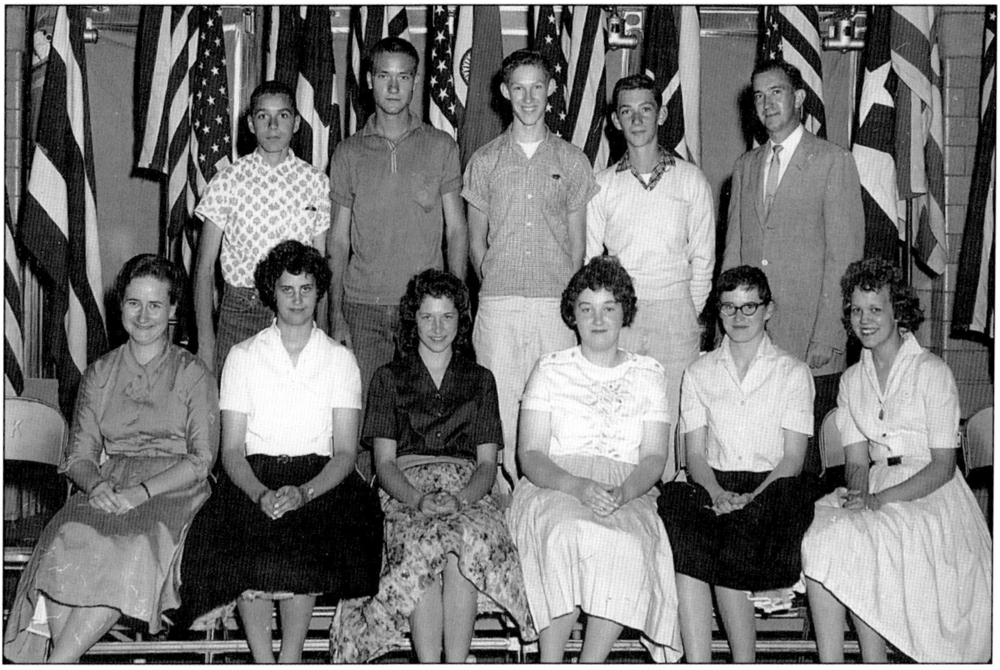

Lewis County youth have long been active in 4-H activities. At state competition at the University of Kentucky in 1960 were, from left to right, (front row) Geraldine Cowan, Avanell Kidwell, Patty Martin, Sue Denham, Shirley Lewis, and Sharon Nolen; (back row) Ed Kennedy, Wendell Sparks, Mitchell Truesdell, Kenneth Fannin, and Fred Watson.

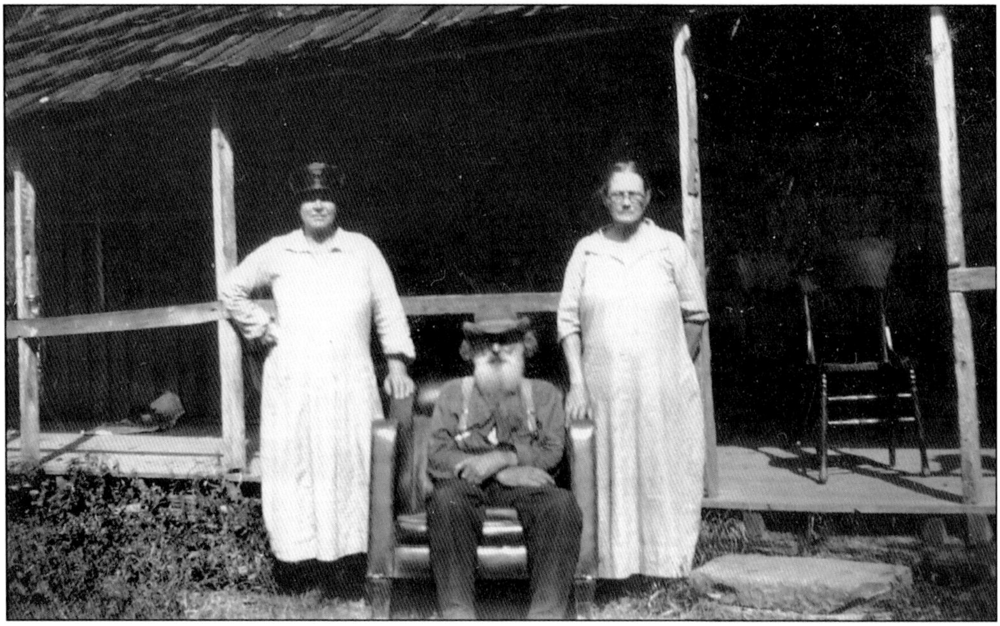

Malinda Elizabeth Bloomfield Lewis (left) is shown here with her father, Henry Bloomfield, and sister, Nicie Bloomfield Lewis (right), at Henry's home on Trace Creek.

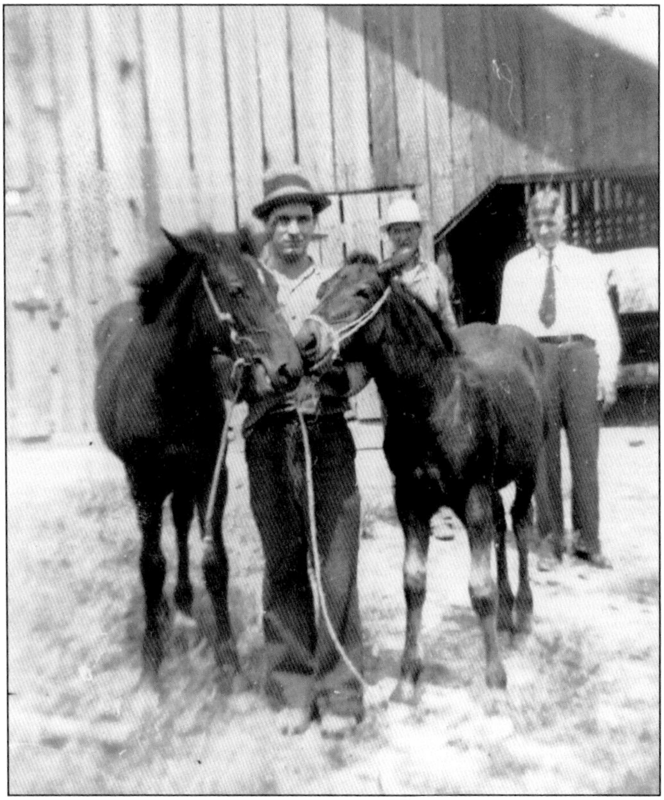

Mules were common work animals in Lewis County. Albert "Buck" Carver holds two mules while Albert Carver (left) and Edward Lewis (right) look on. Buck was a twin brother to James Ellis Carver. Buck married Avanelle Johnson and lives in Garrison.

Seven

Mother Nature and Disasters

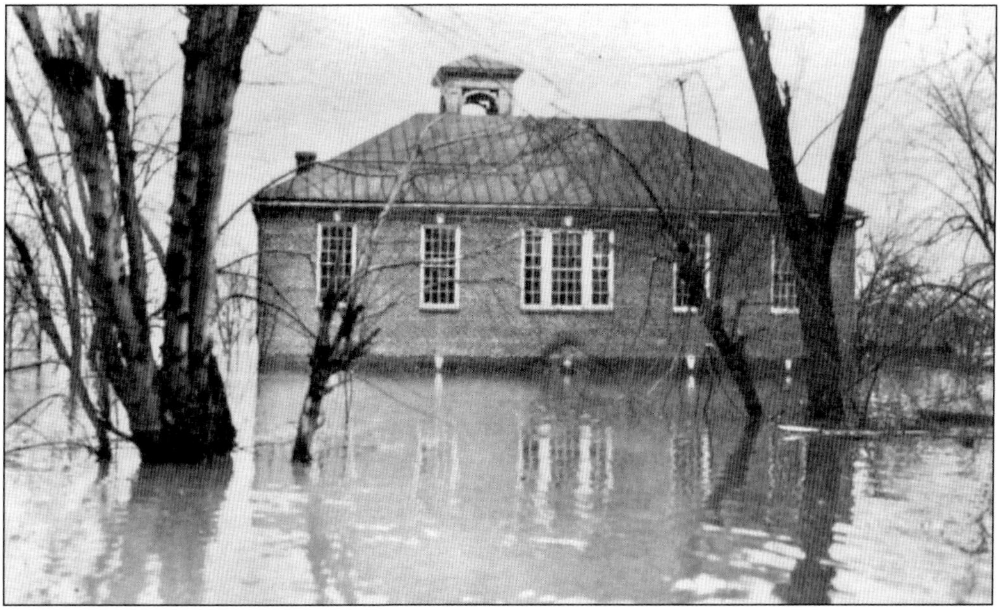

Lewis County has had many inundating floods during its history. During the historic flood of 1937, the Ohio River crested at around 70 feet above flood stage, turning many buildings into islands, including the Vanceburg Grade School.

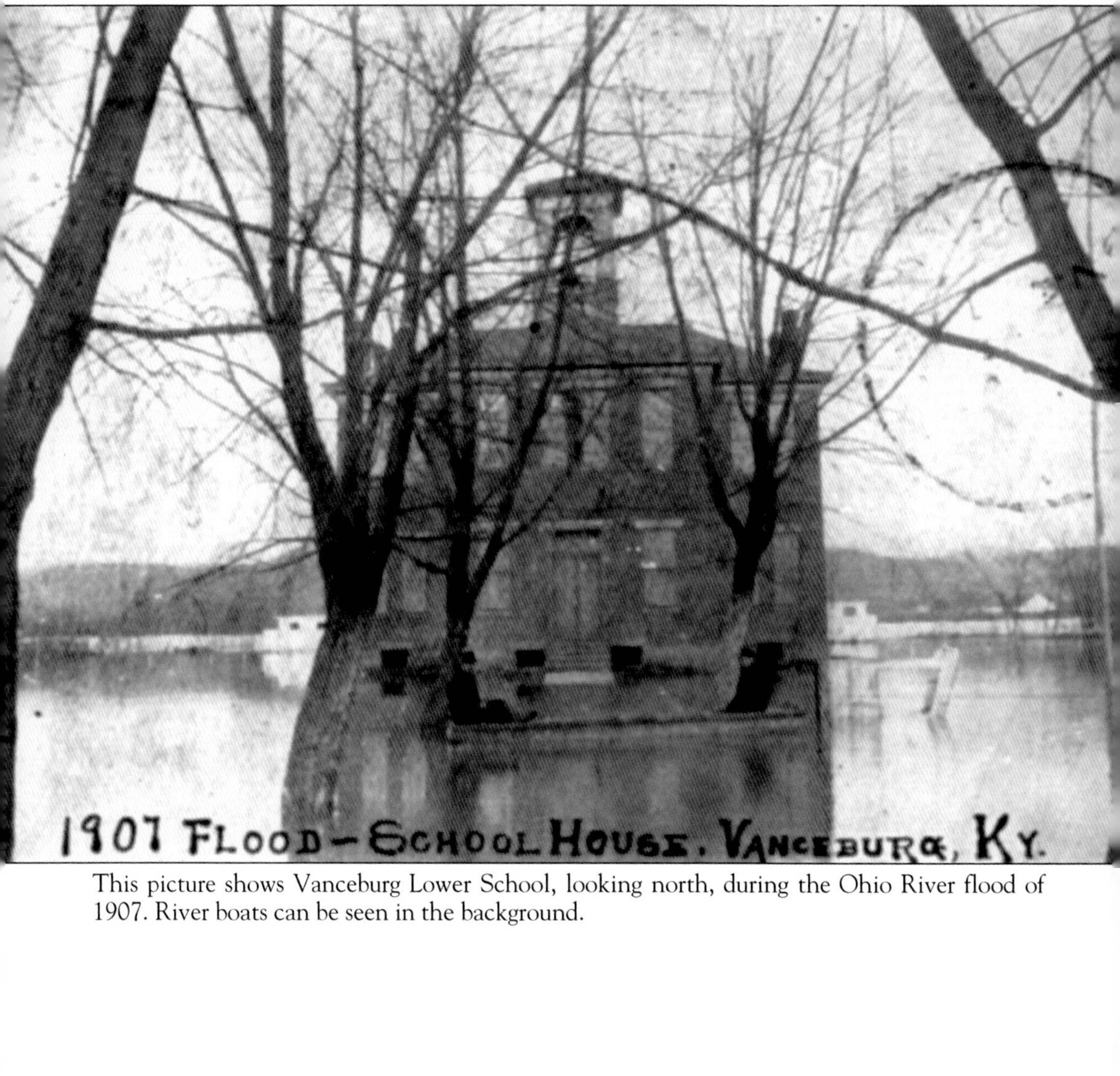

This picture shows Vanceburg Lower School, looking north, during the Ohio River flood of 1907. River boats can be seen in the background.

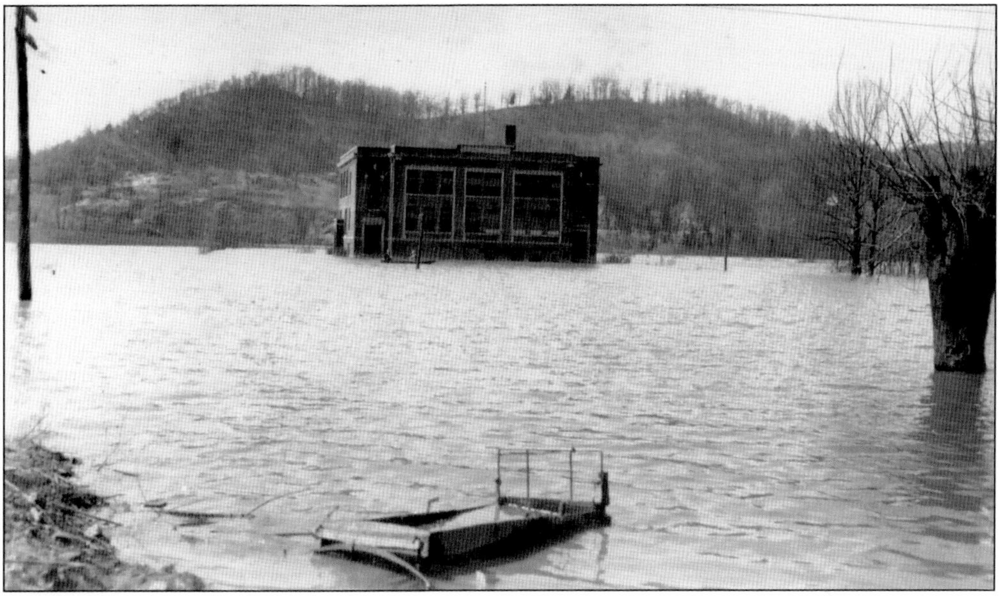

The old high school on Lexington Avenue, which burned in the 1950s, was surrounded by water in an Ohio River flood in 1933.

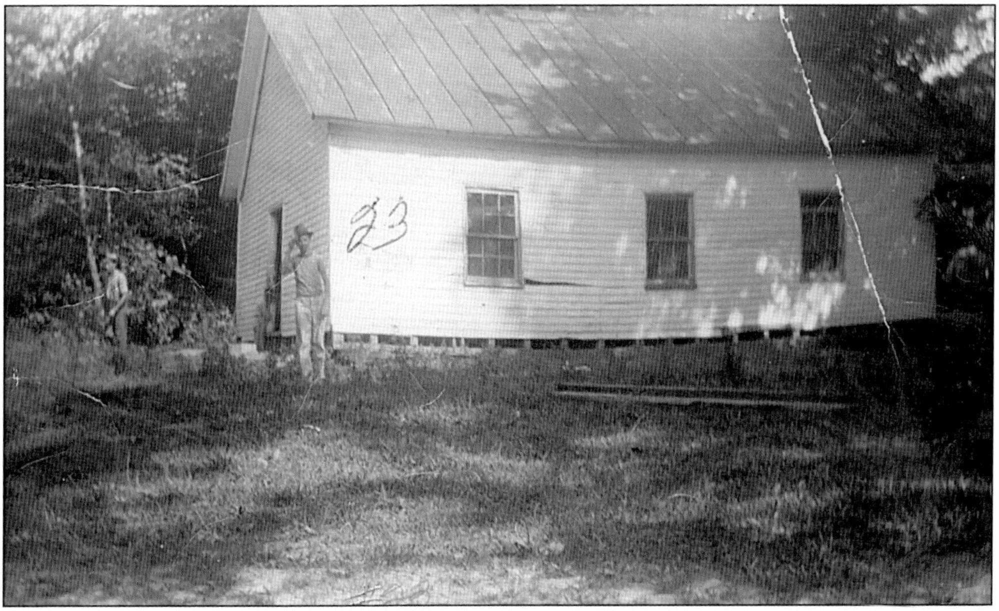

This picture shows the Tannery School after the flash flood of July 4, 1939, when the school washed over the bank. It was later moved back into the school yard. School was held in it for one year, until a little cinder-block building was constructed, which is still standing. The school was closed about 1951 or 1952.

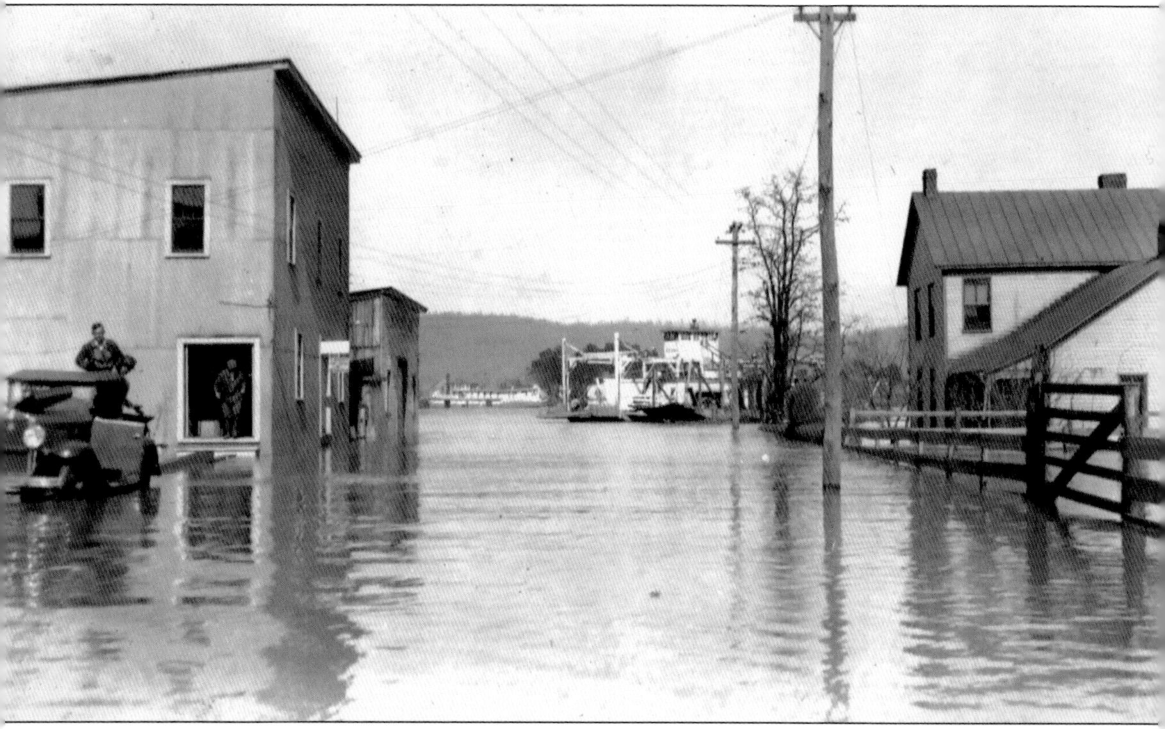

The foot of Main Street in Vanceburg is shown here in 1933, with the old mill and the Kimble/Jarrells house partly flooded. Some boats are in the background.

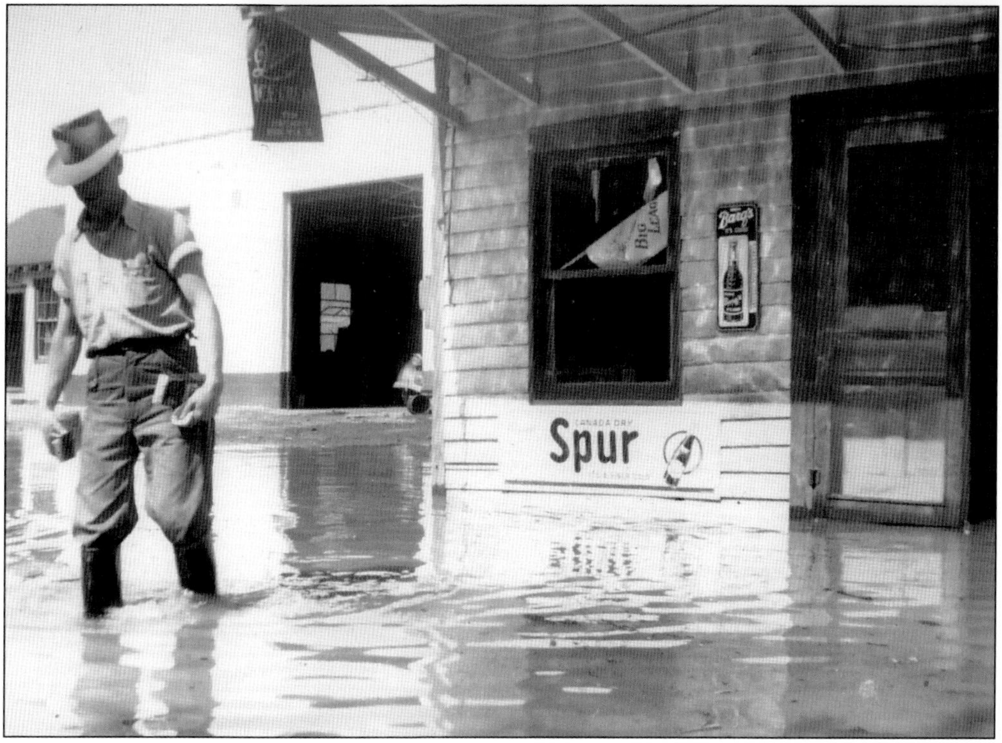

This 1945 picture shows the flood waters surrounding the little grocery that once stood on Lexington Avenue between Gilbert's Service Station and the Christian Baptist Church. The Spur Cola ad is of interest. The man is unidentified.

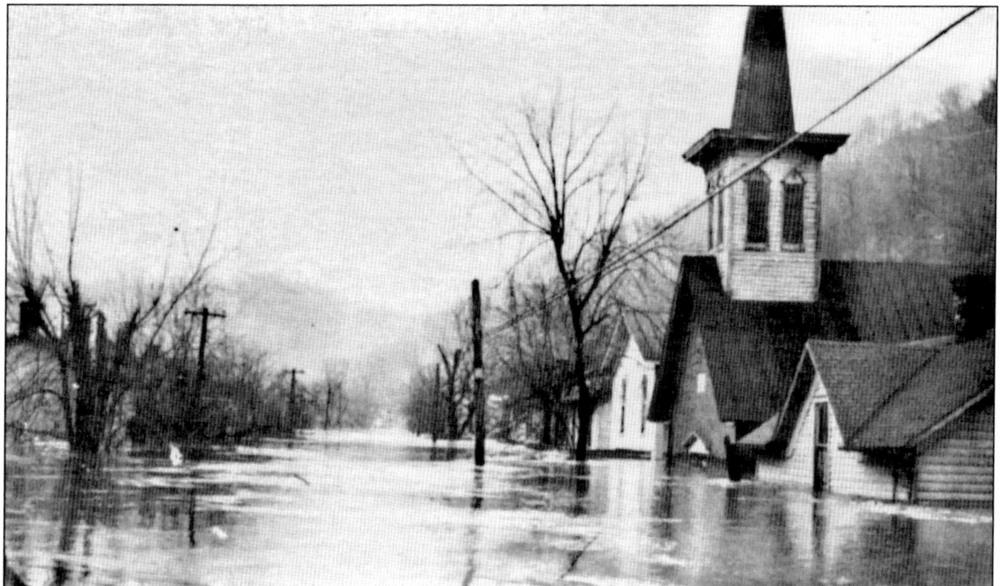

This is East Second Street in the 1937 flood. In the foreground is the Methodist Episcopal Church, South, which is still standing, and beside it is the old home of Miss Anna Davis, a local teacher. Her house has been gone for many years.

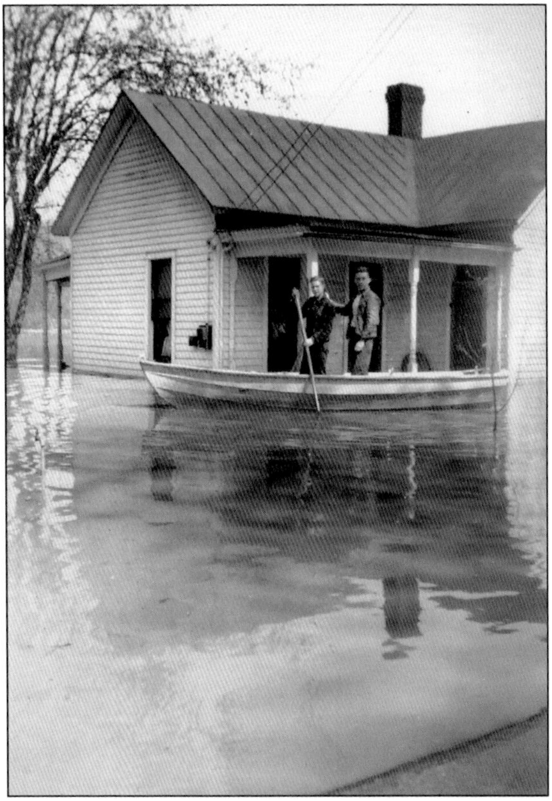

A house at 512 Lexington Avenue in Vanceburg was flooded in the spring of 1945.The house is still standing and has been flooded several times in its history.

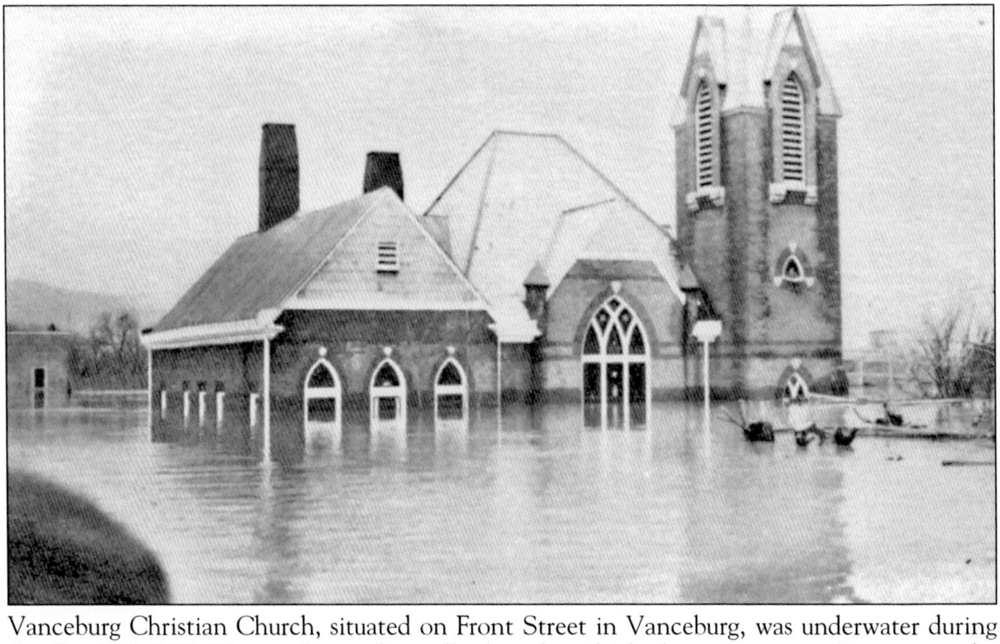

Vanceburg Christian Church, situated on Front Street in Vanceburg, was underwater during the flood of 1937. The marks on the walls show how high the water came. Damage to the church and parsonage cost $3,000. A humorous note written February 3, 1937, states, "Had wedding in boots and beard."

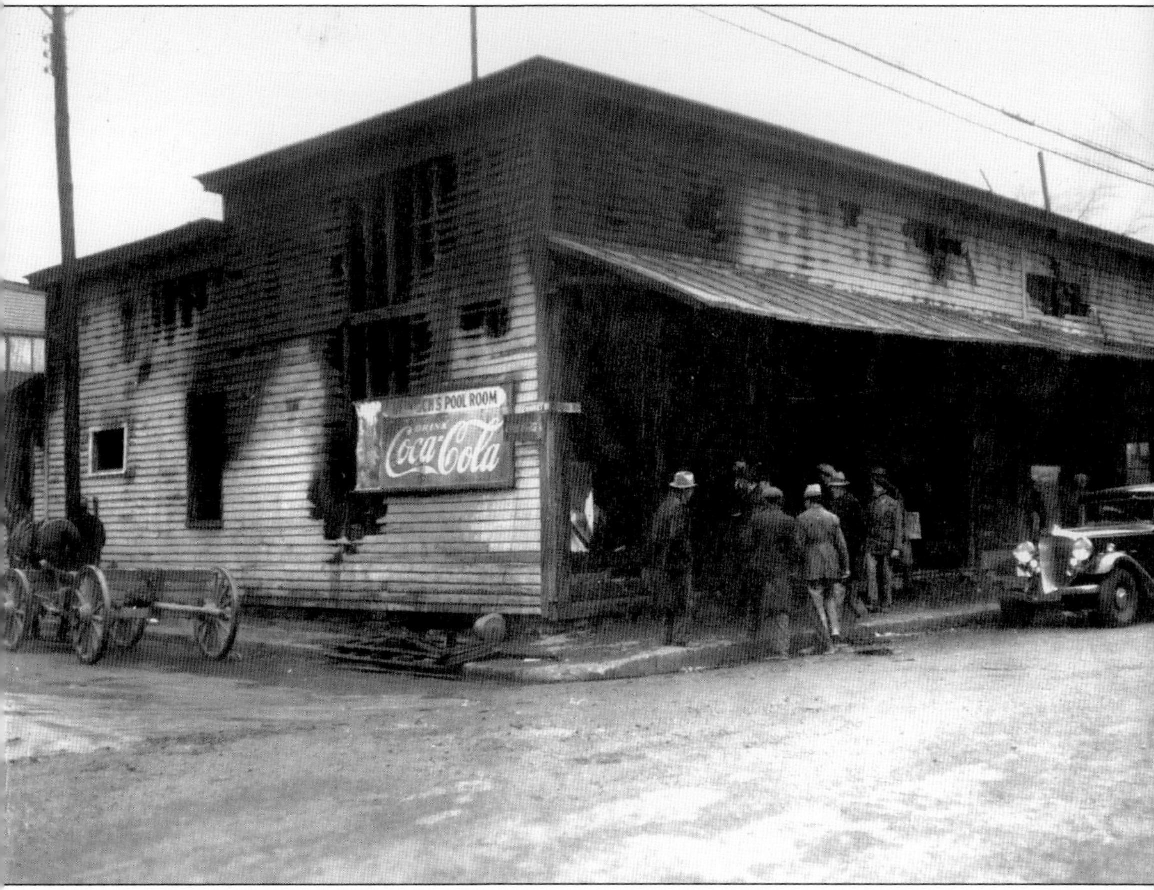

The Heinisch Pool Room fire, which took place on November 13, 1933, destroyed the building on the southwest corner of Second and Market Streets, where the Lewis County (Helen Rayburn) Library now operates.

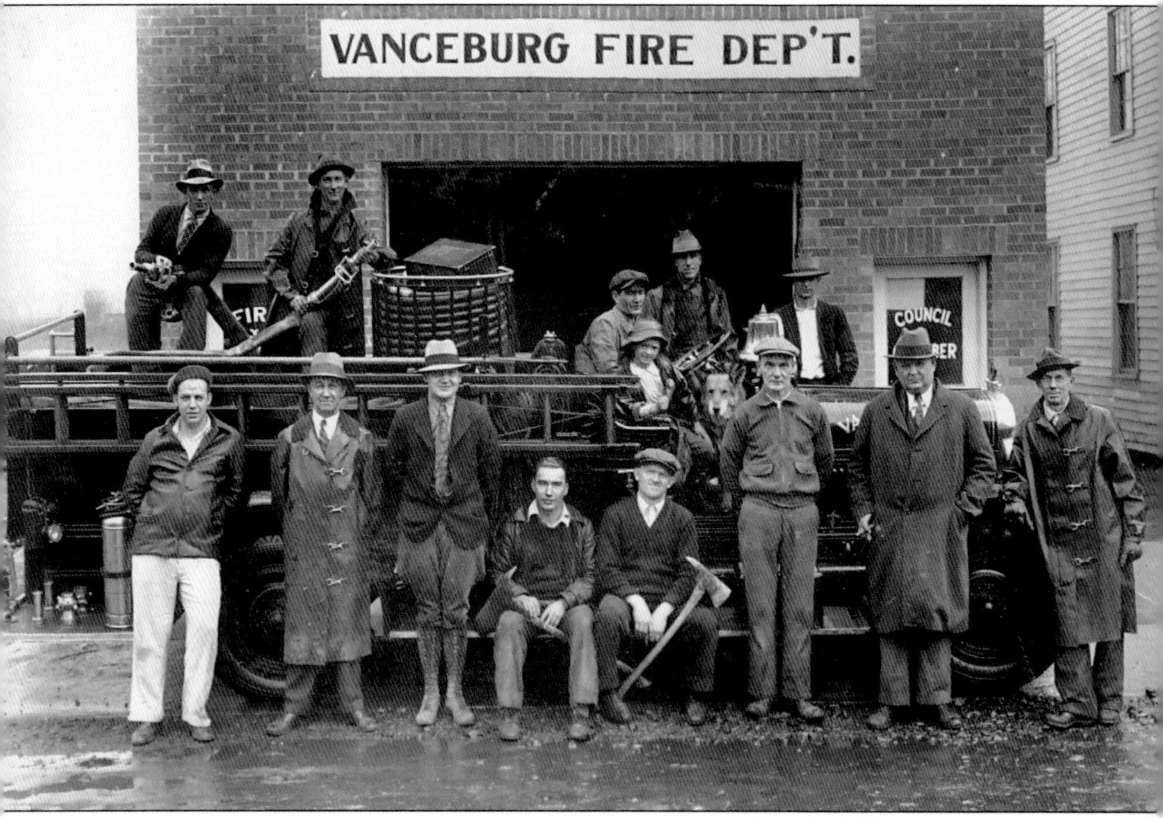

The Vanceburg Fire Department members were photographed in 1933 in front of the newly built station on Front Street. From left to right are (front row) Harry Edwards, Maurice Burriss, Orville Setters, Chester "Bear" Boyd, Bill Brown, Chief Allen Edwards, Mayor John Mann, and Bill Cox, in front of the engine; (back row) Johnny Hasler, Harry Shepard, Engineer Herb Hickle, seated with Bud Kennard and Bud's dog, Sam Ruark, and Hal Copens.

The Ohio River froze in 1939. Taking a walk on the ice, from left to right, are Dolly Smith, Simon Bruce, Marie Bruce, and Agnes Bruce.

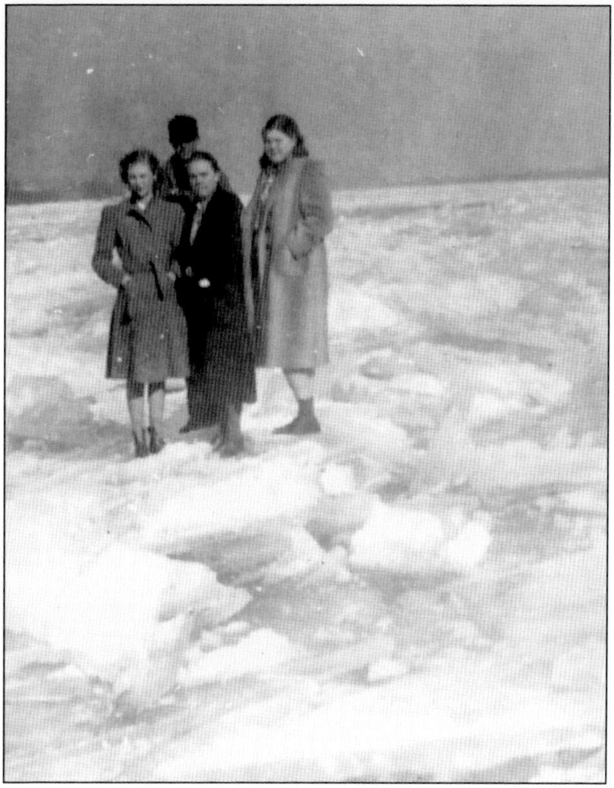

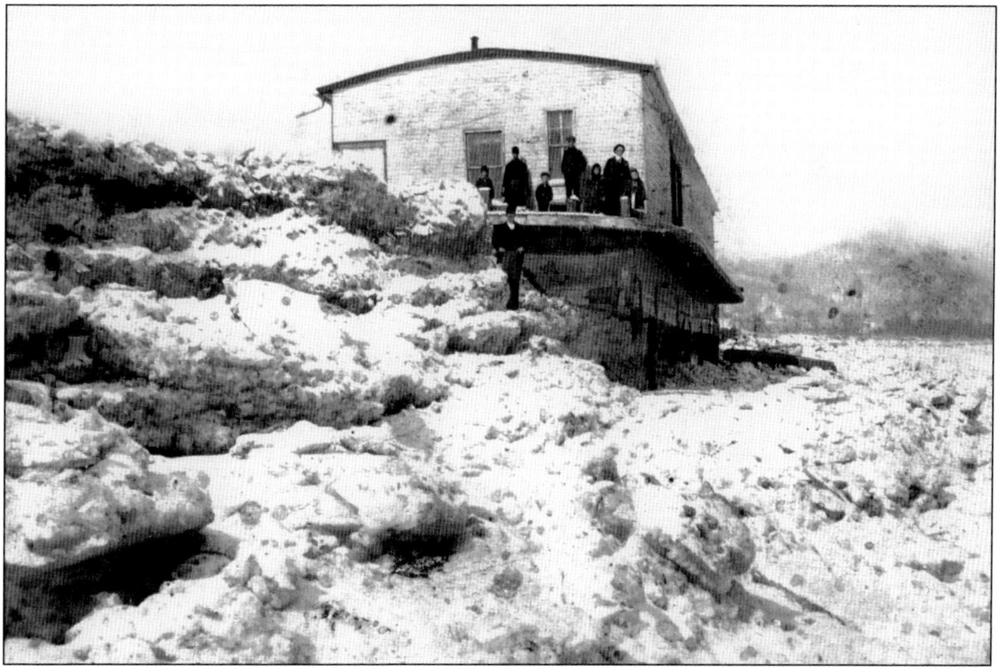

This wharf boat was caught and stranded in the ice of the Ohio River in 1904. The boat usually sat behind the city park at Front and Court Streets. The man standing on the ice is Bert Adams, who owned the boat in partnership with his brother, Ted Adams.

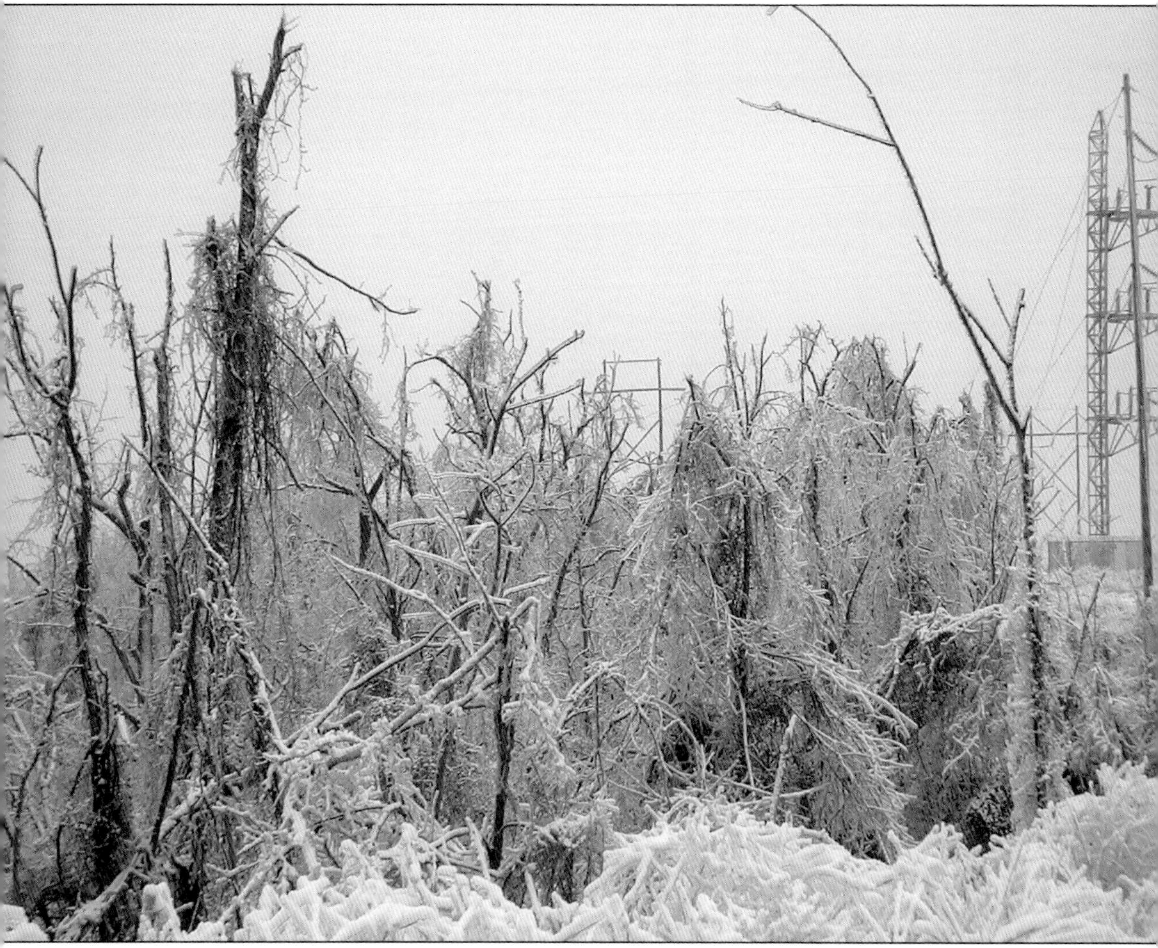

The ice storm of 2003 was one of the worst natural disasters to strike Lewis County. Widespread damage to timber was especially devastating for a county that relies on logging for employment.

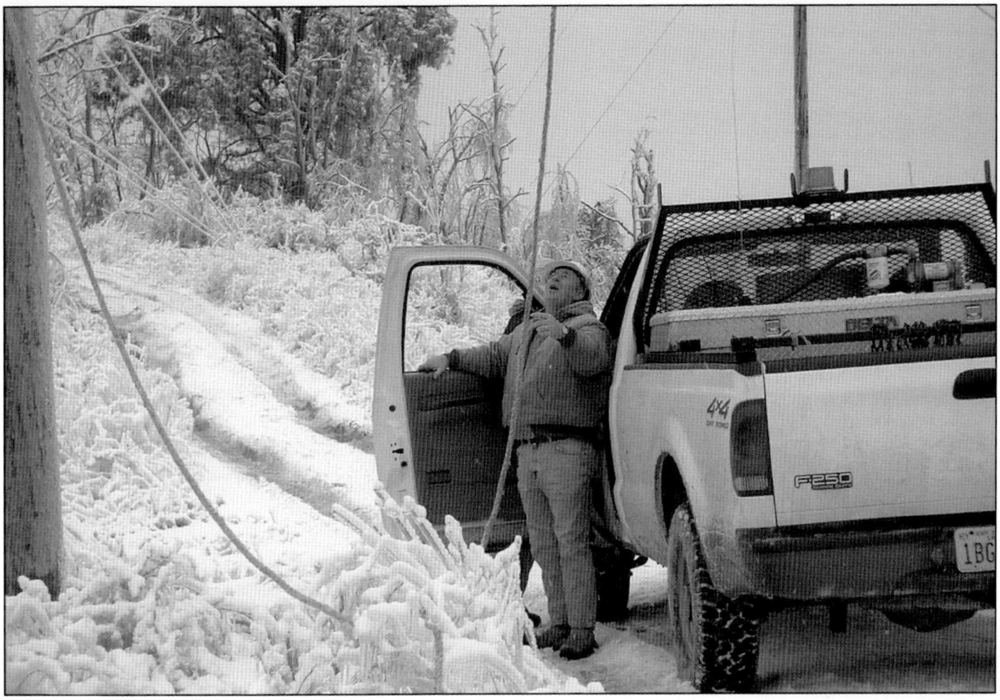

The ice storm took down power lines throughout the region. Some customers were without electricity for up to two weeks. That is ice, not snow, on the ground in this picture.

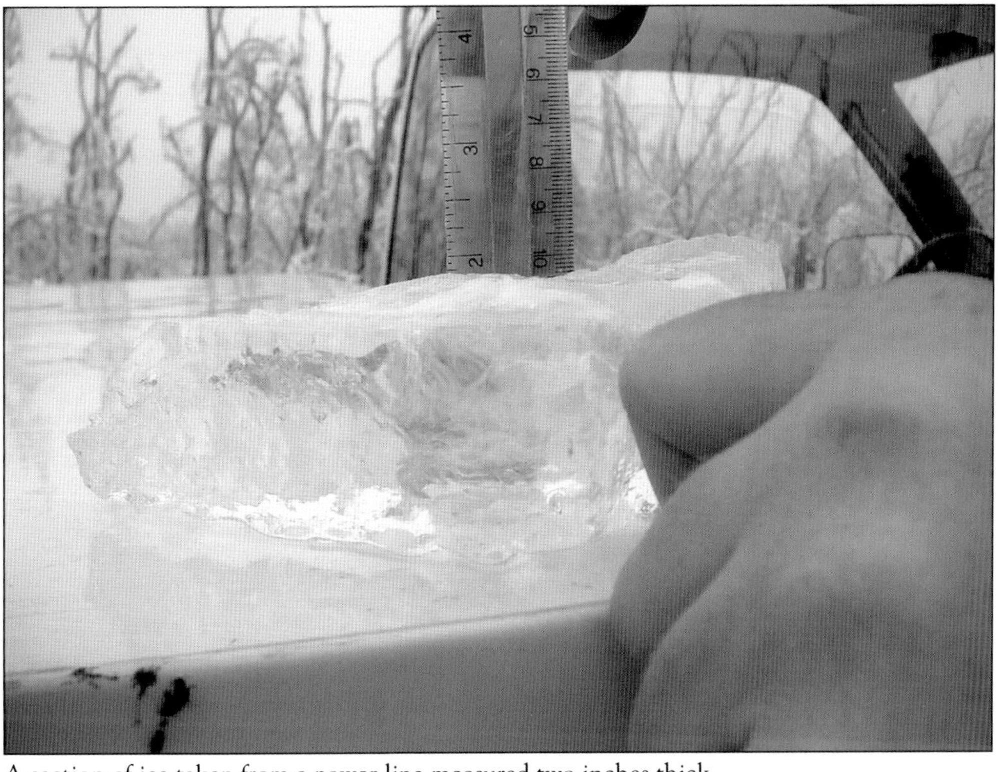

A section of ice taken from a power line measured two inches thick.

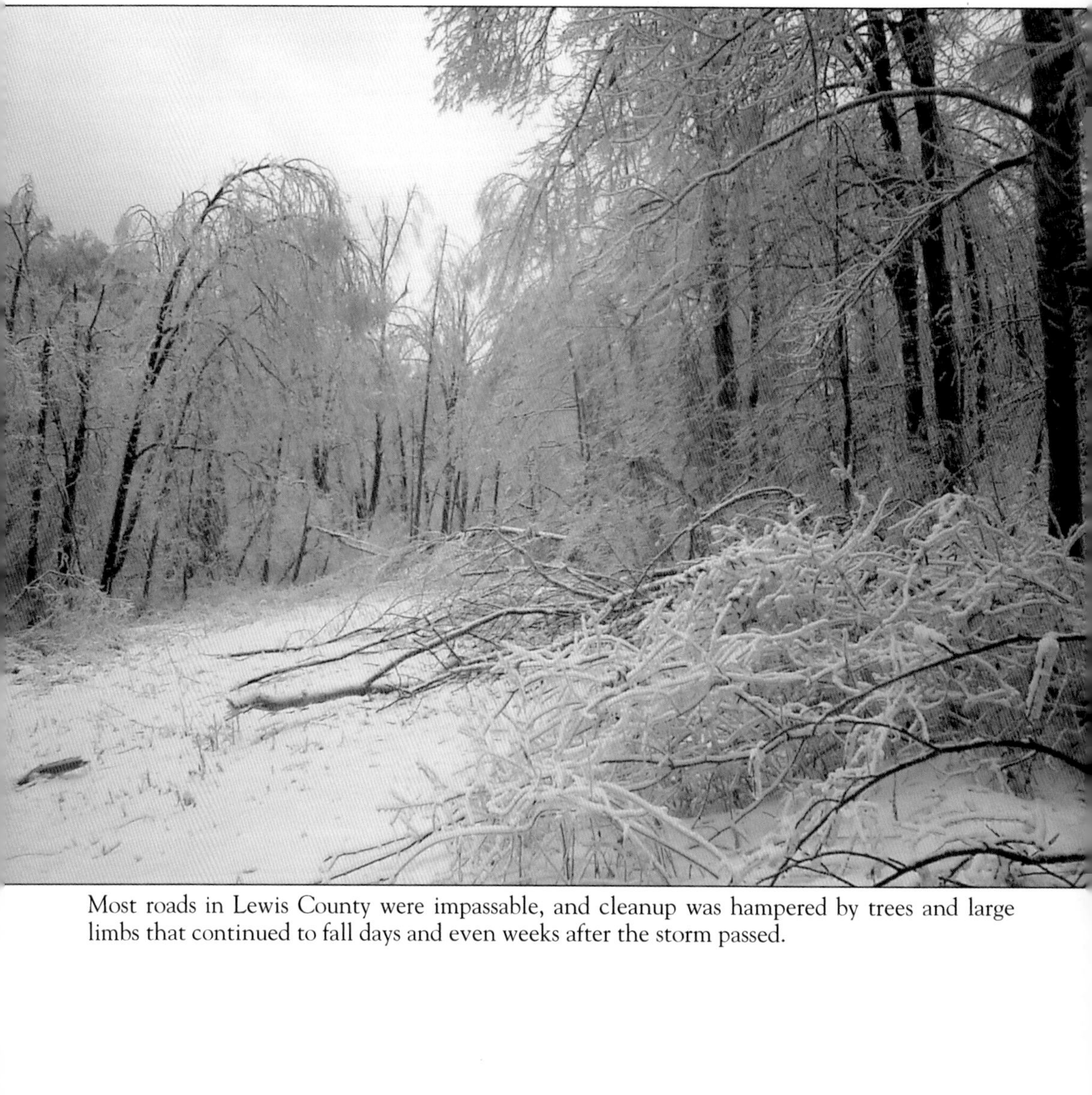

Most roads in Lewis County were impassable, and cleanup was hampered by trees and large limbs that continued to fall days and even weeks after the storm passed.